Total Quality Management Practices and Municipalities Performance in Developing Countries

Abdullah Sulaman Alnasser holds a PhD in University Utara Malaysia. He is a Researcher at University Utara Malaysia. His main area of expertise is total quality management practices. His articles have been published in a wide range of various journals. He is interested in doing research in international trade, marketing, import-export performance, tourism, migration, quality management.

Rabiul Islam holds a PhD in Environmental Economics under the Institute for Environment and Development at University Kebangsaan Malaysia (UKM). He is a Senior Lecturer in the Department of Economics at University Utara Malaysia. He was Post-Doctoral Fellow in Institute for Environment and Development, UKM. His main area of expertise is the application of Global Forest Products Model (GFPM). His articles have been published in a wide range of various journals. He is interested in doing research in international trade, trade and environment, tourism, migration, water, poverty and food security, urban agriculture, sustainable development, climatic hazards, and green economics.

Dr. Ahmad Bashawir Abdul Ghani is currently an Associate Professor in International Business Management with the College of Law, Government and International Studies at University Utara Malaysia, where he has taught international business for 15 years and has supervised about 10 business research projects. He holds an MBA in Financial Management from the University of Hull, UK and a PhD in Commerce from Murdoch University, Australia. His research and consultancy interests cover the theoretical and applied aspects of international business, business research, strategic alliances, strategic/policy modelling, and business economics. He has also published in a wide range of international, Australian and New Zealand journals. In addition, he has spoken at conferences throughout the world on matters dealing with international business management. Prior to joining University Utara Malaysia, he has previously worked in a number of public and private sector organizations in Malaysia and abroad, where he has been involved in economic, strategic and business research projects spanning most sectors of the economy. He is currently the Dean School of International Studies, College of Law, Government and International Studies at University Utara Malaysia.

Total Quality Management Practices and Municipalities Performance in Developing Countries

Study of Egypt, Jordan, Qatar, Saudi Arabia and Turkey

Abdullah Sulaman Alnasser
Rabiul Islam
Ahmad Bashawir Abdul Ghani

SHIPRA

Price: Rs. 995; US$ 49.75

ISBN: 978-81-7541-820-2

First Published in India in 2015

Total Quality Management Practices and Municipalities Performance in Developing Countries

Published by:
SHIPRA PUBLICATIONS
LG 18-19, Pankaj Central Market, Patparganj,
I.P. Ext., Delhi-110092, India
Tel: 91-11-2223 5152, 2223 6152, 9810522367
E-mail: info@shiprapublication.com
www.shiprapublication.com

Preface

We are grateful to the Almighty Allah for giving us the opportunity to complete this work. The purpose of this study is to investigate the effect of National Culture (NC) on the relationships between Soft Total Quality Management (Soft TQM), Hard Total Quality Management (Hard TQM) and the Organizational Performance (OP) in the municipalities of five developing countries—Egypt, Jordan, Qatar, Saudi Arabia, and Turkey. This study is motivated by the inconsistent findings in the contemporary literature regarding the relationships between Soft TQM, Hard TQM, and the Organizational Performance. Due to these inconsistencies, a new research stream emerged which suggests investigating the effect of a third variable that may better explain such inconsistencies, namely culture, where it becomes necessary to establish the correlation between culture and intended strategies as a key success factor. Accordingly, this study integrates many theories such as the contingency theory, organizational change theory, and the congruence model, to study the effect of National Culture (NC) on successful strategy implementation.

To name all the people who have contributed over the years toward the completion of this research with their support, encouragement, advice, data and facilities is very difficult, we are eternally grateful to all. First and foremost, we express our sincere gratitude to Professor Dr. Rushami Zien Yusoff who has been very helpful and supportive throughout our research process. We thank him for all the help provided and his continuing patience in reviewing the countless revisions of our write up. We have learned a lot and are totally indebted to Professor Yusoff.

Contents

One
Introduction

BACKGROUND

Total Quality Management (TQM) has become a universal strategy for the existence and enhancement of various firms and organizations in today's untamed global competitive scenario. Based on strategic criticality, TQM has gathered enhanced attention from many academic scholars towards small medium enterprises, manufacturing, higher education and public organizations administrator.

Numerous firms and organizations have put into use TQM strategy for the purpose to continually desire enhanced performance, and in return garnered competitive advantage. Haplessly, not all TQM implementers have tasked their TQM successfully. Kaplan and Norton (2000) elaborated that 70 to 90 per cent of organizations experienced failure organizational strategic implementation of TQM worldwide. To overcome the non-uniformity of the learnings with respect to the relationship between TQM and organizational performance, many researchers suggested that the effect of some influential organizational variables on these relationships should be investigated and some other organizational variables should be given more attention to better explain the relationship between TQM and organizational performance.

However, for many years performance measurement as one of the major tools in the package of the New Public Management reforms has remained a significant 'management fashion'. The fashion gradually comes to the developing countries which learn from the experience of more 'advanced" countries in different areas of public administration. The most developing country's public sector organizations including municipalities, also take part in the experience transferring process and although, up to now, performance measurement practices are poorly institutionalized or do not exist at all, it is likely that in the nearest future significant changes will take place in this area. Therefore, there is requirement for research on public sector performance measurement of applicable nature that could provide guidelines for development of performance measurement systems, and suggest prospective model performance measurement practices in public sector organizations and municipalities are not sufficient in these developing countries throughout this research.

Situationally, throughout the developing world, citizens are seeking enhanced government accountability and responsiveness as well as higher public services. Economic inequalities is increased by globalization, falling behind public sector reform efforts, implant corruption, and recurring issues about the entire legitimacy of government decision making at all degrees have led to such requirements, creating an intense sense of insistency about budgeting and service delivery limitations.

Albeit, Communities must now showcase the effectiveness of the public services they render. As such, the communities' structure must now also encompass a way of responding to the public (the end-users) demands. Moreover, the social and urban consequences in the existing political-economic scenario will lead to the evolution of new needs such as garbage removal, giving away potable water, and installing public lighting, at which the municipalities will have to respond back. At last, developing countries' people are at large scale promoting the avoidance of substandard public services and they are more and more seeking about the quality of the public funds usage. Not going into the details faced regarding the obstacles by developing countries municipalities, few questions underlie our problem. As such, we must challenge the nature of the measurement systems used for deriving the performance of the municipal public services in developing countries (Avelé & Fillion, 2011). In the literature of organizational studies, significant degree of attention has been put to scrutinize for the determinants of the organizational performance. That is because of the significance of the subject in showcasing the way of development for any firm and organizations.

Nevertheless, the research on organizational performance has long been of central interest to management accounting scholars. Moreover, management accounting literature has inclined to restrict to include only financial performance (Otley, 1999). While financial performance is of significant prominence in establishing the performance of profit organizations, non-financial performance might be more relevant for governmental organizations (Kaplan & Norton, 2000). As such, non-financial measures of organizational performance are critical in assessing the organizational performance effects of TQM strategy in local government. As can be seen in the TQM literatures, Sila and Ebrahimpour (2002) elaborated past studies on TQM and had scrutinized the relationship between TQM and organizational performance in multiple parameters such as financial performance and customer satisfaction. The implementation of TQM had also majorly rendered financial and non-financial performances (Yasin, 2004; Dent, 1990).

However, Overcoming poor organizational performance is one of the most difficult chores public managers face, in part because several factors prohibit or at least impede organizational improvement efforts. Barriers toward improving public sector performance may exist both within the organization and also be present externally. Internally, ineffectiveness and inefficiency are viewed as the primary causes of poor government performance. Ammons (1985) identifies several barriers impacting organizational performance. Among the barriers he describes that the impact of adoption and implementation of performance measures is a lack of creativity and innovation by public managers.

Numerous firms in various sectors of the economy such as manufacturing, service, health care, education, and government have been putting into use TQM practices to enhance their performance and effectiveness. In addition, the TQM practices and organizational performance link has been significantly scrutinized by many researchers.

Besides that, there is anecdotal evidence that the majority of studies in the literature investigating the TQM practices—organizational performance relationship focused on the role of TQM in the improvement of the production point in manufacturing organizations. At any case, many studies have clearly detected that substantial improvement in various organizations can be happened by institutionalizing TQM. TQM strategy has contributed to the improvement of general performance, of municipalities, services organizations, and financial companies.

Although, there are lack of studies in relationship between TQM and performance in the light of national culture, instead most of researches dealt with organizational culture. Prior studies regarding successful organizations revealed that they carried out TQM implementation based on their organizational characteristics, organizational culture, structure and surroundings. In regards with the topic, the municipalities are also considered part of local governments with their activities varying from one country to another. There are few researches dealt with the municipalities' performance problems and solutions. However, there are differences in these countries in the stage of improving their public sectors performance by implementing Total Quality Management (TQM). This research aims to compare between five public sectors in five developing countries; Egypt, Jordan, Qatar, Saudi Arabia, and Turkey. The objective is to discover differences and similarities between them and to measure the effect of national culture on the relationship between soft-hard TQM and performance.

Whatever the case, some features are notable in those countries' municipalities. With regards to Egypt, there are many researches in Arabic language concerning the lack of effectiveness in the performance of the Egyptian public sector including universities, municipalities and other service agencies among others. However, there is lack of research in English language in the area of performance in Egypt's public sector, particularly its municipalities. Most researches in the context of municipalities regarding Egypt are dedicated to e-government or using Information Technology (IT) generally in public services. In addition, there are many problems facing the Egyptian government sector, particularly concerning municipalities (Moawad, 2011).

With regards to Jordan, the Jordanian government strives to achieve performance through the allocation of quality awards; for example, Jordan Quality Award—King Abdullah II Award for Excellence (Rawabdeh, 2008). There are some studies that talk about TQM and performances in the Higher Education, Service Industry, Industrial Sector, Commercial Banks, and Vocational and Technical Training Institutions but there is lack of studies examining the TQM-performance relationship in the public field. One of the rare studies is in the context of municipalities' performance.

In Jordan, the study by AL-Tahat & Daradkeh examined the TQM-performance relationship in the Greater Irbid Municipality (GIM) and concluded that there is a complicated relationship between GIM factors and quality activities. In another study by Takruri (2011), the author examined Al-Basha Municipality in the above relationship's context and he mentioned that Municipalities in Jordan face a set of socioeconomic and administrational problems which negatively affect its performance.

In Turkish municipalities, the quality of service delivery to citizens is a concern to the government. The government has introduced a Performance Measurement System which will provide information on the scope and quality of services delivered and is expected to contribute to a more performance oriented management of local public services (Ozcan, Bahloul, 2006). Some researchers studied specific elements of organizational performance in Turkey's private sector and stated that many principles of TQM are applied by companies in Turkey (Demirbag, *et al.*, 2006). On the other hand, similar to the previous countries, there are only few studies that studied performance in Turkey's public sector. Performance measurement system is a new concept for the municipalities in Turkey although a radical change in the government processes is notably taking place (Hüseyin, 2011).

PROBLEM STATEMENT

Performance measurement systems of the municipality's public services points to salvage local public services which are challenged with crisis of legitimacy and identity. It appears that developing countries people have significant needs. They see themselves as customers' queuing on line for a service. There was a vivid concurrence that theory development in TQM should favour researchers and practitioners similarly to better understand why TQM implementation had frequently failed in spite of its popularity (Dean & Bowen, 1994).

Organization theorists guided further proof that organizational structure and organizational culture have relevance to TQM implementation success or failure. Albeit, the rich bodies of TQM studies in Organization Theory, there appears to be marginal studies that develop and test TQM implementation values, national culture dimensions, and organizational performance in one suitable model.

In any pretext, researches in cross-cultural studies have credibly established that cultural values may have a major effect on an organization's management practices. Various authors have thus postulated that differences in national cultures may require differences in the management practices of organizations.

As established in past, the body of TQM knowledge developed at start from TQM studies that oriented its attention on advanced countries such as Australia, Japan, UK and the US. In the meantime, research continued with more nations in many parts of the world. Albeit, few attempts have been made to perform TQM comparative or multiple-country studies that use the cultural values of a country as an explanatory variable. Researching this solo field, the Operations Research literature started recently to showcase interest in finding how national culture links to the implementation of TQM values. For instance, Tata and Prasad (1999) put across a speculative model highlighting that national culture leads to organizational culture, which in return affects TQM values. In the same manner, Sousa-Poza *et al.* (2001) developed a quantitative model of complex relationships between organizational culture and TQM values that relies upon the national values of a nation. Though, most of these studies orients primarily on organizational culture), or are solely theoretical or render no theories at all.

However, there are many studies that investigate the relationships between TQM strategy and organizational performance, for example Yong and Wilkinson (1999) reviewed 15 articles that showed positive and negative relationships between TQM strategy and organizational performance. The study found that the reviewed articles were related to studies conducted in different countries investigating the TQM strategy and organizational performance relationship. The study also concluded that the unsuccessfulness of TQM initiatives can be attributed to the partial implementation of TQM strategy and claimed that organization should enhance its performance towards achieving a competitive advantage. Baker (2003) stated that the effect of TQM practices on organizational performance has been empirically supported. Prajogo & Sohal (2001) tried to study the relationship between TQM implementation and innovation performance. They argued that the implementation of TQM will be influenced by the environment in which the organization operates and the strategy adopted by the organization. They studied the literature of the relationship between the TQM and innovation, and then performance. He distinguishes between two claims. The first one states that the TQM establishes innovation-oriented environment and then has a positive relationship with innovation and the subsequent. Whereas others, argued that the implementation of TQM principals may hinder the organizational innovation.

At every situation, Molina-Azorin, Tari, Claver-Cortes, and Lopez-Gamero (2009) debated that the development of quality management theory was specifically dependent on three sources which are, the prescription of the quality gurus, the national quality awards, and measurements studies. They also discovered that majority of scrutinized research work has showcased that the successful implementation can enhance organizational performance. Nair (2006), made an attempt to scrutinize which TQM parameters were positively interlinked with organizational performance. Moreover, he attempted to scrutinize the existence of moderating parameters that may affect the TQM practices and organizational performance relationship. The learnings of the research assured the effect of TQM on organizational performance. The findings of this study, however, stressed the effects of some TQM critical factors such as leadership, people management, process management, and customer focus on the overall organizational performance. This research also upheld the existence of moderating parameters in the TQM practices-performance relationship such as organizational structure, as in Douglas and Judge's (2001) research. He, as such, recommended that many other contextual parameters may be taken into account in future research to fine tune the TQM implementation programmes to particular firms and organizations in specific situation.

While Sila & Ebrahimpour (2002), identified 25 factors as the critical factors for TQM that constitute their study framework. According to this study, customer focus and satisfaction was the most frequently discussed factor followed by employee training and leadership and top management commitment. They stated that the quality management in the service sector may seem to be more difficult because of the intangibility of services. Out of 347 research papers reviewed in this study, only few studies were conducted in the developing countries, however the Middle East region including Saudi Arabia, UAE, and Qatar constituted less than 2 per cent from these studies.

Tari (2005) identified nine critical factors of TQM based on reviewing the TQM literature. These nine factors are: (i) customer-based approach, process management which are the most important; (ii) management commitment and leadership; (iii) quality planning; (iv) management based on facts; (v) continuous improvement; (vi) human resource management including training, (vii) work team and communication; (viii) cooperation with supplier; and (ix) finally organizational social and environmental issues-related awareness. He also pointed out that the literature has revealed that TQM and HRM are highly correlated and the latter found to be the basis of the success of the former.

It is found by researchers that the environmental characteristics influence the implementation of TQM and this in turn influence the financial, operational, and human-aspects of organizational performance. Feng *et al.* (2006) tried to examine the relationship between TQM strategy and quality performance and innovation by comparing the performance of companies in two countries. The results showed that leadership and people management are related to innovative performance while customer focus and process management are related to quality performance.

Brah, Tee & Rao (2002) emphasized on the importance of the behavioural factors of TQM strategy, such as top management leadership, customer satisfaction, human resource focus, quality focus. In addition to that, this study emphasized the importance of intangible TQM techniques such as strategic planning and information and analysis, to the organizational success and effectiveness. This study also suggested that there should be longitudinal studies and in-depth case studies as future streams of research in exploring the TQM practices and organizational performance relationship.

Researchers examined the relationship between TQM and performance, their empirical results were corroborating the findings of many previous researches by supporting the positive relationship between TQM and organizational performance. The results generated by Pinho's (2008) analysis confirmed that TQM practices are the major contributors to organizational performance. This study, moreover, showed that measuring results, quality assurance system, and top-management training and leadership initiatives factor are among the most influential factors on performance. Moreover, while it was found that innovation and customer orientation significantly impacted the performance and innovation respectively, the relationship between TQM and customer orientation, innovation and performance was not supported by the results.

It has been vivid from the past assessment of the quality management literature that significant majority of research work related to TQM showcase that TQM strategy can have positive relationship with the organizational performance. Alternatively, many other researchers highlighted the failure of TQM in organizational effectiveness. Albiet, many researchers have ascertained the failure of TQM performance implications to various reasons. To start with, devoid of strategic focus of an organization enables wishful thinking that TQM implementation can address short-term issues and will have spontaneous outcome. On other hand, devoid of the top management commitment with respect to products and service in a firm influences the quality performance. At last, devoid of supportive culture influences the successful implementation of TQM strategy as a change strategy towards enhancing the entire organizational performance.

Almost all TQM definitions differentiate between "soft" and "hard" sides. The "soft" side is related with management concepts and principles such as leadership, employee empowerment, while the "hard" side is related to quality improvement tools and techniques (Vouzas & Psyhogios, 2007; Thiagaragan *et al.,* 2001). Categorizing the TQM factors into hard and soft factors has been a direction in the literature when studying TQM and performance relationship. In this line of research, Gadenne & Sharma (2009) tried to investigate the relationship between hard and soft quality management factors and organizational performance. They identified six critical factors. Moreover, they found that the six factors in their study were benchmarking and quality measurement; continuous improvement; top management philosophy; employee and customer involvement; employee training; and efficiency improvement. More generally, their findings confirmed that for TQM strategy to have effective implications on organizational performance there should be a combination of hard and soft TQM factors to be implemented to positive relationship with the overall organizational performance.

However with regards to national culture, Mathews *et al.* (2001) examined quality systems in three European countries and concluded that differences in approaches exist, and that some of Hofstede's national culture dimensions are appropriate to explain these variations. Sousa-Poza, Nystrom & Wiebe (2001) compared the implementation of TQM values between three countries. They concluded that specific national cultures require different approaches to effectively implement TQM. Mathews *et al.* (2001), stated that no specific hypotheses were developed to test the relationships between national culture dimensions and TQM implementation. One of the rare studies that did develop hypotheses is the one by Lagrosen (2003) Using Hofstede's framework. Lagrosen (2003) found partial to weak support for his hypotheses linking Hofstede's national culture dimensions to TQM values.

As the study stated, since its starting in the early 1980s, TQM has added new dimensions to the management practices worldwide. Moreover, the relationship between TQM and organizational performance has been empirically supported by an increasing number of studies. Besides, it has been widely argued that TQM principles, in support to the contingency model of TQM application, are equally applicable to various environments. Moreover, when applying TQM in the service environment, a modified model with compatible practices should be designed to harvest the utmost potential benefits (Al-Mansour, 2007). However, many researchers emphasized that behavioural and human-focused TQM factors such as leadership, empowerment, customer focus, and involvement are crucial factors in service-oriented organizations.

This study bridges these gaps in several ways. First, the quality management literature showed that the findings regarding the TQM and organizational performance relationship turned out to be inconclusive calling for an extensive research work to be conducted in this area (Nair, 2006). While some studies empirically support the existence of direct as well as indirect relationship between TQM practices and organizational performance. Other studies (questioned the TQM strategy effectiveness, other numerous studies examined the effect of elements of total quality in direct way without distinction between component as Soft or Hard and some studied each element separately.

Second, despite the fact that most of the studies on TQM practices have dealt with developed countries, a little is known about the practices of TQM in the developing countries. Therefore, some researchers such as Al-Marri *et al.* (2007) suggested that there is an urgent need to study the effect of TQM practices on the performance of the service organizations in the context of developing countries, to examine their success factors and drivers of effective performance.

Third, in the literature related to TQM, there has been unresolved debate regarding the relationship between Soft-Hard TQM and organizational performance. This situation drove some researchers to suggest that the relationship with some other organizational variables should be considered. However, in this regard, Ehigie and McAndrew (2005); Douglas and Judge (2001) suggested that more attention should be paid to some organizational variables to better examine TQM and organizational performance relationship. Therefore, this study tried to examine the effect of National Culture (NC), in establishing the fit for these strategies and hence better organizational performance.

Forth, pervious researches in the field dealt with TQM as a whole concept. But it did not study it in the context of Soft and Hard TQM.

Fifth, there are deferent effects between Soft TQM and Hard TQM on Performance (Rahman (2001, 2004), Wilkinson (1992) and Al-Tarawneh (2010).

Sixth, as Reed *et al.* (2000) concluded that there is an agreement among them that TQM strategy requires a supportive culture. Despite the importance of culture as a crucial organizational factor to establish the fit between strategy and environment, it has been widely neglected especially in TQM literature. Therefore, this study will respond to the call to further examine the impact of Soft-Hard TQM practice in the international settings (Parast, 2006).

Seventh, the study's TQM model is firmly embedded in the Organization Theory literature by employing Hofstede's (2001) national culture dimensions, Douglas and Judge's (2001) TQM values, and elements of Lawrence & Lorsch's (1967) contingency theory.

Eighth, the study addresses the call of researchers to focus more on both the role of national culture in TQM implementation and on the need to generate more cross-cultural and multi-country comparative research (Sila & Ibrahimpur, 2002). By testing the model in organizations from a very large number of culturally diverse, predominantly developing countries that differ from one country to others.

Ninth, it furthers a number of Operations Research studies by developing and testing an empirical model and by focusing on National Culture rather than on Organizational Culture.

Finally, in the literature related to TQM, did not link between National Culture and performance. Even most of previous researches dealt with TQM in the context of organizational culture.

The study examines relationships between soft-hard TQM values, national culture dimensions, and organizational performance, the study employs a moderated model. The model basically puts forward two propositions:

(1) National Culture dimensions effect on the relationship between Soft-Hard TQM and performance, and
(2) Soft-Hard TQM values affect organizational performance.

The study's model is a "complete" moderate model, that is, the national culture is proposed to fully moderate the soft-hard TQM values—organizational performance relationship. Thus, the major purpose of this study is to bridge these gaps in the literature by examining the relationship between Soft-Hard TQM, by moderate National Culture and the Organizational Performance. Moreover, investigating these relationships is more interesting in a context of many cultural backgrounds. The emphasis made by this study on the effect of National Culture was in line with the premises of the contingency theory and guided by the congruence model that highlight the fit between strategy and culture as the key success factor.

However, Hofstede's (1980) well-known cultural dimensions of (power distance, uncertainty avoidance, individualism, masculinity) have been selected for this study. Although Hofstede's framework has not been without criticism, it remains the most established in the literature for examining cross-national differences in many aspects of organizational behaviour. Regarding the choice of Soft TQM values, there are five critical Soft TQM value studies i.e., top management commitment, supplier relationship, employee relations, education and training, and customer focus.

Also, there are three critical Hard TQM value studies i.e., process management, quality information and analysis, Anderson and Sohal (1999) and strategic planning.

With respect to organizational performance will measure by four generic diminutions of performance derived from scholarly literature financial performance, internal process performance, customer performance, learning and growth.

Several researchers consider TQM as comprising of two inter-dependent but distinct parts. Soft TQM comprises of elements linked with human resource. Rahman (2001, 2004) stated that TQM deals with long-term natures and is characterized as humanistic. Soft TQM constructs are variables as viewed by many scholars. A review of literature reveals that some prior studies have stressed on the soft and the hard TQM's impact on TQM's success and in turn organizational performance. Based on the study by Thiagrajan and Zairi (1997a; 1997b; 1997c), hard TQM comprise of systems, tools and methods while the soft ones comprise of intangible elements that are almost impossible to measure.

However, Thiagarajan and Zairi categorized the TQM factors into hard and soft quality factors. While hard quality factors are those factors that can be measured and related to the system, tools, and techniques, soft quality factors are those intangible factors that are difficult to measure directly such as top management commitment, customer focus, teamwork, training and empowerment, and effective communication. Although the findings of prior studies are inconsistent and inconclusive (Gadenne & Sharma, 2009), as stated, it is notable that most of them concentrated on the impact of TQM elements directly without distinguishing between components with only a few of them studying the elements individually (Rahman & Bullock, 2005; Christos, *et al.,* 2009). Their study's findings revealed that quality improvement is impacted by the adoption of soft TQM primarily and hard TQM elements secondarily. Moreover, a significant number of definitions place distinction between soft and hard TQM. While soft TQM is related with management concepts and principles including leadership, employee empowerment etc., hard TQM is related to quality improvement methods and tools.

OBJECTIVES

The objectives of the research are:

(i) To determine the relationship between Soft TQM practices and Municipalities performance
(ii) To identify the relationship between hard TQM practices and Municipalities performance
(iii) To investigate the effect of national culture on improving the relationship between Soft-Hard TQM and performance

SIGNIFICANCE OF THE RESEARCH

The importance of this study doesn't only lie in its investigation into the relationship between Soft-Hard TQM factors and their relationship with performance under the effect of the national culture, but also in enabling better theoretical understanding of the underlying mechanisms related to the relationship between Soft-Hard TQM factors and the performance by moderate National Culture between Soft-Hard TQM and performance. The study, in other words, develops and tests the model that considers that National Culture moderate the relationship between Soft-Hard TQM and performance. The model uses (Hofstede's 1980, 1983, 1993) four national culture dimensions and five soft TQM values—top management commitment, supplier relationship, employee relation, education and training, customer focus; and three dimensions of hard TQM—process management, quality information and analysis, strategic planning, derived from previous well-known studies, e.g. Sila & Ebrahimpour, (2003); and Powell (1995). And four items of performance—financial performance, customer performance, learning and growth, and internal process performance, derived from previous studies, e.g. Chan (2004); and Kapalan & Nortorn (1996). The study also adds to the literature related to management practice and cross-cultural studies, as it is a comparative study between different cultures and economies.

The study uses cross-sectional survey in five developing countries (Egypt, Jordan, Qatar, Saudi Arabia, and Turkey) to collect data. Statistical methods such as correlation, regression and analysis of variance (ANOVA) are used to analyze the data to answer the questions previously outlined.

SCOPE

This study focuses on examining the relationship between TQM (Soft TQM and Hard TQM) and national culture as moderator with organization performance. The research questions and objectives of this study will examine the data that will be collected from the Municipalities from five countries—Egypt, Jordan, Qatar, Saudi Arabia, and Turkey. Therefore, this study will be the managers of Municipalities' operation to these countries. The present study selects these five countries because owing to the differences in the stages of improving their performance by implementing TQM, particularly in their public sectors and to the differences in researchers' findings concerning the TQM application in these countries.

Whatever the case, many studies reported that not all critical factors of TQM strategy were found to be significantly related to organizational performance. Although developing countries such as Malaysia and Turkey seemed to be advanced and relatively successful in their application of TQM, the story seems to be different in other developing countries. Also, according to Zakuan *et al.* (2010), the adoption of quality management practices has not applied at a similar rate in different parts of the world. A detailed discussion of the issue is provided in this section.

Researchers have largely failed to touch upon quality management in the context of Arab and Middle Eastern countries in their empirical research. These countries include Saudi Arabia, Qatar, Jordan and Egypt. In the beginning of the 1990, researchers (Aly, 1996 and Zairi, 1996) attempted to examine the issues behind the challenges faced by Middle Eastern organizations and their efforts to employ TQM strategy. Ever since then, increasing attention has been directed to the implementation of TQM in response to the high competition brought about by the global business expansion in the Middle Eastern countries with the inclusion of Saudi Arabia, Qatar, Jordan and Egypt (Al-Khalifa & Aspinwall, 2000; Al-Zamany *et al.*, 2002).

In addition, studies dedicated to the Middle Eastern countries in terms of productivity, efficiency, and implications of organizational competitiveness and TQM strategy are few and quite far (Al-Khalifa & Aspinwall, 2000; Chapman & Al-Khawaldeh, 2002; & Al-Zamany *et al.*, 2002). In Egypt, Salaheldin (2003) tried to investigate the TQM implementation challenges and supporting factors based on the data collected from 84 Egyptian manufacturing firms. The findings of this study revealed that TQM implementation in Egypt has been facing the same challenges as in other developing countries. The main challenges are the lack of top management commitment support, training, resources, and the resistance to change.

In the context of Jordan, as mentioned, the Jordanian government strives to achieve performance through the allocation of awards for quality. Some of the researches contributing to the TQM implementation literature in Jordan include Chapman and Al-Khawaldeh (2002), but they failed to discuss TQM in the context of municipalities and in terms of its relation with performance under the light of culture. In addition, one of the rare study in the municipalities' performance in Jordan was conducted by Al-Taha, & Daradkeh, who studied performance and TQM in Greater Irbid Municipality (GIM) and concluded that there is a complicated relationship between GIM factors and quality activities. GIM must constantly be aware that these factors, which are critical to a quality activities success, may change with time, vary for each quality activity, and vary depending on the stage of quality activity development. They also concluded the following; education and training, municipality communication, customers focus and top management commitment have positive effects on the municipality quality of service; GIM employee participation and scientific approach to decision making do not have a positive effect on GIM employee satisfaction; GIM customer focus and top management commitment have a positive effect on municipality customer satisfaction; employee satisfaction in municipality has positive effects on service quality and customer satisfaction in GIM; GIM quality of service has positive effects on its customer satisfaction; and finally, employee satisfaction, service quality, and customer satisfaction have positive effects on GIM TQM implementation.

Another study concerning the municipalities was conducted by Takruri (2011) who applied his study on in Al-Basha Municipality. According to him, municipalities in Jordan face a set of socioeconomic and administrational problems which affect negatively on its performance. He used 21 measures to investigate the extent of implementing the corporate governance in measuring the efficiency of the municipality and these include rendering services, staff, contingencies and the interaction with its local community. He recommended adopting and implementing the objectives only if the corporate governance of the Municipality is part of its culture, and updating legislation and doing the necessary modification in the organization chart. In a similar study, Al-Shobaki, *et al.* (2010) studied the implementation of Total Quality Management (TQM) in Jordan's Banking Sector. They concluded that there is a high logical relationship between all TQM principles and organizational performance.

In Qatar, one of the first studies related to TQM practices in the Middle East was conducted by Al-Khalifa and Aspinwall (2000). In their study, they tried to reflect the level of TQM implementation in Qatari organizations. However, they found that TQM implementation has been facing major challenges such as the lack of information, top management commitment, and more seriously the lack of quality related education and training. In another context, the empirical findings of Salaheldin's (2009) study of 139 Qatari SMEs categorized the TQM critical factors into strategic, tactical, and operational factors. While strategic factors include factors related to the top management practices and support, tactical factors relate to the employees and suppliers. Moreover, operational factors include factors related to products, resources, and customers. The findings of the study revealed that there is a significant effect of TQM factors on operational and the organizational performance of SMEs. The study concluded by emphasizing the crucial role of the strategic factors in the successful implementation of TQM strategy and programmes in SMEs.

Tennant and Wu (2005) scrutinized the crucial success parameters in TQM programmes in the Gulf Cooperation Council (GCC) and Qatar and noted the impact of cultural values on the success and failure of TQM measures in the region as well. Culture sways to be a critical element and a dominant factor in the success and failure of TQM programmes. The research figured out that there is a sound interlink between crucial success factors of TQM and performance of oil and gas industry in the State of Qatar. This relationship recommended that foreign companies functioning in Qatar are inclined to refer to the implementation of crucial success factors as necessary elements of their TQM and that crucial success factors are not rendering the failure of TQM programmes in the Qatari oil and gas industry. The research also gave foundation to the recommendation that cultural elements are key factors to the failure of TQM programmes in large oil and gas companies. These conclusions are consistent with those of Appelbaum and Steed's (2005) learnings in a research that scrutinized the crucial success factors which guides in establishing elements leading to organizational performance enhancements. As a result, these conclusions supported Hsien *et al.*'s (2002) findings that cultural characteristics are key parameters in the buildup of firms and are contributing factors to the success or failure of TQM programmes (www.tijbmr.org & www.ijbmr.org).

Meanwhile, Al-Musleh (2011) studied TQM in the construction companies in the state of Qatar and concluded that the perception of the concept of TQM, which is taken as a "totality" concept, does not exist and the implementation of TQM in Qatar is still weak. This is also contended by Zairi (1996) who revealed that the region, comprising Middle Eastern countries in general, is a long way from maturity in terms of the total quality practices and organizational culture and climate that are needed to implement TQM. Misunderstanding and lack of awareness towards the TQM concept in construction companies in Qatar could lead to the rejection of the idea and build obstacles that could again lead to adoption failure.

In Saudi Arabia, one of the first studies related to TQM practices in the Arab Region was conducted by Curry and Kadasah (2002). The authors tried to explore the problems facing TQM implementation and key TQM factors in Saudi Arabia. The findings revealed that a clear and thorough understanding of TQM concept and philosophy is critical for successful implementation of TQM.

Alternate research by Alhwairini and Foley (2012) was oriented towards scrutinizing Not-For-Profit (NFP) organizations in the Kingdom of Saudi Arabia in the given background of TQM. Their conclusions pointed that significant number of managers in these firms have a traditional management technique whereas leadership is required towards customer focus, continuous improvement, innovation, motivation, development, involvement, and empowerment. Practitioners could also take into account how management by process could help enhance employee participation (for instance, by manner of teamwork and problem-solving) and commitment—these results pointed towards the lack of TQM practices in Saudi Arabia.

As a matter of fact, TQM concept is comparatively new to the Arab world. As such, there has been a lack of knowledge with respect to the key components and the implementation processes of TQM practices and how they should be handled. In addition, significant portion of the research performed in the Arab region linked to TQM practices were conceptual and descriptive nature showcased the lack of empirical studies scrutinizing the TQM effects on organizational performance. The well-known literature in developing countries are eminently dispelled, rarely available, and mainly conceptual or case study-dependent, unlike the detailed and empirical literature of TQM strategy in Japan, US and European countries. As such, the research performed in other developing and newly industrialized counties can render a means for TQM implementation research.

With the given background of Turkish SMEs in Turkey, Demirbag *et al.* (2006) showcased a solid positive link between TQM practices and non-financial performance, while there is only delicate effect of TQM practices on financial performance. In a relative research, Clegg *et al.* (2012) performed a comparison between TQM practices and its link with performance within firms in UK and Turkey in a desire to elaborate the interlink between crucial success factors of quality management and performance. They quoted that quality management is majorly put into use in manufacturing and service industries but has more statistical deployment in the manufacturing sector. The key challenge for making quality management practice more suitable lies in an adequate balanced use of the various means of the tools and critical success factors.

In the background of Turkeys' Municipalities, Arslan (2011) deep dived the impact of innovative management (TQM, Strategic Planning, Performance Measurement) on local e-government performance of Turkish provinces. His results showcased that the provincial local governments which embraced innovative management practices sway to have greater local e-government performances. He also discovered that TQM was thought to be single handedly as QMSs certification by majority of the local officials. He scrutinized the statements of the Turkish local governments; 47 out of 208 had ISO certificates and the total quality activities of local governments were started simultaneously with e-government efforts.

This study contributes to the TQM literature by understanding TQM practices and their performance implications in the light of effect of national culture in these five countries which are believed to have different cultural, social, and economic environments. Additionally, most of the previous research works conducted to examine the TQM implementation in the public sector are lacking and are theoretical/conceptual in nature. Furthermore, such studies in the public sector lack the systematic empirical evidences exploring the TQM strategy and municipalities performance relationship.

This study attempts to examine the cultural effects on TQM practices and its performance implications in five countries (Turkey, Egypt, Jordan, Saudi Arabia and Qatar). In other words, this study contributes to the TQM literature by understanding TQM practices and their performance implications in the five countries which are believed to have different cultural, social, and economic environments. Additionally, most of the previous research works conducted to examine the TQM implementation in the public sector are lacking and are theoretical/conceptual in nature. Furthermore, such studies in the public sector lack the systematic empirical evidences exploring the TQM strategy and municipalities performance relationship.

Thus, this study is one of the first attempts to understand TQM practices in the context of the five countries and is believed to be the first empirical study to examine the Soft and Hard-TQM practices and municipalities' performance relationship. This study is expected to help enrich the global theory of quality management through examining the effect of national culture upon TQM strategy implementation with the help of the contingency theory.

In addition to that, this study has employed the quantitative cross-sectional research design in which the questionnaire was the main tool for data collection. The model of this study is developed in consistent with the relevant literature and aim to examine the moderating effect of national culture on the Soft-Hard TQM and organizational performance relationship.

Two
Literature Review

INTRODUCTION

The municipalities around the world have a number of common tasks and functions, such as public hygiene, waste management and control of environmental health. The municipalities are also considered part of local governments with their activities varying from one country to another. For example, in some countries they are responsible for housing and transportation within the cities, water and sanitation. While in other countries these activities are assigned to other sectors of government. Most municipalities rely on government support, self-sources such as taxes and fines, donations and other sources.

Many developing countries suffer from ineffective and poor performance of their public sectors, particularly service sectors that have direct relationship with the citizens such as municipalities. There are many criticisms directed to municipalities' performance in the media. While, there are few researches which have dealt with their performance problems and solutions. However, there are differences in these countries in the stage of improving their public sectors performance by implementing Total Quality Management (TQM) as mentioned earlier. This research aims to compare between five public sectors in five developing countries; Egypt, Jordan, Qatar, Saudi Arabia, and Turkey. The objective is to discover differences and similarities between them and to measure the effect of national culture on the relationship between Soft-Hard TQM and performance. The background of these sectors in each country is described as follows:

EGYPT

Egypt's population is about 78 million surviving on 5 per cent of its entire area. 97 per cent of the population lives in the Nile valley. The United National Development Programme (UNDP) has estimated that 23 per cent of the labour strength is in the governorates of Cairo and Alexandria.

Significant amount of the power is governed by central and not the local government (Abdelsalam *et al.*, 2010).

Egypt is a unitary nation that is a collage of 29 administrative sections, called Governorates, each of different sizes, populations, and resources. Governorates are administratively further clustered into cities and districts which are, further, clustered into smaller entities called neighbourhoods in cities and villages in the districts (Abdelsalam *et al.*, 2012).

Based upon official government statistics, there are 4,496 village municipalities and 199 town municipalities in Egypt. These comprise of more than 1,762 local councils, with about 53,000 total seats nationally. Local councils are accountable for many dimensions of local governance, like sewage, sanitation and roads (most of these municipalities are not considered full object).

The widely-criticized Local Administration's Law 43/1979, which essentially submitted local councils to Cairo's control, gives less power to the elected local councils than it does to the executive councils, since it only authorizes elected members of the local councils to supervise governorates and municipalities. Elected members of the local councils also have the right to oversee district budgets and make suggestions, comments and inquiries to governors. However, these powers are subject to constraints by the central government. The major problems include the provision of small budgets to executive municipalities and the rampant corruption within. According to Zaman website (2012), in comparison with Turkey, *Egypt's* as on date scenario is like or may even be more deteriorating than the ambience in Turkey during its 2001 economic crisis. *Municipalities* in Egypt are on the stage of bankruptcy. The local entities have some level of administrative freedom. Nonetheless, they are financially and politically controlled by the central government. Local governments represented in governorates, handle their operations depending on rules, regulations and legal needs developed by the central government. Alternatively, they have autonomy in how they render their service to citizens and how they handle their processes. As a result, governorates might be structured in various manners. They have a level of administrative autonomy, which when appropriately used, can render sound administration, entirely relying on the personality and abilities of the governor (Abdelsalam *et al.*, 2012).

There are many researches in Arabic language that evidences the lack of effectiveness in the performance of the Egyptian public sector such as universities, local governments and other service agencies. However, there is a scarcity of English language in the area of performance in Egypt's public sector, particularly municipalities. Most researches in the field of municipalities are dedicated to e-government or using information technology (IT) in public services such as municipalities in Egypt (Darwish, 2008; Abdelsalam, 2010; Kanungo & Jain, 2011)—for example, El-Messery *et al.*'s (2009) study indicated that municipal solid waste collection and management in the Egyptian areas recorded very poor performance levels.

There are many problems facing the Egyptian government sector, particularly the municipalities as evidenced by Moawad (2011) who highlighted the fact that in the presentation of world water week in Stockholm in August 2011, it was stated that many problems are faced by water and sanitation sector in Egypt.

JORDAN

The Kingdom of Jordan is located in the heart of the Middle East. According to the year 2011 census, the population of Jordan is more than 6.5 million. Jordan is categorized as a lower middle-income country with the average per capita gross national income of up to US $3730, according to the census of 2009. The Kingdom's economy is based mainly on the services sector, trade, tourism, and some extractive industries such as fertilizer and medicines. There are multiple ethnicities and religions in Jordan. Today, Jordan is divided into 12 administrative areas or Governorates—Amman, Irbid, Zerqa, Balqa, Karak, Mafraq, Ma'an, Tafiela, Jerash, Madaba, Ajloun, Aqaba. Each Governorate is managed by a Governor (Mouhafiz) who is designated by the Council of Ministers based on the recommendation of the Minister of Interior. Each province is divided into brigades and districts and Jordan has a total of 90 municipalities. Many researches in Jordanian Public Sector performance dealt with e-government or solid waste in municipalities as part of local government. Some of these studies dealt with Information Technology (IT) (Al-Habeese *et al.*, 2012), e-government (Al-Omari, 2006; Mrayyan & Hamdi, 2006), TQM and performance in health sector (Alolayyan *et al.*, 2011; Ababaneh, 2010; Al-Zu'bi & Judeh, 2011), e-services in government sector (Al Nagi & Hamdan, 2009; Alhyari *et al.*, 2012), high education performance (Forrester, 2011; Al-Tarawneh & Mubaslat, 2011), vocational and technical training institutions (Al-Fawwaz & Badah, 2012), private sector service industry performance (Zigan & Zeglat, 2010; Aboyassin *et al.*, 2011), industrial sector (Chapman & Al-Khawaldeh, 2002) and finally, in commercial banks (Jaafreh, & Al-abedallat, 2012).

In consideration of Jordanian municipalities, Bal'arabi research (2002) found the relationships among the determinants of the organizational hierarchy and the task outcome of the local administration at the governorate of Irbid Greater Municipal. He inferred that the lesser financial support rendered to the municipality guides in inability to cater towards the duty and handle the projects, and dilutes the administrative decision making. He linked such deficiencies to the scantiness of the firm's hierarchy of the municipality. In an alternate study, Al-Momani (2002) displayed that the solution of the local rule in Jordan has to be given critical priority, and the system of the municipality functionality should be reviewed again. Alternatively, there will be lacunae when changes take place in other firms. Considering on a positive angle, Jordan has been significantly putting their share of money in enhancing its sector, orienting at developing the performance of its public and private sector firms in terms of service provision, efficiency, accuracy, time and satisfaction (Obeidat, & Abu-Shanab, 2010).

QATAR

Qatar is an independent state in the Southern Arabian Gulf and is one of the Six Cooperation Council for the Arabian Gulf Countries (GCC) in addition to Saudi Arabia, Bahrain, Oman, Kuwait and the United Arab Emirate. Qatar is a peninsula located east of the Arabian Peninsula, surrounded by the West and is surrounded by the Arabian Gulf from the rest of the sides. It is approximately 11,437 square kilometers with a population of about a million and a half, according to estimates by the General Secretariat for Development Planning for the year 2009. It is inhabited by 83 per cent of the population in Doha. According to the Ministry, the web of municipalities and urban planning comprises of seven Municipalities—that is Doha Municipality, Al Rayyan Municipality, Umm Salal Municipality, Al Khor and Dhekra Municipality, Al Wakrah Municipality, Al Daayen Municipality, and Al Shamal Municipality.

Qatar's citizens are considered one of the highest income individuals in the world where per capita income is more than $85,000 a year, according to the International Monetary Fund (IMF) bulletin for 2008. According to Blanchard (2010), Qatar holds the third largest proven natural gas reserves in the world, and its small population enjoys the second highest per capita income in the world. In April 2011, the International Monetary Fund (IMF) ranked the country as second in the world with regards to GDP per capita, estimated at US$ 109,900. The IMF predicts Qatari GDP growth to moderate to 6 per cent in 2012. With regards to TQM and performance in Qatar, it has one of the lowest populations around the world and almost one of the highest booming countries, and it aims to solve the population problem which is not fit for rapid development of the construction movement. Therefore, Qatar seeks to increase their population by facilitating the immigration to the state. The main issue of this immigration is the entry of a number of cultures which are different from the Qatari society.

In tandem with other nations in the Middle East, there is lack of TQM studies in the context of Qatar—for instance, Chaker & Jabnoun (2010) who studied Barriers to service quality in Islamic banks in Qatar signified lack of empowerment, centralization, and transformational leadership as major obstacles to service quality in Islamic banks in Qatar with the "No" culture not found to be major. Expatriates perceived dearth of empowerment to be a major obstacle to service quality than nationals did and this may be elaborated by the high power distance among nationals.

Al-Musleh (2011) investigated TQM in the construction companies in the state of Qatar and revealed that the employee(s) are familiar with the quality issues Quality Assurance, Quality Control (QA/QC) but the concept of TQM, which is taken as a "totality" concept does not exist. It needs to be designed, implemented and more importantly, the employer needs to make the employee aware of the benefits it can bring to the working ethics and make life easy for everyone, rather than becoming a barrier. In general, the findings of this thesis suggest that the TQM can be successfully implemented in construction companies in Qatar. According to Al-Musleh (2011), the implementation of TQM in Qatar, a country recognized and classified as a leading liquefied natural gas exporter worldwide, is still weak.

In a similar study, Al-Khalifa and Aspinwall (2000) found that the awareness and understanding of the TQM concept was at a very low level and the TQM critical success factors were not well-known and practiced. In addition to this, they found a large gap between the number of respondents who are aware of TQM and those who correctly understand what it is. They, therefore, concluded that it is essential to study TQM application and transferability for the benefit of economy in Qatar, where the need is even greater owing to the lack of TQM information and understanding in the country. Zairi (1996) also revealed that the region, comprising Middle Eastern countries in general, is a long way from maturity in terms of the total quality practices and organizational culture and climate that are needed to implement TQM. Misunderstanding and lack of awareness towards the TQM concept in construction companies in Qatar could lead to the rejection of the TQM idea and build obstacles for adoption.

However, many studies in TQM were conducted in the light of private sector, such as construction companies (Al-Musleh, 2011), banks (Chaker & Jabnoun, 2010; Hossain & Leo, 2009), small and medium-sized enterprises (SMEs) (Salaheldin, 2009), industry sector (Al-Khalifa & Aspinwall (2001), steel industry (Pollit, 2010), and petroleum sector (Mellat-Parast *et al.*, 2007). There are also a few studies concerning the public sector such as e-government (Al-Shafi, 2008; Weerakkody *et al.*, 2011) but overall, there is still scarcity of TQM studies in the country.

SAUDI ARABIA

Many researches dedicated to the public sector in Saudi Arabia focused only on e-government and technologies to develop the performance (e.g. Al-Fakhri *et al.* 2008; & Alshehri *et al.* 2012) while others focused in the field of education and health sector performance (e.g. Maroun *et al.*, 2007).

TQM applications in the Saudi public sector are either limited or the researchers failed to examine Soft TQM; for example, Al-Qahtani and Methheb (1999) found that the efforts made to the application of TQM programmes in the Saudi public sector have been facing various problems and difficulties. In the seam vein, Alhwairini and Foley (2012) found similar result in their study on non-profit organizations in Saudi Arabia. There is lack of published articles in TQM and its relation to the national culture in the Middle East countries and particularly in Saudi Arabia.

In addition, there are only few published researches in TQM and performance in Saudi Arabia particularly in industrial sector. These researches include TQM applications in the food sector (e.g. Alsaleh, 2007), service sector with emphasis on education and healthcare (e.g. Abdelmoula, 2011; Darandari., 2009; Sohail and Shaikh, 2004; Al-Hoqail *et al.,* 2010; Hoskins *et al.,* 1994). Moreover, there are only few working papers presented in conferences, symposia and meetings in the field of TQM application in municipalities in Saudi Arabia and all of them are written in the Arabic language. In Saudi Arabia, there are 285 municipalities, of which, 16 are considered to be major municipalities for provinces and 269 other municipalities are for cities and villages. Their budget is largely dependent on the government in addition to their income from fees and penalties and fines. Each municipality has its own municipal council which participates in planning and strategy making. All municipalities are privileged with being decentralized on a large scale.

There is widespread criticism and dissatisfaction with the overall performance of municipalities in Saudi Arabia. Most of these critics appear in the media particularly in the newspapers as well as in many working papers presented in the symposia and conferences (Alriyadh newspaper, 2010). In a study aimed at determining the level of satisfaction with the services provided by governments sectors, the results confirmed the low level of satisfaction with municipal services. On the other hand, municipalities in many developing countries like Malaysian municipalities and Turkish municipalities made considerable progress towards the application of TQM and as a result, their performance has been continuously improving (Arslan, 2007, 2009; & Arawati, 2005).

Perhaps no study has investigated the impact of national culture on TQM in the public sector in KSA. Thus, this study is the first to analyze the effect of national culture on applying TQM approach on municipalities' performance in Saudi Arabia and some developing countries that are at different levels of growth and that reflect diverse cultures (i.e. Egypt, Indonesia, Malaysia and Turkey) as a comparative study.

TURKEY

Turkey has 81 provinces, 1,000 districts, 3,216 municipalities and greater than 35,000 villages (Ozcan, 2006). The Governor oversee the central administration at the provincial level and is accountable among other duties, for deploying the implementation of government policy at the provincial level (some of these municipalities are not considered full object) (Ozcan, 2006). Mayors are brought to power by universal suffrage every 5 years and so are their Municipal Councils. Villages have a Village Head (the muhtar) who heads an executive committee. There are three types of municipalities in Turkey: metropolitan municipalities, district municipalities (within metropolitan areas) and other municipalities (Ozcan, 2006).

Approximately 75.5 per cent of the population lives in the 325 municipalities which are largest according to data gathered by the year (2009). The balance left municipalities have an average population of about 4,000, which by international standards is a minute in number (State Institute of Statistics, Turkey). Reconstructing of public management or new public administration itinerary has been put into the contents in reform agenda started in the millennium. The reform agendas are declared by parameters including "civilianization", "avoidance of bureaucracy", "privatization", "budget reforms", "performance measurements" and "competition" (Demir & Yavuz, 2009). In the beginning of 2000s, multiple regulations had started to lay their foundations accordingly. In addition, in Turkish public sector, ample of alterations have been experienced in the past decade and few applications have been put forward in the private sector such as TQM, strategic management; performance appraisal systems, permanent staff applications, etc. ever since the start of 2000s (Seijts & Roberts, 2011).

Turkish municipalities depend significantly on central government grants which make up 50 per cent of their budgets. Municipalities are not legally given opportunity to increase duration of their local taxes base in order to enhance revenues. Numerous municipalities as such gets disrupted from acumen of resources. Devoid of resources aligned with constrained management capacity frequently signify that municipal services are inadequate and/or of substandard quality. Based on survey performed by TESEV, a meagre 33 per cent of the urban population is happy with the services rendered by municipalities and their associated institutions (AĐCAKAYA, 2009).

The level of service delivery to citizens is a grave botheration to the government. With the backing provided by the World Bank, government has put forward a Performance Measurement System which will render information on the scope and quality of services delivered and is required to lend an enhanced performance oriented management of local public services (Ozcan, 2006). Performance Assessment System has been established for a long period in the private sector in Turkey. A lot of scholars who researched few parameters of firm's performance in Turkey's private sector elaborated that many principles of TQM are well adopted by companies in Turkey (Demirbag *et al.*, 2006). Although, there are only limited research that scrutinize the performance in Turkey's public sector.

Performance measurement system is a latest introduced concept for the municipalities in Turkey. Period later to the regulation of law (Financial Management and Control Law numbered 5018) which made municipalities (populations greater than 50,000) necessary for building the strategic plan, significant change in the government processes has happened (Kýlýç, 2011). Period after regulation laws in 2005, municipalities in Turkey began to prepare their strategic plans for five year timeline. Each year, their strategic plan and performance programmes are revised (Kýlýç, 2011).

These laws render necessary requirement for laying strong foundation of democratic processes at regional and local level, mitigating economic and social bifurcation among municipalities and provinces as well as enhancing public service delivery (Kýlýç, 2011). The giant leap in the performance of Turkish Municipalities and the steps introduced by these municipalities to enhance the performance is one of the key factors for comparison with other countries' municipalities. Ever since the implementation of this chapter, it will showcase a preface of the past literature linked to the matter of performance, soft TQM, hard TQM and culture. The chapter orients to denote the lacunae in literature that has been ignored by past research and in doing so emphasizes the intent beneath the current research.

ORGANIZATIONAL PERFORMANCE

Overview

Despite the assessment of performance by scholars and practitioners for the last three decades or so, there is still no comprehensive model of organizational performance for all types of organizations. In the literature of organizational studies, a great deal of attention has been paid to examine the determinants of the organizational performance. That is because of the importance of the subject in reflecting the path of development for any organization, and because of the implications of these studies on organizational effectiveness and competitiveness.

In the global context, the competition has been significantly increasing in quantity and quality. Essentially, it has been well known in the management literature that the organizational performance is considered to be one of the most important constructs in the field of strategic management and organizational studies (Combs, Crook & Shook, 2005).

Therefore, over the last few decades, both academics and practitioners conducted considerable amount of research work on organizational performance seeking to understand the antecedents, processes, and other factors that can increase the organizational outcomes (Jing & Avery, 2008). Additionally, this bulk of research was driven by the practical importance of the organizational performance concept that comes from top managers who they are always concerning about the long term success and competitiveness of their organizations (Finkelstein & Hambrick, 1996).

The main objective of organizations in the service and public sector is to provide customers and citizen with products and services that meet their needs and satisfy their desires (Al-Marri *et al.*, 2007). Therefore, many researchers have extended their works to explore the determinants of effective performance in the service sector.

Performance Definition

In today's changing and competitive business environment, it has been widely emphasized that measuring organizational performance is very important to evaluate the success of organizational strategy direction (Neely, 1999). Moreover, it is impossible to improve a business entity without measuring its current situation. However, although there has been an extensive research work conducted in the literature regarding organizational performance, there is no universal agreement among scholars on how organizational performance should be defined. Responding to the need to explain the term, Antony and Bhattacharyya (2010) defined the organizational performance as the measure that is used to evaluate and assess the success of an organization to create and deliver the value to its external as well as internal customers. According to Feisthammel & Massot (2005), performance is the evaluation of results whereas Nyhan & Martin (1999) defined performance measurement in the context of public sector as the timely collection and reporting of information regarding the efficiency, quality and effectiveness of government programmes. There are varying measurements of performance, based on their definitions and aims. The successful TQM implementation could enhance over one single dimension of performance including reduced cost, increased satisfaction level etc. (Prajogo & Sohal, 2006).

Performance Measurement

According to Neely (1999) & Williams (2004), Performance measurement is a basic management technique and has been used since 1910. In the 1990s, it was widely developed in large organizations as a means to measure performance and enhance strategic management functions (Micheli & Manzoni, 2010; Rantanen *et al.*, 2007). Based on the study by Sila &

Ebrahimpour (2002), TQM survey research has taken a new direction which is the measurement of the link between TQM factors and prior dimensions of performance. Hence, a single performance measure is not sufficient as a proxy to the whole performance. Prior studies brought forward appropriate measure for performance in TQM application.

Nevertheless, performance measure may be utilized for varying purposes and there is no one suitable performance measure for the entire purposes (evaluation, control, budgeting, motivation, etc.) (Behn, 2003). According to Otley (1980), organizational performance measure should present the significant dimensions of the required organizational or managerial performance.

Performance measurement has been associated with terms such as promotion, celebration, learning and improvement and it has been in existence for a significant amount of time, considered as a critical element of the decision-making process. Performance measurement can be used for many varying reasons such as; monitoring activities within business units through time, diagnosing issues and adopting corrective action, facilitating continuous improvement in important areas and promoting behaviour in such a way that would help sustainability of competitive advantage. On the whole, performance measurement refers to an important portion of management processes that attempts to carry out an identification of the poor performing sections or the opportunities for the purpose of the development of effective plans.

According to Otly (1999), management accounting literature mostly confined to financial performance. While this financial performance is important, it is insufficient on its own. Despite the fact that financial indicators are the widely acknowledged performance measurements, increasing acknowledgement of such on their own leads to a confined view of the organizational performance. The issues related to financial measures are short-term views, imbalance, prior performance information compared with ongoing operation which and other outcomes are highlighted as opposed to managerial efforts. Therefore, financial measures is said to provide superior performance information when utilized along with non-financial measures.

In the past few years, many performance measurement methods were proposed to meet the changing shift from financial measures to the suggestion of non-financial performance measures along with novel financial measures including the Balanced Scorecard (Kaplan & Norton, 1992, 1996, and 2001); the Performance Pyramid (Lynch & Cross, 1991); the Results and Determinants Framework (Fitzgerald *et al.*, 1991); Tableu de Bord (Bourguignon *et al.*, 2004); Epstein & Manzoni, 1997 among others. According to Strohhecker (2007), a significant and strong positive relation exists between the use of multiple performance measures and firm's performance. In addition, some studies make use of both financial and non-financial performance measures. Moreover, Chakravarthy (1986) & Martinez-Costa (2009) stated that organization performance is a phenomenon full of complexity as it requires over a single criterion to describe it. In actuality, literature acknowledges performance as a construct covering multiple intentions and phases within the organization. This is the reason why the performance measurement is a challenge particularly when the elements to be measured are ever-changing.

Performance measurement is considered as a process that assesses progress to achieving pre-planned goals, such as information on efficiency with which resources are made into goods and services, the quality of outputs and their outcomes, the effectiveness of government operations in the light of particular contributions to programme aims (Amaratunga *et al.,* 2001). According to Pavlov & Bourne, 2011, performance measurement can be used to provide information about past performance and to inform and communicate future direction and performance, intensifying the cycle of reflection of performance and behaviour.

Nevertheless, there is an absence of consensus regarding the most suitable approach to measure organizational performance. This is evidenced by a study conducted by Richard *et al.,* (2009) who reviewed a total of 213 articles concerning performance variable in four main academic management journals published from 2005-2007 and they revealed that 207 performance measures were utilized. The differences in the methods was compounded by the differences in the utilization of single, multiple and aggregated measures; differences that imply ambiguity in the theoretical definition of performance and the lack of consistency in the methodological formulation of the used constructs. Hence, an effective positive scientific comparison between the researches becomes a challenge and it is difficult to justify the normative suggestions and their degree of prescriptive validity in the use of varying performance measures. Moreover, as performance is just one type of effectiveness indicator, earlier studies disagreed on the definition of organizational effectiveness (Moynihan & Pandey, 2005). Therefore, attempts at measuring organizational performance calls for the initial explicit recognition of the reasons behind the choices and the trade-offs outcome.

In the context of government sector (municipalities), the non-financial performance part of performance is suitable to be measured in governmental organizations (Kaplan & Norton, 2000). This type of performance is critical in the evaluation of organizational performance attempts at TQM implementation in local government. TQM literature including the study conducted by Sila & Ebrahimpour (2002) evidenced the relation between TQM and organizational performance in many dimensions like financial performance, customer satisfaction and operational outcome. TQM implementation has also positively resulted in financial and non-financial performance improvement (Yasin *et al.,* 2004).

According to Dent (1990), a serious utilization of non-financial measures of performance would lead to a complete indictor of achievement of the strategic goal of the organizations.

In the context of the public sector, many studies in literature have concentrated on performance measurement as a tool in the assessment of performance and in the demonstration of accountability through the reporting of programme processes. A variety of applications has been brought forward in literature and their uses in performance measurement in the context of healthcare delivery like wait times (Kelman & Friedman, 2009), measuring the degree of citizen satisfaction of government agency services (Wichowsky & Moyhinan, 2008), the programmes efficiency and effectiveness like education and other services in the municipal level including policing, and public organizations delivery (Sanger, 2008).

Researchers such as Abas & Yaacob (2006), Ballantine *et al.,* (1998), Gomes & Miranda Gomes (2011), Haubrich & Mclean (2006) and Padovani & Orelli (2010) proposed some dimensions of organizational performance variables in the context of public organizations according to the differences in performance dimensions in prior studies. Moreover, Kloot & Martin (2000) investigated two main levels of local government namely, local government in nature and local government in similar municipalities. Initially, public organizations have different and diversified stakeholders with many differing interests; this includes government, local community, public organizations, voluntary sector partner, business community, consumer and government services' clients, employees, suppliers and political leaders etc. Secondly, public organizations stress on community as opposed to certain group of customers. The policies of the municipality and their decisions impact the community at large and not just those who are availing their services. Varying principles should be available as ways to base measurement on, such as the following seven principles of performance measurement design offered by Maskell (1989):

(i) The measures must be related to the firm's manufacturing strategy in a direct way.
(ii) The adoption of non-financial measures is a must.
(iii) Measures should be acknowledged to differ between locations while one measure is not appropriate for the entire department or sites.
(iv) It should be kept in mind that measures change with the circumstances.
(v) The measures must be user-friendly.
(vi) The measures should follow a fast feedback mechanism.
(vii) The measures designs should encourage continuous enhancement as opposed to just simply monitoring.

Moreover, several authors have proposed various components of the performance measures; for instance, Bititci (1997) contended that there are five main components which consider measures as well as people. They are stakeholders, control criteria, external measures, objectives of improvement and internal measures. On the other hand, Otley (1999) proposed five differing components including objectives, strategies, targets, rewards and flows of information in the form of feedback and feed-forward loops.

Various models of organizational performance measurement were brought forward by studies such as Keegan *et al.,* (1989), Brown (1996), Azzone *et al.,* (1991), Olve (1999), Eccles (1991), Neely (1999), & Van de Van (1980). However, in today's changing and competitive environment, it has been widely emphasized that measuring organizational performance is very important to evaluate the success of organizational strategy direction (Neely, 1999). Moreover, it is impossible to improve a business entity without measuring its current situation. However, although as we stated there has been an extensive research work conducted in the literature regarding organizational performance, there is no universal agreement among scholars on how organizational performance should be defined (Ford & Schellenberg, 1982; Johannessen, Olaisen, & Olsen, 1999). Responding to the need to explain the term, Antony & Bhattacharyya (2010) defined the organizational performance as the measure that is used to evaluate and assess the success of an organization to create and deliver the value to its external as well as internal customers.

Models of Organizational Performance Measures

As it has been mentioned earlier, due to the concern shown regarding the survival of organizations in today's ever-changing marketplace, both academics and practitioners have conducted huge research studies investigating the organizational performance term and its determinants (Johannessen, Olaisen, & Olsen, 1999). However, the question regarding what is the most appropriate measure of organizational performance has been the issue of growing importance among researchers and practitioners alike (Jusoh, Ibrahim, & Zainuddin, 2008). To say the same in different way, there has been a lack in consensus among researchers about the meaning of the organizational performance term that, despite the extensive research work, remains a debatable issue (Johannessen, Olaisen, & Olsen, 1999). Murphy, Trailer & Hill (1996) in their review on the measurements of performance identified 71 different measures using both financial as well as non-financial indicators to measure the organizational performance. In the following Table (2.1), some of the studies regarding Dimensions of Performance Measures.

Table 2.1: Some of Dimensions of Performance Measures

Studies	*Year*	*Dimensions of performance measures*
Sink and Tuttle Performance Measurement model (S&T; Sink and Tuttle, 1989, 1990)	1985	Effectiveness, efficiency, quality, productivity, quality of work life, innovation, and profitability/ budgetability,
The Strategic Measurement Analysis and Reporting Technique system (SMART; Cross and Lynch, 1988)	1988	Market, financial, customer selection, flexibility, productivity, quality, delivery, process time, cost
World Class Manufacturing Performance Measurement system (WCMPM; Maskell, 1989, 1991)	1989	Quality, delivery, production process times, flexibility, costs
The performance measurement matrix (Keegan *et al.,* 1989)	1989	Financial and non-financial, internal and external.
The performance pyramid system (PPS) Judson (1990).	1990	Quality, delivery, cycle time and waste.
Dixon *et al.,* (1990) The performance measurement questionnaire (PMQ),	1990	The questionnaire consisted of four sets one each for the Supplier, Manufacturer, Distributor, and Customer.
Azzone *et al.,* (1991), framework based on time.	1991	R&D engineering time, Operations through-put, Sales and marketing Sales, order processing, lead time
SMART performance pyramid (Lynch and Cross, 1991)	1991	Market, financial, customer satisfaction, flexibility, productivity, quality, delivery, cycle time, waste
Skandia Business Navigator (SBN; Edvinsson and Malone, 1997)	1991	Financial, customer, human, process, and renewal and development focus
Results and Determinants Framework (RDF) (Fitzgerald *et al.,* 1991)	1991	Financial performance, competitiveness, quality, flexibility, resource utilization, and innovation.
Balanced Scorecard (BSC; Kaplan and Norton, 1992)	1992	Financial, customer, internal processes, and learning and growth perspectives
Multi-model Performance Framework (MMPF) of Weerakoon (1996)	1996	Motivation performance, market performance, productivity performance and societal performance.
Knowledge-based Measurement Model (KBM; Sveiby, 1997)	1997	Three sets of measures—growth and renewal, efficiency, and stability—for three intangible asset categories—employee's competences, internal structure, and external structure
Comparative Business Scorecard (CBS; Kanji, 1998)	1998	Stakeholder values, process excellence, organizational learning, delighting stakeholders
Bititci *et al.,* 1998, dynamic performance measurement system	1998	External monitoring system, internal monitoring system, review system, an internal deployment system.
Otley (1999), performance dimensions	1999	Objectives, strategies, targets, rewards and information flows (feedback and feed-forward loops).
European Foundation for Quality Management's Business Excellence Model. EFQM Business Excellence Model (EFQM, 1999),	1999	Two distinct subsets of performance factors, classified as enablers (leadership and process) and results (people results, customer results, society results)
Performance Prism (Neely *et al.,* 2002), (Kennerley and Neely, 2003; Neely *et al.,* 2001)	2000	Stakeholder satisfaction, strategies, processes, capabilities, stakeholder contribution
Dynamic Multi-dimensional Performance framework (DMP; Maltz *et al.,* 2003)	2003	Financial, market, process, people, and Future
In Municipalities (Chan, 2004)	2004	Financial Performance, customer perspective, Operation Efficiency, employee performance
Fuentes-Fuentes (2004)	2004	Financial performance, operational performance, employee performance

Some of the Models of Organizational Performance Measures are as follows:

a) Performance Pyramid SMART: Lynch & Cross (1991); Cross & Lynch (1992) stated that the Strategic Measurement and Reporting Technique (SMART) pyramid was created by Wand Laboratories. It reinforces the requirement of both internal and external focused performance measures which adds the rationale of cascading measures down the organization to enable the measures at department and work-center level to reflect the corporate visions along with the internal and external business units' aims.

The aim behind the performance pyramid is to relate organizational strategy to its operations through the translation of its objectives from top to bottom while it is measured from bottom to up. It encapsulates four degrees of objectives addressing the organization's external effectiveness depicted on the left side of the pyramid and its internal efficiency depicted on the right side. The process begins with the definition of the overall organization vision at the initial level, which is transformed into individual business unit objectives. This is followed by the second level of business units which have short term targets of cash flow and portability along with long-term aims of growth and position in the market. Meanwhile, the business operating system fills the gap between top-level and daily operational measures. Finally, four main performance measures namely, quality, delivery, cycle time and waste are utilized at the department level and work centers level from day-to-day. The advantage of the performance pyramid model is its attempt to fuse organizations objectives with operational performance indicators (Ghalayini *et al.,* 1997). It disadvantage lies in the fact that it fails to provide any method for key performance indicators identification and it fails to integrate the concept of continuous improvement.

b) Balanced Scorecard (Kaplan & Norton, 1992, 1996, 2001): The BSC perspectives represent three kinds of stakeholders of any business (shareholders, customers and employees), thereby ensuring that a holistic view of the organization is used for strategic reflection and implementation, the success of these perspectives depends on the fact that the perspectives themselves and the measures chosen have to be consistent with organizational strategy Bevanda *et al.,* (2011).

In the current times, the Balanced Scorecard (BSC) is the most widely used performance measurement framework in both profit and non-profit organizations. Its widespread use is evidenced by the adoption of 80 per cent of large US companies in 2004, making it the most widely used management tool for performance improvement (Hillstrom, 2009). Currently, BSC is no stranger to public and non-profit sectors (Niven, 2003).

The BSC framework is created to reinforce financial accounting measures along with performance criteria from three non-financial dimensions or views (customers, internal business processes and employee learning and development) providing effective indicators that reinforce long-term planning. Organizations are enabled through the balanced score card to keep abreast of financial outcome while at the same time to monitor the progress in developing capabilities and purchasing the intangible assets needed for future development (Kaplan & Norton, 1996). The framework is superior to traditional measurement systems in that it relates long-term strategy with short-term targets and hence enabling the budget process to lead to superior resources allocation (Norreklit, 2000). The BSC is the most commonly utilized performance measurement framework in profit as well as non-profit organizations in both developed and developing nations (Sinkovic' *et al.*, 2011). The implementation of BSC directs to the following conclusions:

1. The implementation of performance measurement systems like the BSC entails challenges whatever the implementation method employed.
2. Implementing such systems in a developing country entails problems that may not be faced in developed countries.
3. The implementation issues faced in the developing country have been largely ignored and unexamined.
4. The assumptions characterizing the system may be contradictory to the culture of management in the developing country.

According to Kaplan & Norton (1993), the BSC implementation process comprises of four of the following phases:

1. The translation of the vision and the achievement of consensus,
2. The communication of objectives, setting of goals and relating strategies,
3. The establishment of targets, allocation of resources and establishment of milestones, and finally
4. The provision of feedback and learning.

The basic BSC advises managers to consider their organizations from many facets which are encapsulated in the following four main questions: (Kaplan & Norton, 1992; Kaplan & Norton, 1996a)

1. How do we look to shareholders (comprising the financial perspective)?
2. How do customers see us (the customers' viewpoint, along with customer satisfaction measures)?
3. What must we excel at (the perspective of internal processes and the stress on performance measures, it is a description of organizational operations and shareholders' and customer satisfaction)?

4. Can we continue to improve in value creation (the development of staff and learning viewpoint, stressing on knowledge creation and innovation)?

In sum, Kaplan & Norton (1996a) provided four BSC viewpoints: financial, customer, internal, learning and growth; measures that are basic, precise, in which financial perspective is measured through Return On Investment (ROI), with economic value added, customer perspective is measured by satisfaction, retention, market and account share, internal perspective is measured by quality, response time, cost and novel product offers and finally, learning and growth perspective is measured by employee satisfaction and the availability of information systems. Kaplan (2001) concluded that BSC is a useful tool in the management of not-for-profit organization as it facilitates.

Bridging the gap between unclear mission and strategy statements with daily operational measures, enabling a process in which an organization can develop strategic focus; shifting the organizational focus from programmes and initiatives to the desired results of these programmes and initiative;, assisting organizations to bypass the vision that they possess strategy because they are managing a differing non-united group of programmes and initiatives; and finally, allowing organizations to create an alignment of initiatives, departments, and individuals in such a way that they support each other in an attempt to achieve dramatic performance enhancements.

(c) *Multi-model Performance Framework (MMPF) of Weerakoon (1996):* The Multi-model Performance Framework (MMPF) is a model developed by Weerakoon in an attempt to measure organizational performance. It contains four dimensions of organizational performance namely, motivation performance, market performance, productivity performance and societal performance. All these dimensions have been appropriated to measure items. The measurement of every item through these dimensions is described as follows:

The motivation performance measures the equity of the company to employees, the training function offered to the employees, employee job satisfaction, employee job security, environmental factors impacting the job. The market performance measures the success level of the introduction of novel or modified products for customer satisfaction, product/service competitiveness, and the ability to satisfy customers. The productivity performance measures the material usage efficiency, labour and capital use. The societal performance measures the rights of consumers, acknowledgement of the need for environmental protection, extension of the product/market, and provision of opportunities to employees.

Fitzgerald *et al.*, (1991) published a research concerning performance measurement that considers performance at six dimensions. According to them, their framework (RFD) considers six performance dimensions namely, financial performance, competitiveness, quality, flexibility, resource utilization, and innovation. They presented the RDF and provided example of performance aspects throughout the six dimensions. In detail, there are four kinds of financial performance which are profitability, liquidity, capital structure, and market ratios; three types of competitiveness which are relative market share and position, sales growth, measures of customer base; twelve factors of quality which are reliability, responsiveness, aesthetics/appearance, cleanliness/tidiness, comfort/friendliness, communication, courtesy, competence, access, availability and security; three factors of flexibility which are volume flexibility, delivery speed flexibility and specification flexibility and two factors for resource utilization which are productivity and efficiency and finally two factors for innovation which are performance of the innovation process and performance of individual innovation.

Chan (2004) conducted a survey of US and Canadian municipal governments and utilized various organizational performance measures. Despite the inapplicability of all his measures to other municipal governments, he summarized performance perspectives in the following way:

Financial Performance: This is measured by cost per unit, bond rating, debt ratio, debt management standards, property tax revenue as a percentage of the total city revenues, increase accessible tax base, cost of municipal services as the percentage of the income of median household, budget documents, financial trends, office management and finance.

Customer Perspectives: This is measured by the rate of customer satisfaction, customer satisfaction index, the rate of customer service, complaints, increased dependability in leadership, rate of service delivery by citizens as relayed by the citywide phone survey, national magazine/ survey ranking of the best cities for business, and your city your choice survey.

Operation Efficiency: It is measured by productivity, response time, cycle time, cost per capita, cost per kilometer of road maintenance, cost for water and sewage treatment, average ridership trips for the entire transit services, city support programmes and services increased awareness, and parks bureau-budget document or parks bureau.

Innovation and Change: It is measured by employee satisfaction index, rate of turnover, saved hours, performance contract, number of fragile neighbourhood, threats to or stability of city's quality of life index, and job increase.

Employee Performance: It is measured by customer service ratings, data of employee suggestion, percentage of training dollar in comparison to base salaries, number of departments applying annual training plans and completing goals, high quality employees' increased retention, representation of female workforce.

Based on the usage of self-rating assessments (Govidarajan & Gupta, 1985), Fuentes-Fuentes (2004) created ten items of perceptual statements in an attempt to measure organizational performance which is divided into financial performance including profit growth, profitability growth; operational performance including sales, growth, market share growth, reduction of customer complaints, customer satisfaction level, defects in the products/services level, the meeting or exceeding of customer demands by products/services; employee performance including employee satisfaction level, and absenteeism level. Fuentes-Fuentes (2004) evidenced a significant correlation between the objective and subjective measures in his attempt to validate the perception of the financial performance items collected with the objective information.

After the findings of correlation were obtained, he revealed a positive and significant correlation between subjective financial performance and objective data of performance. The selection of suitable elements to measure performance of municipalities is carried out from the review of prior studies.

Organizational Performance and Culture

Several researchers have dedicated their studies to the relationship between culture and performance. Among them are Abu-Jarad *et al.,* (2010) who provided an overview of the prior studies concerning the relationship between culture and performance, the prior studies are summarized as follows:

Lee & Yu (2004) examined the Corporate Culture and Organizational Performance of 72 manufacturing, hospital and insurance companies in Singapore through a stratified random design. They aimed to investigate the possible existence of a relation between firm culture and organizational performance of the organization with the help of the Organizational Culture Profile (OCP) (Chatman & Jehn, 1994) which was developed by O'Reilly *et al.,* (1991). They revealed that culture affected many organizational processes and performance.

Kotter & Heskett (1992) investigated the relation between Corporate Culture and Performance in 207 firms from 22 various industries through different methods. They revealed that corporate culture significantly affects the firm's long term economic performance and firms having cultures that stress on customers, stockholders and employees and leadership at all levels, displayed superior performance to their counterparts by a huge difference. Denison (1990) also dedicated his study to examining the relationship between corporate culture and performance. He based corporate culture on the perceptions of the influence of corporate culture on organizational practices and conditions. He revealed that organizations employing participative culture had superior performance to other cultural types and he showed that organizational culture directly impacted organizational performance. Zehir *et al.,* (2011) examined the association between leadership culture and performance through the use of data collected from national and global firms in the manufacturing, finance and telecommunication sector in Turkey.

They distributed a survey to 295 employees and conducted analyses. The statistical analyses outcomes revealed the impact of culture and leadership upon firm performance. The study established a connection between types of organizational culture, leadership types and firm performance. The study concludes that organizational culture is the key to leadership types and performance as a positive relationship was revealed between organizational culture and firm performance. Van der Post *et al.,* (1998) investigated the association between organizational culture and financial performance of South African organizations. They revealed a positive relationship between the two and those firms that are more effective financially are distinct from other firms that are not effective in light of their organizational culture dimensions. They utilized 15 dimensions in their measurement of corporate culture as opposed to cultural typology. Either Ng'ang'a & Wesonga (2012) examined the effect of organizational culture on performance of educational institutions through the Organizational Culture Assessment Instrument (OCAI) developed by Cameron & Quinn (1999). It is an assessment instrument that is validated to examine organizational culture. The OCAI is a questionnaire having six categories wherein 100 points are distributed between four sub-items with each representing four competing values culture; type A represents a clan culture, type B represent an adhocracy culture, type C represents a market culture and type D represents a hierarchy culture.

They revealed that culture is a crucial element of effective performance of institutions. They also found a close association between culture and performance and emphasized that the culture type in the institution greatly affects its performance. In other words the development and perpetuation of a strong culture within an institution is imperative to support its high performance. Zhou *et al.,* (2011) attempted to measure the perceptions of organizational culture among employees working in China's public hospitals to show whether these perceptions are related to the hospital's performance. Data was collected from 93 public hospitals through survey questionnaire.

The observations were contradictory. While some organizational culture dimensions were related with performance, others were not. Nevertheless, these associations were parallel with hospital culture and performance expectations. For instance, hospitals having strong culture of social responsibility were inclined to have shorter-length of stay while those stressing on customer focus had longer-length of stay although they faced pressure to reduce length of stay from the government and medical societies. The concluded that organizational culture of public hospitals lack the ability to respond to environmental changes and hence, hospital managers and health policy makers should make it a point to stress on organizational culture and its significance in the performance of hospitals. Denison & Mishra (1995) created a model of organizational culture and effectiveness on the basis of four traits of organizational culture namely, involvement, consistency, adaptability and mission. They conducted their study through two associated qualitative case studies of five firms and a quantitative study providing an exploratory analysis of CEO perceptions of the four traits and their association to subjective and objective measures of effectiveness. Their study involved a total of 746 organizations whereby every trait was found to be a significant predictor of effectiveness criteria including quality, employee satisfaction and overall performance. They also found cultural strength to be linked significantly with short-term financial performance. They concluded that all cultural dimensions relate to different performance indicators.

Lenartowicz & Roth (2001) in their study investigated the impact of within-country subcultures upon business outcomes. Their data is based on four regional subcultures in Brazil and the findings indicate that subcultures are present and their variations affect performance. They also observed that strong subculture impacts business performance. Saxenian (1994) in his study involved the discussion of regional advantage involving culture and competition factors in two of US leading technology areas namely, Silicon Valley and Route 128. Through the comparison of the companies between the two areas, he expounded on the different performance of the two regional clusters and highlighted the local sources of competitive advantage. He concluded that there exists an association between regional culture and regional advantage. Tseng (2010) investigated the association between organizational culture and knowledge conversion, and corporate performance in the context of Chinese-centric set of societal, cultural and linguistic attitudes and behaviours. He made use of questionnaires and the findings revealed that a culture of adhocracy facilitates the conversion of knowledge and improves corporate performance as opposed to clan or hierarchy cultures. Gordon & DiTomaso (1992) examined the link between culture strength and two substantive cultural values and corporate performance. The data was collected through management surveys distributed to 11 US insurance companies in 1981 which were linked to asset and premium growth rates from 1982 until 1987.

The findings showed strong culture despite the content and substantive value of adaptability. Both are related with better performance in the two to three years based on both criteria measures. The result is consistent with Denison's (1990) findings implying that culture is a predictor of short-term impact upon organizational performance. Chatman & Jehn (1994) in their study examined the association between two characteristics of industry, technology, growth and organizational culture. They showed that technology is linked to organizational forms and performance. They made use of 15 firms that represent four industries in the service sector. They revealed the presence of the dimensions of stable organizational culture and they differ throughout industries.

In addition, particular cultural values were linked with degrees of technology and growth in the industry. They also revealed that industry is a moderator in the relation between corporate culture and performance. The results highlight an advanced understanding of the firm culture's determinants and performance impacts. Rashid *et al.*, (2003) conducted an examination of the impact of corporate culture and organizational commitment upon financial performance in the context of Malaysian companies through a structured self-administered questionnaire. The study involved 202 managers working in public listed companies and the findings revealed a significant association between corporate culture and organizational commitment. Both the types of firm culture along with organizational commitment impacted financial performance.

Khan & Afzal (2011) in their study attempted to expound on the cultural construct dimensions in various sectors organizations in the context of Pakistan. The study involved ten organizations with 478 questionnaires distributed to them. Based on the findings, organizational performance increases from negative (56%) to positive (92%) owing to organizational culture. In addition, core organizational values were shown to stress on particular themes including performance excellence. The findings revealed that organizational culture impacts outcomes including productivity, performance, commitment, organizational goal achievement, and the core value agreement. It was also revealed that organizational culture impacts organizations in the areas such as performance and commitment and it is a crucial part of organizational success.

Denison, Haaland & Goelzer (2004) in their article provides an overview of two studies examining the association between corporate culture and effectiveness in various national settings. The first one conducted a comparison of the results from 230 organizations in Europe, North America and Asia and shows an unexpected degree of similarity of results.

The second study, on the other hand, showed the results of target samples of 218 supermarkets in Canada, Australia, Brazil, US, Japan, Jamaica, and South Africa. Denison *et al.*, (2004) developed a theory of organizational culture and effectiveness with empirical support. It identified four cultural traits as positive relating to organizational performance: involvement and participation, consistency and normative integration, adaptability, and mission. Lau & Ngo (2004) studied the link between Human Resource System and the development of new products and services. They distributed a survey to a total of 332 Hong Kong firms and the findings from the survey revealed that organizational culture is a mediator between the HR system of firms and product innovation. They also revealed that organizational culture having development and innovation orientation directly impacts the performance of firm's innovation. Chow *et al.*, (2003) revealed exploratory evidence concerning the association between corporate culture and company size, competitive environment and corporate performance in the context of US companies. They revealed that environmental uncertainty considered as an aspect of industry dynamics—did not provide any impact in Taiwanese firm's corporate culture.

However, aspects of corporate culture differ from one country to the other and Chow *et al.*, (2003) related this aspect to corporate performance in various ways. Robbins (2001) in his study examined the organizational behaviour in terms of concepts, controversies and applications and he advocates that the stronger the culture, the greater will be the effect of organization perceptions upon performance. Various variables' intervention impacts employee satisfaction which in turn, affects performance. HR Marketer (2005) explained that prior studies have revealed organizational culture's direct impact on significant performance outcomes of organizations, such as customer satisfaction and business growth. In addition, organizational culture also impacts a wide array of businesses and industries ranging from educational institutions, churches, automotive sales and service, and fast-food retailing to home construction and computer manufacturing. In sum, corporate culture can impact the organization's bottom line.

Mercer (1996) stated that after his examination of cultural, behavioural and performance traits of over 1000 companies in the world, Denison revealed that corporate culture can impact sales growth and business performance. Azhar (2003) in his study examined strategic management in the context of Indian organizations. He claimed that corporate culture is the phenomenon that distinguishes good from bad organizations. It is one of the important ways in which organizations can improve their performance. He also stated that organizational culture is considered to have wide impacts on performance, and hence relegating it to the important topics that organizations should understand. Values are the basic substance of organizational culture which is considered to be unique to an organization. In sum, the prevailing culture in the organization greatly impacts its performance. Lim (1995) studied the relationship between organizational culture and performance through the review of research dedicated to this area. He claimed that the causal association between culture and performance is still ambiguous. Other researchers such as Kreitner & Kinicki (2008) & Damanpour (1992) tackled the relation between performance and culture in their studies.

Organizational Performance and Total Quality Management

In the literature of quality management, there has been a plethora of research work conducted in relation to TQM strategy. Regarding the performance implications of TQM strategy, the majority of the research work confirmed that the adoption of TQM philosophy will eventually benefit all types of organizations in which it is applied (Sila & Ebrahimpour, 2002). To explore how TQM strategy had been studied, analyzed, operationally defined, measured, and its implementation evaluated, many researchers have conducted comprehensive literature review about the previous research work.

In studying TQM strategy, Ahire *et al.,* (1995) and Thiagarajan & Zairi (1997a; b;c) used MBNQA criteria as the framework. While Ahire *et al.,* (1995) reviewed 226 research works such as conceptual as well as empirical articles and case studies related to the quality management literature between 1970 and 1993, Thiagarajan & Zairi (1997a;b;c) focused only on case studies papers. However, Ahire *et al.,* (1995) found that the majority of the literature was conceptual and the published empirical work was inadequate. Based on that, his suggestion was to intensify the empirical work in relation to TQM strategy. Similarly, Thiagarajan & Zairi (1997a; 1997b; 1997c), after review of previous literature, categorized the TQM factors into hard quality factors and soft quality factors. While hard quality factors are those factors that can be measured and related to the system, tools, and techniques; soft quality factors are those intangible factors that are difficult to directly been measured such as top management commitment, customer focus, teamwork, training and empowerment, and effective communication.

From different perspective, Fynes (1998; 1999) reviewed the TQM literature that was focussed on validating the TQM construct and defining its critical factors. He, therefore, examined 20 empirical studies using the critical factors of TQM strategy that was previously identified by Flynn, Schroeder & Sakakibara (1994) as the framework for judgement. In other words, as the critical factors of TQM strategy, he used the following seven factors:

> (1) top management commitment; (2) quality information; (3) process management; (4) product design; (5) work management; (6) supplier involvement; and finally (7) customer involvement.

As an attempt to review the TQM literature related to the relationship between TQM strategy and organizational performance, Yong & Wilkinson (1999) reviewed 15 articles that showed positive and negative relationships between TQM strategy and organizational performance. In this study, it was found the reviewed articles were related to studies conducted in different countries investigating the TQM strategy and organizational performance relationship. Although, some of these studies mentioned positive relationship, others mentioned negative relationship. The study also concluded that the unsuccessfulness TQM initiatives can be attributed to the partial implementation of TQM strategy and claimed that for organization to enhance its performance towards achieving a competitive advantage, TQM strategy should be implemented fully and to be an integral part of the organizational operations.

In the same vein, Sila & Ebrahimpour (2002) conducted a comprehensive review of the literature related to the quality management. They reviewed 347 articles published in several journals between 1989 and 2000. Throughout their work, they identified 25 factors as the critical factor for TQM that constitute their study framework. According to this study, the review of the literature stated that customer focus and satisfaction was the most frequently discussed factor followed by employee training and leadership and top management commitment. Next to that was the teamwork followed by employee involvement, continuous improvement, and innovation. Finally, the quality information and performance measurement was the last major element of TQM discussed in literature investigated by this study. In addition to that, they stated that the quality management in the service sector may seem to be more difficult because of the intangibility of services. Therefore, they suggested that a comprehensive questionnaire and framework that include all the major elements of TQM should be expanded and tested to suit the context of service organizations. Out of 347 research papers reviewed in this study, only six studies were conducted in the Middle East including Saudi Arabia, UAE, and Qatar which constituted about 1.7 per cent.

In his meta-analysis for studies about TQM during the period 1987-2002, Baker (2003) stated that the relationship between TQM practices and organizational performance has been empirically supported. As previously mentioned, manufacturing organizations were the first to design and implement TQM practices whereas services-based organizations were far behind. Further, TQM adoption in the service sector has been growing rapidly in the global competitive business arena.

More recently, Tari (2005) identified nine critical factors of TQM based on reviewing the TQM literature. These nine factors are:

(i) customer-based approach, process management which are the most important;

(ii) management commitment and leadership;
(iii) quality planning;
(iv) management based on facts;
(v) continuous improvement;
(vi) human resource management including training;,
(vii) work team and communication;
(viii) cooperation with supplier; and
(ix) finally organizational social and environmental issues-related awareness.

He also pointed out that the literature has revealed that TQM and HRM are highly correlated and the latter found to be the basis of the success of the former.

In relation to that, Prajogo & Sohal (2001) tried to study the relationship between TQM implementation and innovation performance. They argued that the implementation of TQM will be influenced by the environment in which the organization operates and the strategy adopted by the organization. They studied the literature of the relationship between the TQM and innovation and then performance and they distinguish between two claims. The first one states that the TQM establishes innovation-oriented environment and then has a positive relationship with innovation and the subsequently performance (Dean & Bowen, 1994; Kanji, 1996; Mahesh, 1993; Roffe, 1999; Tang, 1998). Whereas others (such as Harari, 1993; Samaha, 1996), argued that the implementation of TQM principals may hinder the organizational innovation.

The mediating role of TQM has been studied by many researchers. For example, Fuentes-Fuentes, Albacete-Saez, & Liorens-Montes, 2004; & Prajogo & Sohal, 2006 studied the relationship between environmental characteristics, organization strategy and performance. Fuentes-Fuentes *et al.,* (2004) collected the data from 273 Spanish firms' from quality managers' level. They used casual model and to test the model by structural equation modeling. They found that the environmental characteristics influence the implementation of TQM and this in turn influence the financial, operational, and human-aspects of organizational performance.

Similarly, Prajogo & Sohal (2006) investigated the mediating role of TQM on the relationship between organization strategy and organizational performance. They used the data collected from middle and senior managers from Australian companies. The structural equation modeling techniques were used to test the casual model. Their finding supported the partial mediating role of TQM between business strategy and performance. In the same stream of research, Molina-Azorin, Tari, Claver-Cortes & Lopez-Gamero (2009) argued that the development of quality management theory was mainly based on three sources namely, the prescription of the quality gurus, the national quality awards, and measurements studies. They also found that the bulk of the reviewed research work has revealed that the successful implementation can improve organizational performance.

In the literature of TQM, there has been various trends identified by both academics and practitioners. First, the focus, initially, was directed to define the concept and identify its critical success factors. Later, researchers paid more attention to conduct empirical studies to examine the relationship between TQM and organizational performance and sustainable competitive advantage (Nair, 2006; Reed, 2000).

Apparently, the empirical research related to TQM and organizational performance relationship generated varying and opposite results. While some studies attributed the superior performance of some organizations to the adoption of TQM, other studies highlighted the failure of TQM practices to deliver the desired performance. Due to the mixed findings regarding the TQM and organizational performance relationship, many researchers carried out a literature review to examine the previous research work. Alongside with that many other empirical research works have been conducted to further the examination of the TQM-performance relationship. For example, Nair (2006) conducted a meta-analysis study based on the research published between 1995 and 2004. In his meta-analysis he tried to investigate which TQM factors were positively correlated with organizational performance. In addition, he attempted to examine the existence of moderating variables that may influence the TQM practices and organizational performance relationship.

Findings of the study emphasized the influence of TQM on organizational performance. These findings, however, emphasized the relationship with some TQM critical factors such as leadership, process management, people management, and customer focus and the overall organizational performance. This study also supported the existence of moderating variables in the TQM practices-performance relationship such as organizational structure, as in Douglas and Judge's (2001) study. He, therefore, suggested that many other contextual variables may be considered in future studies to put the TQM implementation programmes to specific organizations in specific context.

In this connection, Sila & Ebrahimpour (2005) tried to review the previous literature and then empirically investigate the relationship between TQM critical factors and business results based on a survey data collected from 226 US manufacturing companies. Based on an extensive review of the relevant TQM literature, they extracted the following seven factors: leadership; customer focus strategic planning; human resource management; information and analysis; process management; supplier management; and business results. Their findings showed that the number of articles empirically supported the existence of positive relationship were much more than the number of articles reported negative or no relationship.

On the other hand, their empirical results showed that TQM factors are holistic in that they must be implemented in whole and not on piecemeal basis to achieve the desired performance results. They also found that while leadership and information and analysis have strong performance implications, leadership and process management are the only TQM factors that have direct relationship with business results.

In the same line of research, Kaynak (2003) proposed a research model based on the previous studies to examine the relationship between TQM practices and organizational performance. However, his proposed model encompassed management leadership, training, employee relations, quality data and reporting, supplier quality management, product and service design, process management, and firm performance. The empirical results, based on the data collected from 383 business units operating in 48 States in US, supported the existence of positive relationship between TQM implementation and firms' performance. In relation to that, in their attempt to explore the relationship between TQM practices and firms' performance of 250 high tech manufacturing firms, Kaynak & Hartley (2005) used the cluster analysis to compare the performance of 250 high tech manufacturing firms based on their extent of TQM implementation. They found that high performing firms were extensively implementing TQM compared with low performing firms. According to that, they suggested that TQM implementation can be considered as a source of competitive advantage.

In their empirical study, Samson & Terziovski (1999a, b) examined the relationship between TQM implementation and organizational performance based on 1200 manufacturing firms of Australia and New Zealand. However, their findings showed that almost all the TQM practices found to be significant predictors of performance. They also found that the TQM behavioural factors, or soft TQM factors, such as leadership, people management, and customer focus were stronger determinant of performance than hard TQM factors. In the same vein, Rahman and Bullock's (2005) study conducted on 261 manufacturing firms in Australia showed the result that there is a positive relationship between soft and hard elements of TQM. In addition to the direct relationship found between soft TQM factors and organizational performance, they found that soft TQM factors affect indirectly the organizational performance through hard TQM factors.

Similarly, in an earlier study aimed to empirically examine the relationship between TQM practices and organizational performance. Lemak, Reed & Satish (1997) found that based on 60 companies, TQM strategy was associated with superior performance. In other words, their study showed that TQM strategy improved the financial performance of the studied firms. This was later supported by the empirical results obtained by Agus & Abdullah's (2000) study in the Malaysian manufacturing companies where they found that customer satisfaction resulted from the implementation of TQM strategy was positively related with the financial performance.

In a comparative study, Feng *et al.*, (2006) tried to examine the relationship between TQM strategy and quality performance and innovation by comparing the performance of companies in Australia and Singapore. The findings of this study were based on the data collected using a survey questionnaire returned from 194 Australian and 58 Singaporean companies. The results showed that leadership and people management are related to innovative performance while customer focus and process management are related to quality performance.

In connection to this vein of research, Brah, Tee & Rao (2002) conducted a study to examine the relationship between TQM and the performance of 185 companies in the Singaporean context. Their findings supported the causal relationship between TQM practices and organizational performance. Furthermore, the study also emphasized the importance of the behavioural factors of TQM strategy, such as top management leadership, customer satisfaction, human resource focus, quality focus. In addition to that, this study emphasized the importance of intangible TQM techniques such as strategic planning and information and analysis, to the organizational success and effectiveness. This study also suggested that there should be longitudinal studies and in-depth case studies as future streams of research in exploring the TQM practices and organizational performance relationship.

Since the area of the TQM-performance relation remained under researched, many other recent studies exerted huge efforts in exploring the relationship between TQM practices and organizational performance in developed as well developing countries. However, the results of many studies suggested that TQM strategy has been gaining a universal importance as a main driver of business excellence. This can be justified by the consistent results obtained by researchers. For instance, Lakhal, Pasin, & Limam (2005) examined the impact of TQM on performance of 133 Tunisian plastic transformation sectors. Their empirical results were corroborating the findings of many previous researches by supporting the positive impact of TQM on organizational performance. Following the same research stream, Kumar, Choisne, Grosbois & Kumar (2009) studied the TQM-performance relationship on the basis of the data collected from 15 Canadian firms. The findings of this study supported the positive effect of TQM strategy implementation on organizational performance.

It has been clear from the previous review of the quality management studied that the vast majority of research work related to TQM reveals that TQM strategy can positively impact the organizational performance. On the other hand, many other researchers reported the failure of TQM in organizational effectiveness. However, many researchers, such as Brah & Lim, 2005, have attributed the failure of TQM performance implications to many reasons. First, the lack of strategic focus of an organization creates the wishful thinking that TQM implementation can fix short-term problems and will have immediate results. Second, the lack of the top management commitment towards products and service in an organization affects the quality performance. Finally, the lack of supportive culture affects the successful implementation of TQM strategy as a change strategy towards improving the overall organizational performance. Categorizing the TQM factors into hard and soft factors has been a trend in the literature when studying TQM and performance relationship.

In this line of research, Gadenne & Sharma (2009) tried to investigate the relationship between hard and soft quality management factors and organizational performance of SMEs in the Australian context. They identified six critical factors based on the data collected from the top management of 119 returned questionnaire. Moreover, they found that the six factors in their study were benchmarking and quality measurement; continuous improvement; top management philosophy; employee and customer involvement; employee training; and efficiency improvement. More generally, their findings confirmed that for TQM strategy to have effective implications on organizational performance there should be a combination of hard and soft TQM factors to be implemented to positively affect the overall organizational performance.

In line with the previous studies, the results generated by Pinho's (2008) analysis confirmed that TQM practices are the major contributors to SMEs' organizational performance. His study used the data collected from 135 Portuguese SMEs to examine the direct relationship between TQM practices and organizational performance and the indirect relationship through customer orientation and innovation. This study, moreover, showed that measuring results, quality assurance system, and top-management training and leadership initiatives factor are among the most influential factors on SMEs' performance. Moreover, while it was found that innovation and customer orientation significantly impacted the SMEs' performance and innovation respectively, the impact of TQM and Customer orientation on innovation and SMEs' performance was not supported by the results.

At any case, the demand on high quality service increases as the society becomes higher in income, more knowledgeable, and matured culturally (Al-Mansour, 2007). Since its starting in the early 1980s, TQM has added new dimensions to the management practices worldwide. Moreover, the relationship between TQM and organizational performance has been empirically supported by an increasing number of studies. Besides, it has been widely argued that TQM principles, in support to the contingency model of TQM application, are equally applicable to different environments. Moreover, when applying TQM in the service environment, a modified model with compatible practices should be designed to reap the utmost potential benefits (Al-Mansour, 2007). In addition to that, many researchers emphasized that behavioural and human-focused TQM factors such as leadership, empowerment, customer focus, and involvement are important factors in service-oriented organizations.

TOTAL QUALITY MANAGEMENT (TQM)

Overview

TQM plays an important role in the improvement of private as well as public organizations and profit or non-profit organizations. It is also considered as a key aspect of the survival of the organization (Noronha, 2003). Despite its introduction in the manufacturing sector of Japan in the early second half of the previous century following WWII as brought forward by notable management leaders like Deming, Juran among others, there is a lack of comprehensive TQM definition in literature (Reed *et al.*, 1996). Reeves & Bednar (1994) highlighted that during the long history of TQM, it was inundated by multiple dimensions and definitions according to varying situations. Crosby (1979), Deming (1986), Juran (1988), Feigenbaum (1986) & Ishikawa (1985) provided definitions encapsulating the concept of quality with a strong emphasis on continuous improvement and customer satisfaction.

Currently, quality management is revealed to have evolved from classical inspection methods, through quality control and quality assurance (Yong & Wilkinson, 2002). Researchers (Mehra, Hoffman & Sirias, 2001; Waldman, 1994) defined TQM as an integrated, systematic, organization wide strategy that continuously aims to improve products services and organizational processes. Other researchers, also stressed on the continuous improvement of products and services in their definition of TQM, but coupled them with the reduction of costs, enhancement of productivity, performance and customer satisfaction. The implementation of TQM carries varying purposes including growth in productivity, environmental improvement, quality improvement, reduction in costs and waste, growth in sales and market share, customer retention and image improvement. TQM purposes can be generally categorized into internal and external purposes. The former is related to the influence of internal functions addressing process improvement such as increasing productivity, quality improvement, and environmental awareness. The latter is linked to the impact of TQM customer satisfaction and the demands of other stakeholders such as improvements of quality and environmental awareness which may lead to corporate image enhancement, increased marketing advantage, and adaptations to customer needs and other stakeholders. TQM also positively impacts solving problems and decision-making processes.

In addition, it is considered as a management integrative system to develop quality of services and goods across all levels and purposes. Arumugam (2011) also agrees that TQM has a key role in organization's continuous improvement. Following the Japanese dissemination of TQM teachings and practices, it gained wide reach in the developed world in the 1980s when the concept's application has disseminated throughout the world in different levels and success rates. They have also infiltrated the developing countries' industrial and service organizations including countries such as, India, China, Singapore, and Malaysia among others.

Although TQM applications had its fair share of attention in the services sector particularly in public organizations, there are still some gaps to fill in literature especially in developing countries. However, there is no doubt about the fact that TQM has become a worldwide phenomenon as more and more countries are applying for quality certificates such as ISO, Six Sigma, and Quality Awards etc. which are over 90 Quality Awards in over 70 countries. Samasn & Terzioveski (1999) gathered more than 1000 articles concerning TQM philosophy and techniques. Its vast literature does not negate the fact that studies concerning the relation between TQM and organizational performance are still few and far between. Additionally, there are only some studies dedicated to TQM and its soft and hard dimensions in relation to national culture and its effect on performance.

Also, TQM has transformed into a globally renowned strategic force in businesses guaranteed to lead to countless of benefits including waste reduction and overall performance enhancement (Juran, 1988). According him "the quality is applicable not only for manufacturing but for other enormous industries, government, healthcare, and academia". He added that in last century's productivity is this century's quality. TQM is more than a measure of competitiveness, it has a widespread effect and it holds the key to the determination of the state governance's and the public sector's efficacy. Wilkinson (1998), states that currently, the world is in the middle of quality revelation. It is accepted all over the world as management practice that is increasingly being adopted by organizations (Dean & Browen, 1994).

Throughout the years since its inception, TQM target audiences have also evolved from producer focus to consumer as citizens along with other stakeholders; hence it has been transformed into a human-centered and stakeholders-focused practice. According to Trompenaars & Hampden-Turner (1997), "technology do work by the same rules everywhere even on the moon". While this statement holds true for machines, it fails to do so for human-machine interaction. It can be stated that technology and culture are not related although technology like information technology that impact human behaviour may just be related to culture. In other words, there is an overlap between the hard elements of TQM linked to technology and soft TQM. The main aspects of TQM are contained within its soft aspects—that are linked to the human aspect and these are viewed as the main engine that controls quality.

Given the fact that organizations are increasingly adopting and implementing TQM and its diffusion is experiencing an increase, despite extensive researches dedicated to the topic, considerable interest still holds and this calls for specialized empirical studies to examine TQM on an in-depth way (Ehigie & McAndrew, 2005). This need is evident in the fact that in the service industry, TQM is still at an infancy stage of theory development (Vozas & Psychogios, 2007). In addition, barriers still exist while implementing TQM in both profit and non-profit organizations owing to bureaucratic culture. Prior studies regarding successful organizations revealed that they carried out TQM implementation based on their organizational characteristics, culture, structure and surroundings.

It is evident from the above discussion of literature that TQM is significant in the public sector and national culture affects TQM elements. However, studies concerning the public sector and the service sector in light of TQM are still lacking owing to their distinct nature from the production sector. Lakhe & Mohanty (1995) provided the following service organization's characteristics:

- Service organization creates either tangible or intangible services and directly provides them to customers.
- In the delivery of service, service organization develops mutual and direct interaction with customers.
- Service organization should always be ready for services delivery anytime the customers require them.
- Service organization should complete the provision of services within a time limit—the duration that is accepted by the customer.
- Services are characterized as un-storable and un-transportable.

The TQM past research done by its founders such as Deming (1986), Juran (1988), & Crosby (1979) changed the philosophy of business worldwide (James, 2008). The growing and intensive literature in the management field reveals that TQM practices have become crucial factor for organizations to achieve a sustainable competitive advantage (Harrington & Williams, 2004).

TQM as a Management Philosophy

Total Quality Management (TQM) is a management philosophy of management of growing interest in the literature of management in today's global competitive environment. As a strategy, TQM has been gaining an increasing attention by many researchers (Ehigie & McAndrew, 2005). TQM strategy, moreover, has been considered as a critical determinant of the success and survival of various manufacturing and service organizations as it is a source of competitive advantage, driver of innovation, and a determining factor for successful shift and cultural development.

A comprehensive review of the literature shows the importance of TQM strategy in manufacturing organizations (Arawati, 2005; Das, Paul & Swierczek, 2008; Sohal & Terziovski, 2000); service organizations (Saravanan & Rao, 2006; Yasin *et al.*, 2004); small and medium size enterprises' (Demirbag *et al.*, 2007; MohdNizam & Tannock, 2005, Sohail & Hoong, 2003); higher education institutions (Cruickshank, 2003; Dahar, Faize & Niwaz, 2010) and in public service organizations (NorHazilah, 2004). According to Prybutok & Ramasesh (2005), quality management had many phases in development started from Quality by Inspection (QBI), Statistical Quality Control (SQC), Quality Assurance (QA), and currently Total Quality Management (TQM).

The increase of importance and consequent implementation of TQM strategy has been the natural response to the demand of consumers' awareness and global stiff competition (Juran, 1995). TQM strategy, however, has been gaining an increasing interest among practitioners as one of the main factors in the creation of sustainable competitive advantage (Williams, Wiele, Iwaardeen & Visser, 2004).

The Quality Prescriptions by the Quality Management Gurus

In the past thirty years, the quality management concept has significantly evolved through the influence of the contributions of the leading authors in the subject including Crosby (1979), Demng (1986), Juran (1988), Feigenbaum (1986), Taguchi (1986), Ishikawa (1985), Groocock (1986) among others. The scenario is such that the TQM discipline has evolved on the basis of the above authors' prescriptions and models. More recently, organizations have a tendency to modify the above authors' approaches to quality adoption so it may suit organizational activities and objectives as opposed to depending on a single model (Motes & Jover, 2004; Yasin *et al.*, 2004).

Among these models is the zero defect proposed by Crosby (1979). Crosby (1979) stressed on prevention as opposed to inspection. He added that a clarified understanding of the quality standards should effectively and continuously be disseminated among managers for high commitment. Moreover, he also emphasized on the management's role in directing successful quality management projects, the employees' awareness as well as their participation. Quality according to Crosby (1979) is an on-going improvement process.

Along the same line, Deming (1986) is considered among the most acknowledged contributors in the field of quality management. He stressed on the utilization of statistical techniques like the Statistical Quality Control

(SQC) in the maintenance of quality processes to the specific standards in the activities of production. He also stressed on the importance of top management support in quality initiatives and the creation of an effective surrounding wherein the quality standards are supported and clear. Additionally, he stated that employees' contribution is a key factor for quality initiative success.

Another TQM pioneer is Juran (1980) where in his study (Juran & Gryna, 1988), the importance of top management support in quality management initiatives was emphasized to be more significant that the employees' role. According to him, managers should be exposed to quality management training in order to enhance communication throughout departments. He also stressed on the importance of the group in the successful design and implementation of quality management initiatives.

Meanwhile, Feigenbaum (1986) stressed on customer satisfaction as the key objective of all the initiatives of quality management. On the basis of this premise, the activities including engineering, production and marketing should be conducted in such a way that they achieve quality objectives to improve customer satisfaction. He added that the importance of quality training lies in four stages of processes of quality control which are standards settings, standards conformation, correcting actions and improvement planning. According to Feigenbaum, quality training should be provided in order for practitioners to be equipped with quality attitudes, skills and knowledge.

In another related pioneering study, Groocock (1986) stressed on quality's role to satisfy customers' expectations and eventually achieve organizational goals. He added that customer satisfaction can be satisfied through 'Chain of Performance' which covers the processes beginning from product design until the culmination with the customer. Similar to other quality pioneers, he stressed on top management role, employees' participation and quality training for successful implementation of quality initiatives.

Crosby's (1986) zero-defect was criticized by Taguchi (1986) by emphasizing that the important role of the quality department in the determination of product quality may be realized through the employment of statistical quality control tools. Moreover, Ishikawa's (1985) contribution to the field included his stress on the quality training's importance through the establishment and dissemination of quality-related knowledge. He explained the utilization of cause-and-effect in the improvement of quality performance. He was among the pioneers to emphasize the involvement of employees and the requirement of training them on the way processes can be monitored with the help of statistical-related analysis methods.

On the basis of the above discussions of pioneering contributions of various authors, it is notable that there are similarities and differences among the quality prescriptions provided by them in light of quality management. Despite the differences in the quality approaches, there is a consensus on some main success factors; for instance, scholars agree on the importance of top management commitment, quality training and participation of employees for quality initiatives success.

Individual approach of quality management has its own advantages and drawbacks and hence organizations have to be flexible in selecting the quality management approach they want to employ (Ghobadian *et al.*, 1994) as several factors may affect the TQM initiatives implementations including organizational structure, culture and environment (Yasin *et al.*, 2004). However, the universal applicability of the critical factors of TQM and the quality proposals introduced by pioneering quality scholars have not been developed on the basis of empirical studies (Saraph *et al.*, 1989) although several researchers have attempted to validate some of these approaches empirically through the development of instruments to measure critical factors of TQM strategy.

Definition of TQM

Although literature concerning TQM practices is rife with extensive work on the subject, no agreement among researchers has been reached on a standard TQM definition. In addition, TQM definitions vary from the method adopted towards quality (Reed *et al.*, 1996). It is evident that convergent and discriminant validity of TQM constructs exist in the extensive TQM literature (Hackman & Wageman, 1995). Various TQM definitions have been proposed. To begin with Dale (2003) defined TQM as the management method ensuring cooperation and contribution of all individuals in the firm to develop products and services that meet customers' needs and go over their expectations. In a similar definition, Flynn *et al.*, (1994) defined TQM as the combination of approaches that lead to high quality outcomes, through the maintenance and sustainability of ongoing improvement processes in an attempt to satisfy the needs of customers.

TQM was also defined as an integrated path in realizing sustainable high quality output while focusing on the maintenance and ongoing improvement of process and prevention of defect at the entire levels and in all organizational functions to satisfy or even exceed expectations of customers (Flynn, Schroeder & Sakakibara, 1994).

Moreover, other researchers like Kumar (2009) & Demirbag (2006) defined TQM as a management philosophy of holistic nature aiming for the ongoing improvement of all the organizational functions and allowing employees under top management leadership to contribute to the production and delivery of services effectively in an attempt to obtain competitive edge from rivals and to satisfy customers' demands and organizational objectives. In a similar manner, Pfau (1989) described TQM as a holistic method towards the enhancement of quality, productivity and competitiveness in the global marketplace and Flynn (1994) along with Kaynak (2003) described it as a management philosophy of holistic nature that improves the quality of the entire organizational functions in an attempt to satisfy or exceed customers' expectations and needs. On the other hand, Dean & Bowen (1994) defined TQM as a management method known for its principles, practices and methods. The principles originate from a set of practices directing customer contact, process analysis, group skills training, collaboration with suppliers among others while sustainable practices stem from many methods like quality function deployment, control charts etc. Despite the above many differing TQM definitions, they reflect particular commonalities in the light of key principles, practices and values.

Furthermore, other TQM definitions provided by researchers have their basis on TQM principles; for instance, Anderson, Rungtusanatham & Schroeder (1994) defined TQM strategy as a holistic approach to the overall quality of the organization built on key principles like leadership, continuous improvement, product/service design, continuous improvement, effective process management, customer satisfaction and involvement, and employees' training and contribution. Consistent with this view but from the perspective of changed management, Yusof & Aspinwall (2000) defined TQM as a management philosophy that can enhance organizational status through change initiatives. The authors added that TQM is a system that assists organizations in realizing excellence.

Along the same line, Kumar, Choisne, Grosbois & Kumar (2009) defined TQM as a management approach having a holistic nature that integrates organizational activities for the satisfaction of customers' needs and expectations and to achieve organizational aims. Meanwhile, Dean & Bowen (1994) recommended that TQM strategy can be viewed in the light of principles, practices and techniques with principles including customer focus, continuous improvement and teamwork. Every principle possesses a set of specific practices like customer relationships, quality and process control, and group training and skills. To guarantee effective employment, the practices should have specific tools including quality functions deployment, control charts and techniques for team building.

Mehra, Hoffman & Sirias's (2001) attempt to review literature for TQM definition highlighted human resources focus, quality tools, supplier support, a management structure and customer orientation as the main critical factors on the basis of which TQM should be defined. MBNQA was also cited by researchers to be the most suitable model upon which TQM should be defined despite the differences among the provided definitions (e.g. Dean & Bowen, 1994; Black & Porert, 1996; Rao *et al.*, 1999; Flynn & Saladin, 2001). Moreover, TQM can also be measured on the basis of some critical factors as recommended by researchers in TQM literature (e.g. Arawati, 2005; Li *et al.*, 2003; Saraph *et al.*, 1989; Sila & Ebrahimpour, 2002). According to Swamidass & Newell (1987), strategy is a series of actions' practices in order to reach organizational goals. On this basis, TQM may be defined as a management system comprising of many interrelated critical factors that assist organizations in developing an effective group of actions to realize pre-established organizational goals.

Popular National Quality Awards

In addition to the quality prescriptions provided by theoretical as well as empirical studies, several models have also been proposed in literature as guidelines of TQM implementation. Specifically, TQM strategy of organizations is mostly based on key national quality awards that have also been used by several studies as their framework (e.g. Tari, 2005; Sila & Ebrahimpour, 2002). Additionally, Chuan & Soon's (2000) review of quality management literature highlighted 17 National Quality Awards (NQAs) with majority of the Awards modeled on the basis of three influential quality awards which are Deming Prize, MBNQA and EQA. And despite the differences among these national quality awards, they are based on the same criteria of quality measurements (Sila & Ebrahimpour, 2002). This section provides a brief discussion of some of the most popular quality awards; the Malcolm Baldrige National Quality Award (MBNQA) in the US, the European Quality Award (EQA) in Europe, and the Prime Minister Quality Award (PMQA) in Malaysia.

The Malcolm Baldrige National Quality Award (MBNQA)

The MBNQA was passed by the US Congress in 1987 with the aim of helping companies to achieve long-term effectiveness. Following its initiation by the Congress, the award is presently employed by the National Institute for Standards and Technology (NIST) (Peschel, 2008). MBNQA considered the main factors of TQM strategy in its quality criteria (Kartha, 2004). It is widely utilized as a framework benchmark of national awards in many countries including Hong Kong, New Zealand, Singapore, and Sri Lanka (Chuan & Soon, 2000). The MBNQA comprises of seven categories and several items. These categories are explained below (Davis, Marcos & Stadning, 2005; Peschel, 2008):

(a) *Leadership*: looks into the director practices of top management.
(b) *Strategic Planning*: is concerned with the organization's development of its strategic plans.
(c) *Customer and Market Focus*: is concerned with how organizational policies determine customers' needs and expectations.

(d) *Information and Analysis*: it looks into the effective utilization of information to improve capabilities of planning.
(e) *Human Resource Management Focus*: it looks into the organizational strategies utilized for the entire development and use of potential workforce capabilities.
(f) *Process Management*: it looks into the design, management and enhancement of processes.
(g) *Business Results*: it looks into the overall performance of the organization against its rivals.

European Quality Award (EQA)

The European Organization for Quality along with the European Commission backed the creation of the European Quality Award (EQA) in 1991. EQA comprises of the European Quality Prize (EQP) and the European Quality Award (Conti, 2007). It consists of nine criteria and concentrates on resource management, employee's satisfaction and the way operations, products and services affect society (Chuan & Soon, 2000). These nine EQA criteria are briefly described below:

(a) *Leadership*: it examines the leader's role in the development and facilitation of the achievement of organizational goals.
(b) *Policy and Strategy*: it examines the manner in which organizational strategies can be employed through procedures and programmes.
(c) *People*: it examines the organizational plans and policies pertaining to the development and the use of employees' full potential.
(d) *Partnerships and Resources*: it examines the plans developed by organizations for the management and support of its effective operations.
(e) *Processes*: it examines the manner in which processes are designed and managed by the organization to produce maximized customer values..
(f) *Customer's Results*: it examines the performance of the organization in terms of its customers.
(g) *People's Results*: it looks into the organizational performance in terms of its people.
(h) *Societal Results*: it looks into the performance of the organizational in terms of society.
(i) *Key Performance Result*: it examines the organizational performance excellence in terms of its developed plans.

Prime Minister Quality Award (PMQA) in Malaysia

In order to improve quality and efficiency of the public sector organizations' performance, the Malaysian government set up many awards pertaining to management, innovation, and efficient employment of information and communication technologies (The Malaysian Government Official Portal, 2010). They include the Prime Minister's Quality Award (1990), the Public Service Innovation Award (1991), the Innovation Award for Joint-Research between Public and Private Sector, the Quality Control Circles Award (1984), the District Office Quality Award (1992), the Premier Information Technology Award and the Financial Management Quality Award (2001).

Among them, the Prime Minister Award is quite popular and it has a total of seven evaluation criteria for performance excellence; leadership in quality management, use of information and data in quality management, strategic planning process, human resources utilization, quality assurance output, quality innovation improvement project and finally, customer satisfaction.

Critical Factors of TQM

Researchers have consistently debated on the TQM practices categorization (Samson & Terziovski, 199a). Initially, the Malcolm Baldrige National Quality Award (MBNQA) was utilized as the most popular framework and was considered as a reliable TQM measure. In the present research, four out of five TQM soft factors and all hard TQM factors are adopted from the seven factors categorized in the MBNQA. The selection of soft and hard TQM factors is based on their significance to the public sector—other soft and hard TQM factors are more suitable to the private sector. On the basis of literature reviewed pertaining to quality management in the service sector organizations, some TQM factors have been investigated. The TQM critical factors that are commonly examined by researchers in their attempt at studying the TQM-organizational performance relationship are listed in Table 2.2.

Soft Total Quality Management

Soft TQM comprises of: the utility of HRM-style personnel policies to product commitment to quality and a management ideology that supports cultural change maxims, continuous improvement and customer satisfaction. Several researchers consider TQM as comprising of two interdependent but distinct parts. Soft TQM comprises of elements linked with human resource. Rahman (2001, 2004) stated that TQM deals with long-term natures and is characterized as humanistic. Soft TQM constructs are

Table 2.2: Critical Factors of Soft-Hard TQM

Critical Factors of TQM strategy	*Authors*
Management commitment	Ahire *et al.*, (1996); Anderson *et al.*, (1994); Anderson *et al.*, (1995); Arawati (2005); Black & Porter (1996); Crosby (1979); Deming (1986); Flynn *et al.*, (1994); Khairul Anuar *et al.*, (2001); Li *et al.*, (2003); Powell (1995); Saraph *et al.*, (1989); Silvestro (1998); Sureshchander *et al.*, (2001).
Customer focus	Arawati (2005); Brah *et al.*, (2000); Flynn *et al.*, (1994); Khairul Anuar *et al.*, (2001); Li *et al.*, (2003); Sila & Ebrahimpour (2005); Samson & Terziovski (1999); Yang (2006); Hoang *et al.*, (2006); Singh & Smith (2006); Gotzamani *et al.*, (2006); Drew & Healy (2006); Prajogo & McDermott (2005); Sila & Ebrahimpour (2005); Prajogo (2005); Tari (2005).
Process management	Wu *et al.*, (1997); Lee & Quazi (1999); Zhang *et al.*, (2000); Black & Porter (1996); Ahire *et al.*, (1996); Anderson *et al.*, (1995); Flynn *et al.*, (1994); Saraph *et al.*, (1989).
Education and training	Anderson *et al.*, (1995); Flynn *et al.*, (1994); Saraph *et al.*, (1989); Ahire *et al.*, (1996); Wu *et al.*, (1997); Rao *et al.*, (1999); Zhang *et al.*, (2000); Tamimi (1995); Drew &Healy (2006); Yang (2006); Hoang *et al.*, (2006); Hafeez *et al.*, (2006); Armstrong-Stassen *et al.*, (2005); Miyagawa &Yoshida (2005); Tari (2005).
Employee relations	Zhang *et al.*, (2000); Rao *et al.*, (1999); Saraph *et al.*, (1989); Anderson *et al.*, (1995); Black & Porter (1996); Drew & Healy (2006); Yang (2006); Hoang *et al.*, (2006); Singh & Smith (2006); Gotzamani *et al.*, (2006); Hafeez *et al.*, (2006); Armstrong-Stassen *et al.*, (2005); Prajogo &McDermott (2005); Sila & Ebrahimpour (2005); Prajogo (2005).
Quality data and information	Ahire *et al.*, (1996); Black & Porter (1996); Flynn *et al.*, (1994); Khairul Anuar *et al.*, (2001); Powell (1995); Saraph *et al.*, (1989); Sanchez-Rodriguez & Martinez-Lorente (2004); Sureshchander *et al.*, (2001); Wu *et al.*, (1997); Hoang *et al.*, (2006); Singh & Smith (2006); Gotzamani *et al.*, (2006); Armstrong-Stassen *et al.*, (2005); Prajogo & McDermott (2005); Sila & Ebrahimpour (2005); Prajogo (2005); Lagrosen & Lagrosen (2005); Miyagawa & Yoshida (2005).
Supplier relationship	Ahire *et al.*, (1996); Anderson *et al.*, (1994); Black & Porter (1996); Deming (1986); Flynn *et al.*, (1994); Powell (1995); Sanchez-Rodriguez & Martinez-Lorente (2004); Drew & Healy (2006); Yang (2006); Singh & Smith (2006); Gotzamani *et al.*, (2006); Sila & Ebrahimpour (2005); Miyagawa & Yoshida (2005); Tari (2005).
Strategic planning	Black & Porter (1996); Li *et al.*, (2003); Samson & Terziovski (1999); Sila & Ebrahimpour (2005);Wu *et al.*, (1997)' Drew & Healy (2006)' Yang (2006)' Hoang *et al.*, (2006); Gotzamaniet al. (2006); Prajogo & McDermott (2005); Sila & Ebrahimpour (2005); Prajogo (2005), Miyagawa & Yoshida (2005); Tari (2005); Bou-Llusar *et al.*, (2005).

variables as viewed by many scholars. A review of literature reveals that some prior studies have stressed on the soft and the hard TQM's impact on TQM's success and in turn organizational performance.

Based on the study by Thiagrajan & Zairi (1997a; 1997b; 1997c), hard TQM comprise of systems, tools and methods while the soft ones comprise of intangible elements that are almost impossible to measure. Although the findings of prior studies are inconsistent and inconclusive, it is notable that most of them concentrated on the impact of TQM elements directly without distinguishing between components with only a few of them studying the elements individually (Rahman & Bullock, 2005; Christos *et al.*, 2009). Their study's findings revealed that quality improvement is impacted by the adoption of soft TQM primarily and hard TQM elements secondarily. Moreover, a significant number of definitions place distinction between soft and hard TQM. While soft TQM is related with management concepts and principles including leadership, employee empowerment etc., hard TQM is related to quality improvement methods and tools. Soft-TQM elements are characterized by their long-term nature and hence must be stressed on and referred to, based on the organization's TQM implementation plan. The effective handling of the soft elements is only possible through reinforcements by the hard elements (Zairi & Thiagarajan, 1997). However the case, the hard element reflects the production orientation of the systems, data collection and measurement stressed on by the quality gurus. It relates to varying production methods such as statistical process control, layout changes, design processes and organizational procedures and the utilization of basic TQM tools for data clarification while the soft side works on human resource management and stresses on the requirement of culture change (Al-Tarawneh, 2010). Various studies concerning TQM call for future efforts to conduct a diachronic evaluation of TQM elements, the adoption outcome and the kind and level of relationships. There are five main factors of Soft-TQM that are acquired from many studies from literature:

(a) *Top Management Commitment:* TQM implementation in any organization calls for top management commitment as it is the core requirement to the driver of TQM application and results cannot be reached without it. It is also imperative for top management to comprehend TQM applications in a comprehensive way and guarantee that employees' responsibilities are clarified. TQM calls for the shift from 'management by control' to 'management by commitment' (Yusuf & Dang, 2007). The latter involves participative management and members' empowerment to concentrate on and realize total quality objectives and commitment to organizational systems that are developed to guarantee total quality (Ugboro & Obeng, 2000).

There is a unanimous agreement among researchers when it comes to the important role played by senior management commitment in the TQM application as their commitment is criterion to the entire strategy and action plan (Al-Trawneh, 2010). It is responsible for providing direction and motivation to organizations (Shores, 1992) to employ and implement quality improvement programmes (Idris, 2011). It is essential for organization's quality development as with support and contributions from them, ample resources will be appropriated to the improvement of training activities leading to better quality measurement, enhanced customer satisfaction and benchmarking (Ramseook-Munhurrun *et al.*, 2011). It is to such level that top management commitment to TQM applications is a critical determinant to TQM applications adoption. The commitment develops appropriate bases for successful TQM applications including values, goals and systems to achieve customer satisfaction, and to go beyond satisfying customer expectations and the development of organizational performance.

The entire TQM practices positively impact the internal and external performance and support from top management displayed the greatest effect upon performance (Jitpaiboon & Rao, 2007). In addition, leaders who are competent are able to carry out significant critical factors of TQM implementation in an effective manner (Idris, 2011; Das *et al.*, 2011; Idris & Ali, 2008; Idris *et al.*, 2003). In reality, everyone in the organization working at various levels either individual or group occupying positions in top management should play a part to enhance their tasks. TQM process can be effectively and successfully implemented on the condition that the whole organization acknowledges the responsibility and commitment to quality management.

(b) *Supplier Relationship:* The adoption of TQM is considered to be the first step that service organizations take to improve their performance. While prior studies stressed on supplier relationship as among the important elements of soft TQM in the manufacturing sector, TQM adoption is considered to facilitate service organizations' achievement of enhanced performance (Ramseook-Munhurrun, *et al.*, 2011).

Some studies dealth with TQM and supplier relationship as two distinct concepts. For instance, Gunasekaran & McGaughey (2003) revealed that TQM facilitates the enhancement of customer satisfaction whereas, Tutuncu & Kucukusta (2008) claimed that supplier chain management is viewed as a method for competitive performance enhancement through the integration of the internal process of an organization and the external operations of suppliers, customers and members of the supply chain.

Several researchers examined supplier relation as a distinct concept while others examined supplier relationship and TQM to be interdependent and integrative concepts. Both concepts have the common goal of achieving customer satisfaction. Despite the different methods of studying both concepts, most researchers deal with supplier relationship as a part of TQM such as Fotopoulos & Psomas (2009); Sila & Ebrahimpour (2002); and Khamalah & Lingaraj (2007), few studies examined both concepts as an integrated concept (Talib *et al.*, 2011). Additionally, literature recommends that both TQM and supplier relations are significant to organizational performance and only a few studied TQM and supplier relationship as one.

In actuality, quality management implementation has provided benefits to different kinds of non-manufacturing organizations such as public organizations (Sila & Ebrahimpour, 2002). There are many studies that tackled this significant factor in non-manufacturing organizations. Among them, is Khairul Anuar (2001) and Sanchez-Rodriguez & Martinez-Lorente (2004). Public sector is characterized by many suppliers particularly the commercial sector including governments, donors, non-governmental organizations, traders and other sectors of different organizations and other social organizations.

(c) *Employee Relations:* Employee relations are considered as employee participation, employee empowerment, employee involvement, employee fulfillment, employee satisfaction, delegation and empowerment, worker-manager interactions (Karuppusami & Gandhinathan, 2006). Many researchers who highlighted TQM critical elements conducted an analysis of the TQM critical factors such as employee relations in different ways or under various ways. Many critical success factors are brought forward by various writers in the light of their varying qualifications and background and work experience (Al-Zu'bi & Judeh, 2011).

Researchers noted that many TQM implementations lead to failure for varying reasons. From the cited reasons is the absence of employee relations, the absence of employee involvement and participation in efforts for quality improvement, resistance to change towards TQM owing to fear of change (Lakhe & Mohanty, 1994) or reasons stemming from individual as opposed to team (Tan, 1997). Moreover, Jones & Seraphim (2008) claimed that other factors hindering successful TQM implementation involves employee relationship such as communication problems or misaligned values. The concept includes staff involvement, fulfillment, empowerment and participation. Employees need encouragement to vocalize their work issues through varying ways. Quality teams, quality circles, inter-department teams and department teams should be created to fulfill this purpose. Employee participation can reinforce employee understanding and commitment to the company's quality objectives.

In other words, it is imperative for both teams and individuals to be acknowledged for their outstanding performance and achievement in quality management. Based on the study by Grandzol & Gershon (1998) and Anderson *et al.,* (1994), employee fulfillment hinges on the way organization continuously achieves employee satisfaction in terms of job satisfaction, job commitment and workmanship pride. According to Kerr (1996), employee fulfillment, commitment, and engagement are the core company requirements. Similarly, Zhang (2000) stated that employee participation results in lasting changes in behaviour, just as participation is core to inspiring action on quality improvement. In addition, Juran & Gryna (1993) claimed that participation results in work attitude and behavioural change. For this purpose, employee commitment to their jobs in the form of organization loyalty is required (Mitchell, 1979).

Based on Deming's (1986) study, employees should be motivated to provide suggestions and great levels of responsibility. Similarly, Anschutz (1995) stated that they have to participate in teamwork and they have to be flexible to be able to bring about partnership between them and their managers. Also, internal cooperation among employees facilitates each of their performance through the creation of beneficial circumstances between the organizational members and the organization as a whole. Moreover, in the context of Malaysian public and private organizations, Karia & Ahmed (2000) examined the effect of empowerment and teamwork in five organizations. They revealed that employees working in cooperation with each other experience enhanced organizational commitment. Silos (1999) also added that the secret behind Japanese efficiency is the way people always work together while Wruck & Jensen (1994) stated that empowerment of employees involves providing them the right to take part in decision making particularly those who are well-informed. Furthermore, Stashevsky & Elizur (2000) and Stone & Eddy (1996) stated that empowering employees improves the quality of product and process and the adoption of TQM without high degrees of empowerment will only result in failure (Gomez-Mejia, Balkin & Cardy, 2004). Hence, employee empowerment comes with employee fulfillment, motivation, satisfaction, productivity and commitment of employees.

(d) *Education and Training:* The importance of education and training is undoubted in the organization's success or failure and a successful organization keeps this into consideration. They not only reinforce the abilities of individual workers, but they also create the basis for sharing skills, abilities and knowledge and their development. Education and training importance are summarized in the following:

They assist organizational workers to comprehend the main process of creating products and/or services, they assist management in appropriating employees in suitable positions, and they decrease the employees' turnover rate. In addition, continuous training and education leads to the improvement of their abilities and the enhancement of their organizational interest and commitment. Continuous education and training may result in a competitive environment within the organization which increases the chances of creativity, education and training assists in the identification of an appropriate position for the right employee.

Several studies highlighted the importance of continuous learning and improvement; among them Ramseook-Munhurrunet *et al.* (2011) stressed on their continuous provision to induce a positive culture wherein required modifications to behaviour are undergone to sustain the TQM climate. Similarly, Jimenez-Jimenez & Martinez-Costa (2009) and Tari *et al.*, (2005) emphasize on the importance of educating and training employees concerning quality control and management along with the technical aspects to enable them to enhance their work methods and to take responsibility for quality (Kaynak, 2003). Other researchers claim that education and training are the key to discover innovative methods to help enhance the performance of the organization. It is evident from the above that many prior studies revealed that importance of education and training as success factors for TQM implementation (Deming, 1989; & Keng *et al.*, 2005).

(e) Customer Focus: Most of the national quality awards in the world advocate the criterion of customer focus in improving customer satisfaction; for instance, the Malcolm Baldridge National Quality Award (MBNQA, 1995), the European Foundation for Quality Management (EFQM Excellence Model, 2003) among others. Arasli & Ahmadeva (2004) claimed that TQM is a philosophy whose objectives involve the provision of a success template for organizations through customer satisfaction. Nevertheless, it is the TQM definition brought forward by most researchers that confirm that the ultimate TQM objective is customer satisfaction in all organizations, profit or non-profit organizations along with government organizations Hence, in attempt to achieve customer satisfaction, customer focus should be stressed on during TQM implementation. In other words, TQM facilitates customer satisfaction and places a stress on it in any organization in each transaction (Kangi, 1998). A close and positive relationship with customers is critical in the determination of their needs and in taking their opinions and feedback into consideration in terms of product and service designs. Moreover, customer involvement is called for in the development of these designs.

Hard Total Quality Management (Hard TQM)

As previously mentioned, the core characteristic of Hard TQM is its stress on production control. Hard TQM was introduced at the onset of the industrial revolution in the earlier years of the past century. During those years, TQM was not as popular as today, although some elements of Hard TQM were being applied. In addition varying schools of TQM were also in existence such as Henry Ford, Frederick Taylor's Scientific Management which all had a significant impact to the achievement of the TQM movement (Ross, 1993). At that time, quality management involved the inspection of products to guarantee that they each achieve the specifications. In the 1940s, when World War II broke out, statistical sampling was utilized in the evaluation of quality control, performance, and the production process monitoring. The quality work was synonymous with the name W.E. Deming. Two decades later, quality spread through the production process into all the organizational parts; the focus shifted to product technology management, quality assurance in design and customer satisfaction. It was evident that the focus was in certain aspects of hard TQM and the scientists attributed to the TQM literature of this caliber was Juran and Crosby. The concept of TQM became widespread in Japan following the World War II and later in the 1980s it reached America and Western Europe. The concept of hard TQM stemmed from the identification and elimination of the causes of quality issues in TQM, continuous improvement and quality awards including ISO, EFQM, Malcolm Baldrige National Quality Award, and the Toyota Way. At the onset of the millennium, the focus shifted from human management to the interconnection between soft aspects of TQM and firm performance (Wilkinson and Redman, 1998).

The pioneering researcher who made a distinction between soft and hard TQM was Wilkinson (1992). On the other hand, Rahman (2001, 2004) stated that hard TQM are more involved in practical, numeric, and systematic quality control techniques while AL-Tarawneh (2010) claimed that hard TQM presents the production orientation of the quality stressing on data collection, measurement, TQM tools application including statistical process control (SPC), flow charts, tally charts, Pareto analysis, scatter diagrams, histograms, control charts and cause and effect analysis. Hard TQM is said to have the following three critical factors:

(a) *Process Management:* Porter & Parker (1993) stated that process management is imperative in total quality strategy and Brah *et al.,* (2002) claimed that process management has to do with the way organizations design and produce products and services, correlates between production and service requirements and oversees the suppliers' performance. Measures such as six sigma and others comes to mind, when the topic of process management is brought up.

Process management involves all processes, production process, process flow management, process control, process control, process improvement, and improvement, process design, flexible processing, advanced systems and the utilization of Just In Time (JIT) principles, use of technology, and process quality (Karuppusami & Gandhinathan, 2006). On the other hand, Mehmet *et al.,* (2010) considers process management as the process control implementation with the help of statistical process control methods. Various statistical process control techniques are present such as control charts, cause-effect diagrams, scatter diagrams and Pareto charts.

According to Juran & Gryna (1993), process is considered as a specific group of machines, tools, materials, methods, Pareto charts, and people involved in production while Chin & Sofian (2011) claimed that TQM tools encapsulates tools including scatter diagram, cause-and-effect diagram, check sheet, histograms, run charts and control charts and stratification. Zhang *et al.,* (2000) are of the opinion that the most critical element in process management is to make sure that process capability meets production needs. In other words, effective process management should encompass accurate documentation of different processes and instructions for operation of equipment in an attempt to decrease the possibility of errors in operations. In addition, Kaynak (2003) & Saraph *et al.,* (1989) claimed that process management target at carrying out a preventive method to quality management and enhancement like designing full-proof, stable production schedules and work distribution to minimize the differences and hence enhancing product quality in the production phase. The improvement of innovation capabilities of human capital maximizes the process quality (Chin & Sofian, 2011).

It is evident from the above discussion that process management is crucial in industrial and productive sectors as several researches and studies were conducted in these specific sectors. Nevertheless, there is a gap in research concerning public and service sectors. This is evidenced by Vouzas & Psychogios (2007) who claimed that TQM in service industry is in its infancy stage of theory development. It is important to stress on the significance of hard TQM in the government sector in terms of national culture. Both tangible and intangible benefits can be reaped from the adoption of hard TQM.

Despite the lack of an ideal model in TQM, quality awards including Deming Price, MBNQA and others along with quality gurus and experts like Deming (1986), Juran & Gryna (1980), Crosby (1979), Ishikawa (1985), Saraph (1989) consider process management as the most critical component of TQM. Motwani (2001) compares TQM to house construction and process management as a critical TQM factors, is considered as one house pillars. In sum, process management has to be integrated with other TQM critical factors for the achievement of a comprehensive successful TQM that is parallel with national culture.

(b) Quality Information and Analysis: The suitable and timely provision of relevant data and information is of significant importance to any firm. The effective flow of communication and information among individuals and teams in an organization is not possible without a system of data and information.

According to TQM gurus, quality information and analysis is a significant TQM factor. Based on the study by Chin & Sofian (2011), easy access to relevant information facilitates the availability of knowledge in a timely manner and enables human capital's utilization of data in their work processes for the purpose of production and continuous improvement and it also enables information sharing regarding operational measures among the organization's employees which would lead to production improvement. The access to quality data and information of all stakeholders through quality tools, dependable user-friendly software and hardware systems are all important in driving and maintaining quality excellence and performance improvement (Sila & Ebrahimpour, 2005). In addition, they revealed that quality information and analysis have direct and indirect effects on customers. Quality data involves quality improvement measurement system quality information, availability of quality information, flow of quality information, quality information systems, quality information usage measurement, and internal quality information usage (Karuppusami & Gandhinathan, 2006).

Similarly, Brah (2002) viewed information and analysis as the main element of any organization in their assessment and understanding of performance. Meanwhile, Hussian (2004) considered knowledge management as a novel strategic method that shifts the paradigm of information systems from processing data and provision of information to harvesting and knowledge capitalization of the whole organization, varying from expertise to documented material. Finally, Melhem (2004) claimed that employees fail to contribute to the improvement of organizational performance if they lack the information of the significant dimensions of performance and training and the way information is interpreted and used.

(c) *Strategic Planning:* Strategic planning is considered to be among the TQM critical success factors (Karuppusami & Gandhinathan, 2006). It includes mission/vision statement, quality policy, quality aims, business plan, communication methods, and control and improvement of plans. It is the driver in an organization, whether profit or non-profit, in order to survive in a competitive market. For the achievement of effective strategic planning, it is imperative to take into consideration the following aspects of the organization; quality goals, effective measurement, clear unambiguous plans, and accurate goals and objectives, and resources. Strategic planning lays down the direction, assists in evaluating and creating synergies, facilitates prioritization, and offers the basis for effective planning, motivation and control (David, 1995). Several researchers consider strategic planning as one of TQM's critical success factors (Black & Porter, 1996; Li *et al.*, 2003; Wu *et al.*, 1997; Drew & Healy, 2006; Prajogo & McDermott, 2005; Sila & Ebrahimpour, 2005).

CULTURE

Definition

The mid of last century marked the increasing definitions brought forward by the researchers of the term 'culture'. However, despite the decade and a half that passed, no consensus has been reached of the concept's definition. It has been varyingly defined by authors and individuals, culture is a concept that is difficult to define and based on Johnston and Klandermans (1995), there are varying definitions of culture but it is easy to note commonalities between them including customs, beliefs, values, artifacts, symbols and rituals. Following their review of over 160 definitions of culture from prior research, Kroeber & Kluckhohn (1952) proposed a definition of culture which states that culture comprise of patterns, explicit and implicit for behaviour obtained, transmitted through symbols, comprising distinctive achievement of human groups, including the embodiment in artifact. The main element of culture comprises traditional ideas and their attached value. On the other hand, Kroeber & Parsons (1958) define culture as "transmitted and created content and pattern of values, ideas and other symbolic-meaningful system as factors in the shaping of human behaviour and artifacts produced through behaviour".

Another take on culture came from Triandis (1972) who viewed the subjective element of culture from its objective artifacts and proceeded to define culture as the characteristic way that an individual perceives certain facets of its environment that is man-made including rules, norms, and values which are all impacted by language, gender, race, religion, place of residence and occupation and which impact interpersonal behaviour. Along this line Lenartowicz & Roth (1999) stated that "culture is better defined as a set of learned characteristics shared by a particular group of people" and that culture influences the individual's core values and evidenced through behaviour which should be acknowledged by the group. Similarly, Kempner (1987) defines culture as, "the sum total of belief, knowledge, attitudes of mind and customs to which people are exposed to during their social conditioning". Another definition came from Mobley *et al.,* (2005) who considered culture as a set of values, beliefs, common understanding, thinking and norms that is revealed through behaviour and is common to all societal members. The element of complexity in defining culture was pointed out by Groeschl & Doherty (2000) who posited that, "Culture consists of several components of which some are explicit and others are implicit. Most often these elements are explained in terms such as behaviour, values, norms and basic assumptions".

Another proposition of culture definition came from Trempenaars & Hampden-Turner (1998) who defined culture as a kaleidoscope of thoughts, feelings and behaviour learned by the person throughout his life since childhood. The most notable definition of culture came from Hofstede (1980), who, following the revision of countless definitions present in the literature concerning the topic and in different fields and periods of time, stated that culture is the, "collective programming of the mind which distinguishes between the members of one group of people from another". He proceeds to state that culture requires the mental programming patterns of thoughts of feelings and possible actions (Hofstede, 1991). From the above definitions of culture, it is evident that its characteristics include: it is relayed through inheritance; it is obtained through a learning process in all walks of life; it signifies an expression and a communication among group members in light of language, rituals etc.; it determines what is accepted behaviour among the members; and finally, it plays a critical role in forming collective values reflecting each individual values that are shared.

Levels of Culture

The widely renowned cultural guru, Hofstede, proposed many layers of culture programming encompassing a set of culture operatives in the behaviour of an individual (Hofstede, 1991). On the basis of these layers, culture is categorized into: national level (belonging to a single country; regional/ethnic/religion/linguistic level, gender level (belonging to one's gender), generation level (separation of generations), social class level (related with educational opportunities and profession), organizational cultural level (belonging to an organization or a corporate culture) and the way employees socialize within the work organization (Hofstede, 1991). In addition, Hofstede added that almost every individual belongs to more than one level at the same time. On closer examination of these levels, there are evidently two levels which are related to the current subject of research; national culture and organizational culture. The reason behind the distinction between the two levels of culture lies in the huge differences between nations and organizations. In the later part of the study, it will shed a light on quality culture as an important element of the study.

National Culture

Various studies have been dedicated to the study of national culture but some of them failed to deal with the following limitations:

A reflection of why cultures differ from one another (e.g. Early & Erez, 1999).

Validity of findings (e.g. Kluckhohn & Strodbeck, 1961).

Insufficient dimensions or the consideration of culture as a single variable (e.g. Hall, 1960; & Triandis, 1995).

Study is confined through specificity and specific purpose or a certain area (e.g. House *et al.*, 1999; Menou, 1983; Ein-Dor, Segeve & Orgad, 1993).

The inability to construct the study at the national level (e.g. Martinsons & Westwood, 1997).

Culture was studied as a limited aspect (e.g. Tricker, 1988).

Incomprehensive study of elements compared to other studies (e.g. Early & Erez, 1999). In the following Table 2.3, some of the studies regarding Dimensions of National culture:

In order to comprehend cultural dimensions, prior studies have put forward several models although only a few of them are currently used in

Table 2.3: Some of the National Culture Studies

Studies	*National Culture Dimensions*
Hofstede's (1980, 2001) Cultural Dimensions	Power distance, uncertainty avoidance, individualism/collectivism; masculinity/femininity and time orientation
Schwartz's (1994) three Pairs of Value types.	Embeddedness versus Autonomy, Hierarchy versus Egalitarianism, Harmony versus Mastery
GLOBE project House *et al.*, (2004) in Cultural Dimensions	Uncertainty avoidance, power distance, performance orientation, future orientation, assertiveness, institutional collectivism, individual collectivism, gender egalitarianism and human orientation
Hall (1976), Culture Dimensions.	High/low or high/medium/low context categories.
Trompenaars Model (1993) THE TROMPENAARS VALUE QUESTIONNAIRE Seven Dimensions	Universalism versus Particularism, Achievement versus Ascription, Individualism versus Collectivism, Affectivity versus Neutrality, Specificity versus Diffuseness, internal-external control, Time perspective
Kluckhohn and Strodtbeck (1961), six culture dimensions.	Human Nature, Relationship to Nature, Time oriented, Human Activity, Relationships among people.
Schwartz's (1994) three Pairs of Value types	Embeddedness versus Autonomy, Hierarchy versus Egalitarianism, Harmony versus Mastery
Smith *et al.* (1996), two culture-level dimensions	Egalitarian Commitment *vs.* Conservatism and Utilitarian Involvement *vs.* Loyal Involvement.
Phatak (1986), Cross Culture Management (Five Culture Management Value)	Individualism, informality, Materialism Chang, Time orientation,
Herskovits (1989) Five culture dimensions	Material Culture, Social Institutions, men and universe, aesthetic, language

an extensive manner. Six studies earned distinction in most of the studies in literature and they are: Kluckhohn & Strodtbeck's (1961) theory of value orientation, Hall's (1976-2000) high context and low context cultural framework, House *et al.*'s (2004) GLOBE group, Hampden-Turner & Trompenaars (1993-1997) study, Schwartz's (1994) study, and Hofstede's (1980, 1983, 1991, and 2001) study.

Kluckhohn & Strodtbeck's Theory of Value Orientations and its Six Dimensions

A model developed to analyze culture based on the following three main assumptions was developed by Kluckhohn & Strodtbeck (1961):

General and common human issues that everyone must find solutions to a range of varying possible solutions.

The variety of solutions displayed by all societies at all times with different choices.

According to them, the method of solving problems presents the community culture. From this, they brought forward a culture framework comprising six main orientations:

1. Human Nature: National culture commonly considers people as good, bad or a combination of both. A good person is traditionally,

socially oriented while a bad one is characterized as selfish. The dimension refers to the goodness or badness of human nature as according to Thomas (2002) "People are inherently good, evil or a mixture of good and evil".

2. Relationship to Nature: The dimension refers to the belief of some human beings of being one with nature while others view nature as a supplier. The relationship of people to nature can either be mastery, subjugation or harmony (Yeganeh & Su, 2007).
3. Time Orientation: Based on the authors' belief, cultural differences lie in its focus on time; some focus on the past and traditions, others focus on the present and short-term, while the rest focus on the future and long-term outcomes.
4. Human Activity: Kluckhohn & Strodtbeck (1961) stated that this dimension of culture focuses on three elements; being, doing and thinking. For instance, some societies put much weight on 'being who a person is' rather than 'what a person does' while some others depend on action-centered belief creating status as opposed to ascribing them.
5. Relationships among People: According to Yeganey and Su (2007), this dimension can be summarized as individualism, collectivism and hierarchical structure. Meanwhile, Darley & Blankson (2008) along with Kluckhohn & Strodtbeck (1961) introduced three categories of relational orientations: the individualistic, the collateral and the lineal. The individualistic principle is said to be dominant when individual goals weigh more than the group goals and the collateral principle is said to be dominant when the goals and welfare of the group in a lateral extension is more prominent. As for the lineal principle, the group goals are of primary importance and the group continuity through time and the laid down succession of the group are very important.
6. Conception of Physical Space: This dimension depict private, public or a combination of both as in some cultures, a strong importance is placed on privacy and personal property of space while other cultures have common property, avoid close doors and people are free to go where they desire. Despite the old element of the study, it has been seminal to most studies in the field of national culture. Hence, it is not surprising that some common elements are evidenced in most studies. For instance, 'relationship orientations' are mentioned in Hofstede's individualism and power distance dimensions (Hofstede, 1980) as well as in Trompenaar's individualism-communitarianism, achievement-ascription, and equality-hierarchy dimensions (Trompenaar & Hamden-Turner, 1993; Yeganeh & Su, 2007). Various researchers have tested the

validity of Kluckhohn & Strodtbeck's above mentioned dimensions (Maznevski, *et al.*, 2002).

Hall (1976-2000)—High Context and Low Context Cultural Framework

Hall (1976) proposed a set of parameters to study cultures comprising a dimension that extends from high-context to low-context and from the low-context to the high-context category. Hall (1976) stated that high-context communication refers to a type of communication that relays not just verbal communication and includes behaviour and para-verbal cues as according to him, "meaning and context are inextricably bound up with each other" (Hall, 2000, p. 36). Hence, for communication understanding, one should examine the meaning coupled with the context and the code. Context is referred to as the situation, background or surrounding that is linked to the event, situation or even the individual. High context communications also entails drawing on the common knowledge of the parties to the communication. According to Hall (1976), cultures from high-context to low-context are represented by the following countries; Japan, France, Greece, Spain, Italy, Scandinavian Countries, Arab countries, England, North America, and German-speaking countries. Hall (1976) added that people from low-context cultures possess a communication style that is consistent with feelings while people from high-context culture allow the relay of message without directly addressing the problem. In case of conflict, high-context cultures are known to make use of indirect, non-confrontational and unclear language, that depends on the listener's or the reader's skill in understanding the meaning from the context. On the other hand, low-context cultures are more inclined to be direct, confrontational and candid approach to guarantee that the listener got the correct message intended.

Similarly, other authors like Gudykunst *et al.,* (1996) refers to high context communications as indirect, unclear, harmonious, reserved and understated while to low-context communication as direct, accurate, dramatic, open, clear and highly dependent on feelings and true intentions. Salleh (2005) added to the explanation by pointing out that high-context and low context communication can be distinguished from their characteristics; for instance, emotions in close-knit relations, direct messages, non-verbal communication and the use of analogous or digital language.

In a related study, Morden (1999) offered significant points in this dimension of culture by stating that high-context cultures obtain information required for decisions and deal within the network of personal information including their friends, business acquaintances and relatives. They tend to ask questions and believe gossip. On the other hand, low-context cultures obtain information from research base and they listen to colleagues and relatives' advice to make use of reading materials, reports, databases and other information sources. In fact, information highways comprising the internet, e-mail and other communication tools are great sources of invaluable knowledge and information.

Global Leadership and Organizational Behaviour Effectiveness (GLOBE) (House et al., *2004) and its Nine Dimensions*

House *et al.,* (2004) conducted the GLOBE study involving 62 different cultures and 127 investigators in societies all over the globe through the years from 1994-1997. The data collection tool used was the survey questionnaire which was distributed to 17,000 middle managers in a total of 951 organizations throughout 3 particular industries namely banking, food processing and telecommunication. The authors were greatly influenced by Hofstede's seminal work in their selection of variables, and in fact, some of their nine societal scales had the same labels as Hofstede's dimensions despite the many evident differences between the two studies.

GLOBE proposed nine cultural dimensions throughout actual society practices and values in varying cultural settings. The dimensions measure different practice in societies 'as is' and values, 'should be' with the 'should be' scores used to gauge the cultural visions and the culture's desire for change. If the two cultures' cultural practices are different then 'as is' is applied while similar values are applied with 'should be'. The nine dimensions of GLOBE are: assertiveness, future orientation, human orientation, performance orientation, gender egalitarianism, power distance, institutional collectivism, in-group collectivism, and uncertainty avoidance. A brief description of these dimensions is presented below (Javidan *et al.,* 2006):

(a) *Assertiveness*: It refers to the level to which an individual is, or should possess the character of assertiveness, confrontational, and aggressiveness in their relation with others. People coming from a culture characterized by high assertiveness are inclined to have a can-do attitude to doing things and are very competitive in business while their counterparts from less assertive countries often opt for harmony, loyalty and unity.

(b) *Future Orientation*: The level to which people engage or should engage in behaviours catered to the future like gratification delay, future planning and future investments. Organizations from future oriented countries are inclined to be averse to risk taking and decision making that is opportunity-centered while those from the less future oriented countries are systematic and more opportunistic in their activities.

(c) *Gender Egalitarianism:* It is the level to which the group decreases or should decrease their perception of gender inequality. Organizations coming from gender egalitarian societies are more tolerant of varying ideas and individuals.

(*d*) *Human Orientation:* It is the level to which the group encourages and should encourage individuals' actions that are fair, altruistic, generous, caring and kind.

(*e*) *Institutional Collectivism:* It is the extent to which organizational and societal practices reward and perpetuate (and should perpetuate and reward) resource distribution in a collective manner. Collectivistic organizations are inclined to stress on group performance and rewards while individualistic ones are more inclined to stress on self-achievement and rewards.

(*f*) *In-Group Collectivism:* It is the extent to which individuals present or should present feelings of pride, loyalty and unity in organizations or families.

(*g*) *Performance Orientation:* It is the extent to which a group promotes or rewards and (should both promote and reward) members of the group judging from their improvement and extraordinary performance. Countries high on cultural practices tend to stress on training and development while those who are low, tend to stress on family and background.

(*h*) *Power Distance:* It is the level to which group members of a collective, look forward to (or should look forward to) equal distribution of power. Societal high power distance present unequal distribution of power and countries scoring high on distribution of power are, based on their economy, society and politics more hierarchical and those in higher positions hold expectations of, and receive subordinates' obedience. They also seem to present hierarchical decision making processes with little or no communication.

(*i*) *Uncertainty Avoidance:* The level to which a society, organization or group depends (and should depend) on societal norms, regulations and procedures to minimize the presence of unpredictability of future happenings. The more they are desirous of avoiding uncertainty, the more orderliness, structure, formal procedures, consistency, and rules govern their day to day lives. Organizations displaying high uncertainty avoidance set up structured processes and procedures and they opt for more iron-clad strategies. On the contrary, those with low uncertainty avoidance opt for simple processes and generic strategies. They are more open to opportunities and enjoy taking risks.

The above GLOBE study received many criticisms. Among them, Minkov (2007) questioned the cultural dimensions measure of the study while McCrae *et al.*, (2008) considered some of their measures as unfounded country stereotypes. The study also failed to regard the distinction between personal values and norms stating that human and performance orientation do not produce convincing arguments. Hofstede (2006), on the other hand, came up with a summary of some of the distinctions of his study from GLOBE's.

GLOBE made use of many volunteer to gather data from in over 950 national organizations and in 62 societies. On the other hand, Hofstede's study has its basis on existing data of employees gathered by IBM Corporations from its branches in a total of 72 countries in the years between 1967 and 1973 and was later extended to 75 countries (Hofstede, 2001).

An individual researcher versus a team of researchers—GLOBE data analysis was brought about by team effort closely monitored by Robert House, its designer while Hofstede work was an individual effort.

> The GLOBE study concentrated on studying managers while Hofstede studied employees.
> The GLOBE study was powered by theory while Hofstede's was driven by action.

The GLOBE network and population comprised of international individuals but both its project design and analysis are more American in nature perpetuated by management, or psychologists holding degrees from US Universities, while Hofstede's study of the IBM Company involved locally recruited researchers with local degrees who contributed to a large extent to the success of the study. Organizational culture versus societal culture—GLOBE's questionnaire was formatted in a way that one half of them were from the organization and the other half from the society whereby both were treated in a similar way. Hofstede's (1980) studied societal cultures from IBM respondents hailing from different countries in a different way. Majority of the researchers are against this difference (e.g. Javidan *et al.*, 2005).

The GLOBE study and Hofstede's study of culture have been receiving many criticisms particularly the latter (MacSweeney, 2002; Shenkar, 2001). The former, owing to its current status, has not been fully analyzed yet and compared extensively with Hofstede's method although the two have commonalities and are therefore similar in process.

Trompenaars (1993) Model—Seven Dimensions

Trompenaars (1993) created a model in his attempt to study national culture and its impact on business practices through gathered data from 15,000 managers from 47 countries. In 1997, Trompenaars proceeded to conduct a study with a fellow researcher on the basis of data gathered from 30,000 managers working in multinational and international companies hailing from a total of 45 countries (Trompenaars & Hampden-Turner, 1997). The study examined the impact of national culture and other factors including occupation (Woolliams, 1997). Each dimension was provided by examples and outcome expectations for both management and organization.

Trompenaars came up with seven cultural valuing dimensions, of which five are—achievemen-ascription, individualism-collectivism, universalism-particularism, affectivity-neutrality, and specificity-diffuseness and were taken from the study conducted by Parsons & Shils (1951) while the remaining dimensions are adopted from other researchers (Kluckhohn & Strodtbeck, 1961; Hall, 1959; & Rotter, 1966). The seven dimensions of Trompenaars model are described as follows:

Universalism versus Particularism: This shows the person's attitude regarding universal principles because people may either view the principles as something that should be applied to a situation or specify the situation to determine the suitability of application. The measurement of this dimension raises questions that help comprehend it and its alternative behaviours.

Achievement versus Ascription: The status of an individual may gained on the basis of either achievement or ascription. In a place catering to individual's achievement, employees are more inclined to be judged based on how they perform and successful individuals reach their goals faster in this environment as opposed to an ascription-centered environment. Their position is in direct relation with the efforts they expend. On the other hand, in an ascription-oriented environment, the background and experience of the manager is the main determinant of his promotion. Elements such as educational background and years of experience are taken into consideration.

Individualism versus Collectivism: According to Trompenaars & Hampden-Turner, this dimension can be defined as an individual's main orientation to himself or to common goals or aims. The measurement for this dimension concentrates on its work environment and its influence on the organization and responsibilities.

Affectivity versus Neutrality: This dimension is based on the expression of feelings in a particular environment. Trompenaars offered questions to measure the dimension such as, "How would you behave if you felt upset about something at work? Would you express your feelings openly?" Responses from each individual in each country differed. The cultural dimension outcome allows the recognition that in some countries, emotions are laid out along with rational arguments and this may offer confusion to individuals hailing from countries were expressing emotions is not the norm but just the laying down of arguments.

Specificity versus Diffuseness: This dimension stresses on the individual's distinct view of private and public spaces. In some cultures, people usually separate their lives into varying categories. For instance, being good colleagues at work does not automatically transform to becoming family friends. In other words, the authority of the individual's position at work does not shift external to the workplace. A manager may meet his subordinates socially outside the office, and he may accept the superior skill of the subordinate in a sport they mutually play and seek some pointers from him. On the other hand, in a diffused situation, the differing categories of life overlap. The manager's status at work influences all other activities he does external of the workplace and his position or status remains.

Internal versus External Control: The dimension of internal versus external control shows the capacity of the individual to control and change his environment or his inability to do so. The management outcomes are shown in the strategic choices it makes through planning and provoking changes or trying to make do with what the situation offers. According to Trompenaar's analysis (Smith, Trompenaars & Dugan, 1995), innate directness shows beliefs in planning, efforts and luck will impact the outcome while outer directness shows beliefs that personal relations, and political conditions make their mark on success with luck being decisive. Business outcomes may be viewed in the employee's success strategies. In an environment of inner directedness, employees plan and work hard to reach their aims but in the outer-directedness environment, employees tend to leverage their personal network and other avenues to achieve their aims.

Time Perspective: Time is considered to be comprised of two themes; the first one being the ability to perform in a particular time frame and the other one in a particular time orientation. In the context of silent language, Hall (1959) proposed the monochromic and polychromic (one time and several times respectively) with the former signifying time perception in a linear, sequential and definite way and the latter, the time perception is viewed in a multiple, synchronic and diffused way. This is evident from the individual's behaviour whether he/she is able to view activities in a polychromic way (at the same time) or in a monochromic way (differentiate activities into phases). Trompenaars (1993) proposed themes concerning the organization's actions that are made either sequentially or synchronically. The first one is the ability of the organization or management to tackle multiple projects and not concentrate on one project at a time. The second theme shows the differences appearing between countries as evidenced by the respondents' views of the present, past and future prioritization. For instance, in an environment focused on the past, the prior year's sales may be a greater benchmark than the expected market growth while gauging new sales objectives. This is similar to Hofstede's long-term versus short-term orientation. Short term is similar to present orientation while long-term is akin to future orientation.

However, Trompenaars & Hofstede have differing views of the core element of culture. While Hofstede's definition has its basis on ideals particularly the values attached to the ideas and considers it the essence of culture, Trompenaars' definition considers meaning as the essence of culture.

Despite their mutual criticisms, both studies have been seminal and both have contributed to a large extent in the improvement of studies in the field of culture.

Schwartz's (1994)—Three Pairs of Value types

Schwartz (1992, 1994) conducted a survey regarding value preferences in 25 countries with the sample categorized into teachers and students. He chose 56 values based on theoretical reasoning concerning value types and prior theoretical and empirical studies from Western as well as non-Western countries. He considered values as concepts that are positive and that act as guidance to social actors (organizational leaders, policy-makers, individual persons) in their action selection, evaluation of people and events and their explanation of actions and evaluations. Hofstede's study may be considered as the most comprehensive study, but Schwartz's study provided greater details regarding value dimensions and he tried to avoid the pitfalls of confined elements of culture that prior researches were characterized with (Hall, 1976; Hall & Hall, 1990; and Triandis, 1990). He considered his values (success, justice, freedom, social order, tradition) as the vocabulary depicting socially accepted aims for motivation, expression and justifications of the solutions followed. He proceeded to highlight three main social issues which are: relations between individuals and groups; positive ways to ensure responsible behaviour and maintain social fabric; and finally, the relations of human kind with their habitat and society.

From the above issues, he obtained three bipolar, culture value dimensions and their analysis provided seven value orientations whereby comparison of cultures is enabled. Schwartz's theory also explained the relationship between the orientations. The seven value orientations proposed by him are discussed in the following paragraphs.

Embeddedness versus Autonomy: On the basis of the first social issue, embeddedness considers culture in which an individual is an entity who is embedded or who is a part of the group and loyal to maintaining the group's harmony, propriety and to avoiding actions that threatens the group's unity or the traditional order. On the other hand, autonomy describes cultures where the person is considered as having autonomy, and someone who is bounded and determines his and her own distinctive qualities and is inclined to express them. There are two types of autonomy; intellectual autonomy and affective autonomy. The former comprises the idea and thoughts, the individual's right to be guided by his intellectual direction while the later comprises the feelings and emotions and the right of the individuals to be guided by his affective positive experience.

This dimension resembles Hofstede's individualism/collectivism dimension although in Schwartz's case, he emphasized the individual's role in the society and the level to which the society bestows the autonomous or the embeddedness quality in the individual. Hofstede's dimension emphasized between the differences of individual goals and group goals.

Hierarchy versus Egalitarianism: On the basis of the second social issue, egalitarianism depicts the way people have an innate commitment to cooperate and to feel concerned for others' welfare. It stresses on the overcoming of selfish interests. Hierarchy on the other hand, appropriates roles to guarantee responsible productive outcome of behaviour and advocates the unequal distribution of power, roles, and resources. It contends that among the ways to ensure socially responsible behaviour is for the hierarchical system to ascribe roles.

Harmony versus Mastery: The dimension of harmony advocates the acceptance of the world as is, and the preserving of it as opposed to changing and exploiting it. On the other hand, mastery is to be the master and change in the world and to shape it to the individual's will, to gain control and get ahead with the help of active self-assertion.

Hofstede's (1980, 1983, 1991, and 2001) Five Dimensions

Hofstede's influential work in the field of culture resulted in the researchers' applications in the field even today. He is successful in highlighting cross-cultural analysis in the field of international business. Despite the criticisms it gained including reliance on old data, lack of inclusion of the Eastern bloc among others (Kuchinke, 1999; McSweeney, 2002; Schwartz, 2008; Oyserman, Coon & Kmmermeier, 2002; Holden, 2002; Fang, 2003, 2005-2006, 2010), it is still viewed as the most comprehensive and most valued work in the culture domain (Sondergaard, 1994) with citations of his work over 54,000 times up until 2010 (Tung *et al.,* 2010). Either, Hofstede's dimensions which have been cited more than (14,700) times in February 2010 (Google Scholar, 2010, accessed 23 February 2010). Other reason for using the Hofstede specific four dimensions is to validate his claim of homogeneity of Arab culture and their effect in their relations between Soft-Hard TQM and Performance in the municipalities. Other reason, Hofstede, 1980, applied all of his four dimensions that is (power distance, uncertainty avoidance, and individualism/collectivism)., while he did not apply the fifth dimension (long term oriented) on these countries. For the previous reasons, his typology of his four dimensions will be used in this research.

Table 2.4: Hofstede's Four Dimensions of Culture in Several Countries/ Region, Hofstede (1980)

Country/Region	*PDI (Power Distance)*	*IDV (Indivdualisim)*	*MAS (Masculinity)*	*UAI (Uncertainty Avoidance)*
Arab countries Egypt, Lebanon, Lybia, Kuwait, Iraq, Saudi-Arabia, UAE	80	38	52	68
Argentina	49	46	56	86
Australia	36	90	61	51
Austria	11	55	79	70
Bangladesh	—	—	—	—
Belgium	65	75	54	94
Brazil	69	38	49	76
Canada	39	80	52	48
Chile	63	23	28	86
China	—	—	—	—
Columbia	67	13	64	80
Costa Rica	35	15	21	86
Denmark	18	74	16	23
East Africa	64	27	41	52
Ecuador	78	8	63	67
Finland	33	63	26	59
France	68	71	43	86
Germany fr	35	67	66	65
Great Britain	35	89	66	35
Greece	60	35	57	112
Guatemala	95	6	37	101
Hong Kong	68	25	57	29
India	77	48	56	40
Indonesia	78	14	46	48
Iran	58	41	43	59
Ireland (Republic of)	28	70	68	35
Israel	13	54	47	81
Italy	50	76	70	75
Jamaica	45	39	68	13
Japan	54	46	95	92
Malaysia	104	26	50	36
Mexico	81	30	69	92
Netherlands	38	80	14	53
New Zealand	22	79	58	49
Nigeria	—	—	—	—
Norway	31	69	8	50
Pakistan	55	14	50	70
Panama	95	11	44	86
Peru	64	16	42	87
Philippines	94	32	64	44
Poland	—	—	—	—
Portugal	63	27	31	104
Salvador	66	19	40	94
Singapore	74	20	48	8
South Africa	49	65	63	49
South Korea	60	18	39	85
Spain	57	51	42	86
Sweden	31	71	5	29
Switzerland	34	68	70	58

Country/ Region	PDI (Power Distance)	IDV (Indivdualisim)	MAS (Masculinity)	UAI (Uncertainty Avoidance)
Taiwan	58	17	45	69
Thailand	64	20	34	64
Turkey	66	37	45	85
Uruguay	61	36	38	100
USA	40	91	62	46
Venezuela	81	12	73	76
West Africa	77	20	46	54
Yugoslavia	76	27	21	88
Zimbabwe	—	—	—	—

Source: Hofested, Geert (1980).

Hofstede's comprehensive, empirical study which investigated 116,000 IBM employees located in 72 countries in the years spanning 1968-1972 revealed significant differences in the employees' behaviour and attitudes between different countries. He concluded that the employees' natural culture held most of the explanation to their differences as opposed to other characteristics including age, gender, profession or position. These dimensions impact all facets of life and on the basis of his findings, he came up with four cultural dimensions namely, power distance, collectivism/individualism, femininity/masculinity, high/low uncertainty avoidance. He added short term/long term orientation later one which he concluded from a Chinese Value Survey (Hofstede, 1991). An explanation of each dimension is provided in the following paragraphs.

Individualism (IDV): It is the level to which individuals can either be integrated either the individualist group or the collectivist group. In the former group, ties between individuals are not tight and individuals look after themselves and their families while in the latter, people are integrated into a strong closely-knit group from birth and have extended families of uncles, aunts and grandparents. The collectivist society is characterized as a society not welcoming to strangers (Fukuyama, 1995) while in an individualistic society, trusting strangers is one of its important aspects.

Power Distance Index (PDI): It is the level to which the weaker members of the organization or institution acknowledge the unequal distribution of power. It represents more versus less inequality viewed from below as opposed to from above. It is considered as the degree of inequality in societies perpetuated by followers as much as leaders and it is evident from Shaffer & O'Hara's (1995) study that individuals from high PDI scores are less inclined to trust service providers.

Uncertainty Avoidance Index (UAI): This depicts the society's tolerance of uncertainty and unexpected situations. Uncertainty is said to have two kinds: the first that avoids uncertainty and decreases the possible situations through rules and regulations and the second type that accepts uncertainty and is tolerant of novel opinions. Rules are not as many as the first kind and based on religion and philosophy, this type of societies have realistic individuals and they allow many situations to occur together.

Masculinity (MAS): It is the role distribution between genders and is considered as crucial in every society in which selective solutions are reached.

Short-term/Long-term Orientation: Originally, this dimension was known as Confucian Dynamism. It is the most ignored dimension in literature. Long-term dimensions implies the encouragement of virtues advocating future rewards specifically perseverance and thrift (Hofstede, 1991) while short-term orientation implies the encouragement of virtues advocating the past and present specifically tradition, face preservation and achievement of social responsibilities (Hofstede, 1991). While long-term orientation advocates persistence, thriftiness, shame as a social modifier and differences in status, short-term orientation stresses on tradition, stability, face-saving, reciprocity and giving gifts.

However, Hofstede's dimensions which applied to the largest number of employees from IBM (more than 115,000) employees. Therefore, his typology of his four dimensions will be used in this research.

Organizational Culture

Up until today, there has been no consensus regarding a single definition of organizational culture (Behery & Paton, 2008) owing to its reflection in varying fields. For instance, in anthropology, the definition of organizational culture differs from that of sociology or psychology or even public administration.

At any case, there are varying definitions of organizational culture (Schein, 2004) although the commonality between them exists in the shared values. For instance, Schein (1992) provides the definition of organizational culture as the basic understanding of the organization's patterns which are developed by a team of people with the objective of tackling problems that are parallel with the external environment and of creating coordination and integrity within the organization while leveraging its high reliability. On the other hand, Denison (1990) defines it as a shared common meaning within the organization that impacts the people's behaviours and Hofstede (1991) defines it as the collective programming of the mind that differentiates one organizational member from the other. Similarly, Ravasi & Schultz (2006) consider culture as a group of common mental perceptions guiding the interpretation and action within organizations through the definition of suitable behaviour in different situations. In addition, Davis (2007) defined it as the shared beliefs and values' patterns providing members of an institution meaning and rules for behaviour. Bate (1995) defined it as a strategic phenomenon while Sathe (1985) defined organizational culture as a set of imperative beliefs, understandings and norms shared among the members of the organization and relayed to new members. Finally, according to Tsui *et al.,* (2006), organizational culture is a set of core values that is acknowledged and adopted by the organizational members.

On the basis of the above varying definitions, Maull *et al.,* (2001) summarized the following points concerning organizational culture: Culture is a system of beliefs in a sense that they are guiding or daily beliefs. The former are universally true therefore, they need little or no modification while the latter are a part and parcel of the corporate culture as evidenced by Davis's definition. Culture is an entity that is learned at a basic level. It is the way people behave and perceive things in their surroundings as evidenced by Schein's definition. Culture is a strategic phenomenon while strategy is a cultural phenomenon as evidenced by Bate's definition. The two concepts are inseparable. Culture is a mental programming as Maull *et al.,* (2001) claims that it is collective and not attributed to a lone individual, and it is a mental software in a sense that it is not tangible and not seen as evidenced from Hofstede's definition.

National Culture and Organizational Culture

In the past three decades, studies have conducted comparisons between national and organizational culture (Ford & Chan, 2003) with emphasis on the relation between them and the level to which one impacts the other (Smith, 1992). However, there are only few empirical researches that measured the influence of national culture upon organizational culture owing to the following main reasons: Different levels of analyses which bring challenges in methodology including challenges in sampling. The research tools used in measuring national culture often emphasizes on the basics, or work values that cannot be employed directly on the organizational level. Both types of culture's measurement tools comprise disparate dimensions (Klein *et al.,* 2009).

Hofstede (1991, 2002) highlighted differences in the nature of national and organizational culture in a sense that the former often arises from consistent values, while the latter arises from consistent practices. According to him, national culture is linked to our dearly held values; for instance, good vs. evil, normal vs. abnormal, safe vs. dangerous, and rational vs. irrational. They are learned at an earlier age and are believed to change gradually through generations. On the other hand, organizational culture consists of general guidelines based on organizational practices that are picked up on the job and he claims that changing organization culture is challenging and time consuming. In this type of culture, an individual learns to adapt to processes and priorities and he can be urged to follow certain behaviours of organizational leaders. Nevertheless, in cases where the priorities and leadership traits go against an individual's national cultural values, the national cultural values will prevail.

In addition, while national culture is tackled by anthropology, organizational culture is dealt with in organizational sociology. According to Cooke & Szumal (2000), different cultural regions display varying ideal organizational profiles. Pun (2002) on the other hand, stated that national culture promotes the creation of organizational culture within organizations and hence, they interlink. Similarly, Noronha (2003) described national culture as a super-ordinate value system and the organizational culture as sub-value system. The former impacts organizational culture as Johns (2006) stated, "National culture constrains variations in organizational cultures".

In addition, Nelson & Gopalan (2003) stated that in case variance in national samples is smaller compared to between countries, this indicates that organizational cultures are constrained by the national cultural environment. Moreover, Sousa-Poza *et al.*, (2001) claimed that corporate culture is a function of ethnological culture and the combination of high power distance with individualism advocates task culture while the combination between low power distance and individuals advocates people culture. On the other hand, low individualism advocates outward culture. They came to the conclusion that individuals are inclined not to follow a certain behaviour that conflicts with ethnological cultural values.

Miroshnik (2002) revealed that national culture may impact the leadership style which influences organizational culture. Leadership is considered to be the most important factor in company culture formation as when leaders apply their vision and business strategy in the organization, people act based on their philosophy. A corporate culture then emerges from this reflecting the leader's vision and strategy and the experiences he had.

Moreover, based on Lok & Crawford's (2004) study, individuals normally employ their values, attitudes and beliefs in the organization and these are reflected in difference national cultures. While leadership is stated to contribute in a significant way to the organization's success or failure, national culture impact show organizations are managed and structured. In conclusion, literature reveals that national culture influenced the organization's leadership style which forms organizational culture and eventually improves employees' satisfaction from and commitment to the organization.

Quality Culture

The previous section provided an extensive explanation of national and organizational culture. It may be concluded that culture is considered as shared beliefs, values, attitudes and behavioural patterns characterizing the organizational or the institutional members with quality being a part and parcel of it (Harvey & Green, 1993). The present section deals with the discussion of quality culture in light of management to develop a supportive good working environment and eventually lead to effective performance and quality enhancement. Commitment of senior management is the engine that drives quality culture.

Quality culture's importance lies in the fact that the success of the TQM implementation in any organization hinges on its quality culture. However, quality culture cannot be studied in separately from organizational culture. Ehlers (2009) stated that quality culture is integrated into the overall organizational culture and they are inseparable as it is embedded in the organization's technology, structure, business strategy and financial decision-making. It is crucial in the enhancement of performance and the success of TQM implementation. According to Mahmood *et al.,* (2006), it is the design of patterns of items of behaviour adopted by the society in an attempt to solve problems and it is a core component of a successful TQM plan. Organizations having quality culture often display clear values and beliefs encouraging total quality behaviour. Similarly, Prajogo *et al.,* (2005) claimed that quality culture often results in successful TQM while Zadry (2005) commented that management leadership has a key role in shaping the organizational quality culture.

Research relating quality to organizational culture is few and far between. Those that do exist are limited to higher education particularly in Europe; for instance, Vidal (2003), Olsen & Maassen (2007), Ehlers (2009) all proposed models for quality culture in the field of higher education. Their models are composed of four main elements:

1. A structural element representing the organization's quality system which can be an existing method to quality management for higher education, or the tools and mechanisms used to improve organizational quality.
2. The enablers which are the factors allowing organizations to integrate quality into their culture.
3. The element of quality culture representing artifacts, symbols and rituals in organizations.
4. Transversal elements liking various components of together with the help of cooperation, trust and communication.

Quality Culture Definition

A quality culture definition hinges on two main elements:

> A cultural element of factors such as shared values, beliefs, expectations and quality commitment and a psychological element of understanding, flexibility, participation, hopes and emotions.

> A structural or managerial element having structured process improving quality and aiming at the coordination of individual tasks—individual, units and services' standards and responsibilities.

The two aspects are to be considered together and related through effective communication, discussion and participatory process at the institutional level (EUA, 2006). Based on the European University Association (EUA, 2006), some quality features provide meanings such as: quality as compliance (having zero errors), quality as fitness for purpose, quality as quality as excellence, customer satisfaction, quality as enhancement in the process of changing the institution, quality as value for money, quality as transformation in the process of changing the customer, and quality as control in the process of punitive/reward of quality assurance.

Quality culture can be defined according to the list as, "an organizational climate in which groups of staff work together to realize their specific tasks" (EUA, 2006). Harvey (2009) stated that quality culture is synonymous to "the development of, and compliance with, processes of internal quality assurance". It can also be stated that quality culture is a value system of the organization resulting in an environment characterized by its continuous quality improvement.

Quality Culture Criteria

According to Lakhe & Mohantry (1994), the criteria for quality culture improvement include: organizational processes, procedures and policies emphasizing quality, employee understanding of the importance of quality in meeting business goals, employee awareness of customer requirements and needs the permission of continuous enhancement attempts by the business structure, the integration of internal and external customer needs with business quality plan, the importance of customer-based performance criteria, the development of a tight communication network, the development of customer loyalty, the emphasis and assistance of top management in clarifying values and beliefs regarding customers.

Moreover, Gordon (2000b) describes quality culture as, "easy to say but hard to do openly, honestly and convincingly" although it is likely to be the important factor that promotes the building of internal and external partnerships that are committed to its development (Gordon, 2000b, p. 76).

National culture and Municipalities: National culture can have a strong control on people's tendency to react towards administrations' responsibility for public sector competency. As such, public sector administration scholars are required to take care of the cultural values possessed by its team players. Researchers are required to be altered to suit the local cultures, specifically when public sector practices enhanced in one culture are equally assigned to public organizational in different culture. For instance, a policy or practice structured for a nation's public sector leaders may require to be altered when assigned in other countries. (Alshaya, 2002, dissertation).

The positioning of national culture appears to be the crux in elaborating national public administration differences because national culture influences organizations' policies and practices (Hofested, 1993). National culture values that further strengthen the human resources in a firm are more appropriate to render predictable behaviour and enhanced performance. One of the reasons is similar firms practices are congrous with current behaviour practices that govern the workplace.

There is valid proof that national cultures and management practices differ relying on the national culture in discussion {Luthans, Welsh& Rosenkrantz (1993); Newman & Nollen, (1996)}. Albeit, culture can be stated not only at the national level, but also at the group, firms, and even international levels, (e.g., "American" culture, "European" culture, "Arab" culture, etc.). All these cultures have influence on the option and efficiency of organization policies and practices.

As such, the difference between national and other types of culture is critical, and has been significantly searched in the literature. However, national culture specific value in understanding management policies and practices (Adler, 1997). Based on this research, Hofestede conducted study among 67 nations and took feedback of over 116,000 employees from multinational firms to enhance a platform for national culture. Based on this data, four key parameters were explored: Power Distance, Individualism, Masculinity, Uncertainty Avoidance, and Long-Term Orientation, (Hofstede, 1993; Hofstede & Bond, 1988; Hofstede & Hofstede, 2005).

Flynn and Saladin (2006) quoted Hofstede's comments that national culture is "collective programming." This collective programming enhances due to the experience contributed by dwellers of the same country from those of another. Hofstede's research on national culture is widely elaborated as milestone and is largely used as a theoretical foundation for swaying cross-cultural comparisons (Lundberg, 1988).

Culture renders a mark of adaptation to people. Significant management study signifies that the ultimate viewpoint of culture is "a set of ideas shared by members of a group" (Jaeger, 1986). National culture is the wholesome programming that happens from instances gathered from values such as family, government, religion, architecture, and even science (Flynn & Saladin, 2006). National culture alters very slowly because what becomes thinking of people of a nation also becomes embedded culture in its firms. Hofstede's work on national culture is widely elaborated as milestone and is significantly used as a theoretical foundation for leading cross-cultural comparisons, especially using the original four dimensions.

These days, cross-cultural studies become significantly critical (Inkson *et al.*, 2007; Tams & Arthur, 2007) and the foundation of the current research can be understood in the viewpoint of the convergence–divergence–crossvergence debate (Ralston, 2008): how much do the direct and indirect associations of culture and career success differ in an increasingly globalizing scenario? Researches emphasized the criticality of nationality to the management of organizations (Faucheux, Amado & Laurent, 1982; Hofstede, 1983; Inzerilli & Laurent, 1983). Also, studies found that organizational behaviour varied as a result of national culture and as a consequence.

Significant studies have been inducted to have an impact upon the national culture in various fields and organizations, more specifically at the degree of the private sector. Wide culture study in international business study and practice started in earnest during the 1980s, after Hofstede's (1980, 1983) pioneering work in classifying national cultures was published, and widely acclaimed on the fundamentals to apply in analyzing, and understanding, national cultures. As this framework rose to significance in culture study in the 1990s, international business researchers learned from developments in cognate disciplines, such as anthropology and organizational behaviour, and enhanced their research of culture with utmost care.

Significant studies elaborated on the effect of country variable on the acceptance of the new manufacturing paradigm. These international comparisons helped to denote whether such practices are dependent on a geographical idiosyncrasy or are applicable in national and cultural settings other than the original.

For any reason, national culture is of importance to the managerial practices or organizational strategic adaptation (Metters, 2008). The pertinence of the national culture in researching variances in manufacturing practices is also concluded by research, such as that of Burgess (1995), who states worldwide manufacturing competitiveness, Pagell *et al.*,'s (2005) research on similar manufacturing plants in the same firms's proximity in different countries, and Metters' (2008) study on outsourcing services. Moreover, in the HRM literature various studies showcase the significance of understanding the key parameters of policies and practices in various regional and national settings that are interrelated to the national culture

(Budhwar & Sparrow, 2002). The research of the European Commission (2002) ascertained this fact in lieu of the new forms of work organizations.

Rivera-Vazquez *et al.*, (2009) in their research was to denote the cultural obstructions that resets knowledge production as (combination of experience, values, expert and contextual facts that help the people or firm in the evolution and absorption of new experience), and sharing in firms of the Municipality of Caguas at the Commonwealth of the Puerto Rico in order to search for dynamic methods to get over them. The objective is to find on how the firm enhances efficiency among people and how they structure a viable ambience for knowledge production. They have found that at managerial level, both private and public agencies have got over with known obstructions that resets the knowledge sharing, while from the questionnaires it is established at the employee level that various cultural obstructions such as organizational environment, emotional intelligence and managers' commitment continues to exist.

Ralston *et al.*, (1997) scrutinized the effect of national culture and economic ideology on managerial work values in four national cultures using the Schwartz value survey. Their conclusions supported the belief that national culture and economic ideology both had an effect on work values in China, Japan, Russia and the USA. Ringov & Zollo (2007), in their research designed to elaborate how national differences in cultural values have an effect on organizations' social and environmental performance. They used dataset consisting of ratings of the social and environmental performance of 1,100 public companies from 34 nations on five continents issued by Innovest Group. They concluded that two of the four dimensions of national culture studied, which are power distance and masculinity, have an effect in high magnitude and in the hypothesized negative direction the intended quality of corporate behaviour. Albeit, no major effect was upheld out in their data for the other two parameters of national culture—uncertainty avoidance and collectivism.

Paul *et al.*, (2006) put to use Hofstede's framework to find the relationship between the cultural values and marketing ethics in the USA and India and learned that these societies varied in how they react to ethical predicament, again emphasizing, like the past research, that national culture have a significance. At last, in the pretext of marketing strategy, Cagliano *et al.*, (2010), in their research were to have an understanding of the relationship between the acceptance of new forms of work organizations and measures of nations impact, in terms of national culture and economic development through data from the fourth edition of the International Manufacturing Strategy Survey, while Hofstede's measures are embraced for national culture. They learned that it is feasible to elaborate various patterns in the adoption of new forms of work organizations practices when taking into fact company size and cultural parameters. Gross national income is instead only major for some practices and does not always positively have an effect on acceptance of new forms of work organizations. Alternatively, cultural variables are interrelated to all the practices, but there is no singled out dimension out of many to elaborate higher or lower new forms of work organizations adoption.

Various international studies have stated national level altering viewpoints with respect to the degree of job satisfaction. The national differences stated are comparable among the researches so it does seem that there is an externally driven national factor affecting the degree of job satisfaction in a nation.

Eskildsen & Kristensen, (2010) scrutinized the correlation between job satisfaction and national culture. For the analysis, the document used data from The European Employee Index from 2008 and 2009 as well as scores in Hofstede's five angles of national culture. Their data used in this research were gathered in 2008 and 2009. A total of 25,411 assessors from the following 22 nations gathered and their findings stipulated that national culture does have an effect on the national level of job satisfaction but not on entire national level evaluations of job related parameter.

Don, Kash (2010) researched the criticality of culture on the invention of technological study. It carried out case studies of the invention of 13 technology products and processes structured around China and other five countries. They found Innovation success in the several technology sectors varies within nation including China in part because of varying national cultures—the norms and values that leads and restricts both the individuals in societies and the societies on an overall view.

Herbig & Dunphy (1998) considered that apt environments for innovation are characterized largely by higher individualism, desire to take risks, willingness to adapt change, long-term orientation, and low on power/status/hierarchy (low power distance). Albeit, these research about the influence of national culture on IT and innovation adoption are for sure a useful analogy to our research of culture and e-government as whether people of country use government web sites and e-services are in certain percentage dependent on their desire of adoption of IT.

Lin, L.H. (2009) in their research was in 14 nations, and their learnings proclaim that uncertainty avoidance and long-term orientation positively affect innovation. In addition, high uncertainty avoidance and low power distance increases reliability of process. Co-operation and member participation is put in front in cultures with low power distance since employees are given decision making power to develop themselves and the processes management in global automakers.

Seleim & Bontis (2009) researched the relationship between the GLOBE project national cultural dimensions of values and practices and the Corruption. The GLOBE project is dependant on the recognition of 18,000 individuals they found. The results render empirical support for the effect of uncertainty avoidance values, human orientation practices, and individual collectivism practices on the degree of corruption after restricting economic and human development, which, on the other hand, adds to the efforts to structure a general theory of the culture angle of corruption. Cultural dimensions may affect one's recognition of ethical situations (Scott *et al.*, 1993); as such, national cultural differences are expected to affect corruption. Understanding cultural dimensions that may affect the degree of corruption is crucial for an organization's and a country's competitiveness (Davis & Ruhe, 2003) and for performing international business abroad (Park, 2003). Past researches have shown that national culture is critical factor that may narrate corruption, but this has not been scrutinized among various nations. Current study is an extended arm of empirical studies that have used Hofstede's (1983) culture dataset. Empirical studies that made use of Hofstede's measures in narrating various phenomena take into consideration that cultural values are stable and are applicable to current ethical situations debates that Hofstede's findings are priceless with respect to applying cultural analysis to practical management problems, even though they were at start reported more than 25 years ago.

Laurent (1983) elaborated that global companies have not overcome in restricting differences in the different cultures found within firms covering employees of different nationalities. Moreover, research analyzing culture and the relationship between the type of national culture and organizational effectiveness found that specific national culture types were related to given organizational effectiveness (Lau & Ngo, 1996; Pettigrew, 1979; Shane, 1992, 1993).

Alajmi *et al.*, (2011) in their study was to scrutinize the effect of national culture in relation of power distance and indecision avoidance on service provision in relation to information flow and communication policy among the Takaful industry (Islamic insurance) in Kuwait and Egypt. Results showcase that: more differences than similarities relies between Kuwait and Egypt in terms of power distance and indecision avoidance, which enforce that the differences in national culture between the two countries are in different perspective to Hofstede's claim of homogeneity of Arab culture, and national culture in relation to power distance and indecision avoidance influence service provision in relation to information flow and communication policy, respectively.

More share of current research has been oriented on studying the influence of culture on service quality from the customer perspective and oriented to comparisons between US and European samples, and Middle Orient samples (Donthu & Yoo, 1998).

Zhao, *et al.*, (2011), in his research made use of E-government Development Index from the United Nations E-government Survey 2010 and Hofstede's culture dimension index scores of 84 nations, to scrutinize whether national culture has an effect on e-government development in 84 nations across the world. He found that there is a linkage to varying level between e-government development and the five culture parameter defined by Hofstede, although only individualism, power distance and long-term orientation are stringly interlinked with e-government development. Numerous researchers have found that cultural parameters play a crucial role in ICT/IT/IS adoption (Dwyer *et al.,* 2005; Srite &Karahanna, 2006; Zhang & Maruping, 2008). Hofstede (2001) elaborates that low-uncertainty-avoidance cultures make enhanced use of a recent technological innovation, the internet, than do high-uncertainty-avoidance societies. The study of Erumban & de Jong (2006) concluded that national culture and the IT adoption rate of a country are interlinked. They conceded that Hofstede's parameters are affecting IT adoption. Specifically, the power distance and the indecision avoidance dimensions of national culture appears to be utmost crucial.

In any case, from the earlier studies and researches in the area of public sector there are proof that the criticality of national culture and its effect on service sectors and the public sector in general and specifically for municipalities. Overall, National culture was found to colour overall aspects in which individuals are engaged (Hall, 1989; Hofstede, 1983), and established their behaviour and attitudes toward such fundamentals as authority, responsibility, autonomy and profit (Graves, 1972).

UNDERPINNING THEORY

One of the main aims behind the present study is to investigate the moderating effect of national culture upon the relationship between Soft and Hard TQM, and organizational performance. Owing to the nature of the variables relevant to the study, there are various underpinning theories that are appropriate to be used as the study framework. The following paragraphs discuss the contingency theories and their supportive arguments.

Organizational Change Management Theory

The theory stresses on the significance of effective alignment between people and culture and the needed changes to facilitate the move towards the expected future state characterized by effectiveness (Jones, 2004).

The goal behind any organizational change initiative is the achievement of a new better position whereby the organization is enabled to use its resources in an efficient way and obtain benefits of its capabilities in an attempt to maximize the creation of value and competitive advantage (Jones, 2004). In addition, factors such as technology, economic factors, legal factors and socio-political factors are critical drivers of organizational change (Ivancevich & Matteson, 2002). Moreover, there organizational forces are influenced by various forces including competition, economic situations, political changes and ethical needs. A change initiative of any kind may face challenges from different organizational levels.

Organizational change is driven by the global competitive environment and therefore, changes may take place in manufacturing, service and public organizations (Diefenbach, 2007). Furthermore, change as stated by Romanelli & Tushman (1994) may take place in five core domains namely, strategy structure, culture and power distributions, which significantly impact organizational activities.

According to McGuire & Hutchings (2006), organizational changes are linked to human resource and process issues within the firm and hence, current organizations adopt human-resource-oriented and process-oriented strategies to help them survive and develop in a competitive environment (Schuler, 2000). TQM may in fact be considered as change initiatives which attempt to produce changes in human behaviour as well as processes in the firm. This is the reason why these strategies hinge on culture (Rad, 2006).

Organizational Development Theory

This theory has its basis on the study by Bennis (1996). The theory postulates a series of methods that are adopted by the organization to maximize its adaptability. Organizational development is considered as the educational strategies that the organization employ to change its values, attitudes and structure for better adaptation to the competitive, IT-driven and volatile business environment.

Jones (2004) stressed on the goal of organizational development theory in improving the organization's efficiency through the use of the organizational members' potential skills. The organization may leverage the same in establishing a beneficial match between the individual's and organizational goals. Moreover, there are various organizational development drivers including leadership development, change management and business process re-engineering. Organizational development is emphasized by Cusick (2005) as a general method of change management where the entire stakeholders are educated as to the way their functioning is enhanced in a continuous manner. The variables of the present study reveal some of the main elements that develop the way to human and process changes and development.

The Contingency Theory

On the basis of the contingency theory, there are many strategic choices that an organization can pursue that are dependent on the environment within which the organization operates (Schuler, 2000). The theory's emphasis lies on the concept of 'fit' as it has been stated in various ways (i.e. consistent with, contingent upon and aligning, (Venkataraman, 1989b). Stated differently, the concept of 'fit' or 'match' is the core premise behind the contingency theory (Lawrence & Lorsch, 1967). Scholars advocating the theory stresses on the requirement of the fit between the strategies of the organization and the organizational variables as the main criteria for critical performance (Selto *et al.*, 1995; and Van de Ven & Drazin, 1985).

As the fit is the main issue of the contingency theory (Van de Ven & Drazin, 1985), the term has been defined through the use of three approaches; selection approach, interaction approach, and the system approach. The first approach considers fit as the correlation between the environmental variables and the organizational variables while the second approach is concerned with the interaction between organizational and environmental variables. Finally, the last approach studies the impact of the interaction upon firm performance. In literature dedicated to contingency theory, scholars have claimed that organizational performance could be enhanced with the realization of an effective alignment between the main organizational variables (Naman & Slevin, 1993). Based on the theory, the relationship between two variables depends on the level of a third variable. Hence, it was highly recommended that the introduction of a moderator variable into the relationship of the two variables may allow a more specific comprehension and prevention of misleading outcome concerning contingency relationships. For the better understanding of the inconsistent findings of the relationship between organizational strategies and organizational performance, this theory made significant contribution to the development of management sciences (Venkataraman, 1989b).

In order to explain and understand the TQM-organizational performance relationship, literature brings forward some potential moderating variables (Lumpkin & Dess, 1996; Prajogo & McDermott, 2005; Sila & Ebrahimpour, 2002, 2005; Zahra & Covin, 1995; and Zahra & Garvis, 2000). Among the most significant organizational variables having the potential of moderating power between organizational strategies and performance is culture (Prajogo & McDermott, 2005; Sila & Ebrahimpour, 2002, 2005; and Zahra & Garvis, 2000). As mentioned earlier, the primary objective of the present study is the examination of the role of national culture in the TQM-organizational performance relationship. Based on literature, it may be stated that national culture may be among the major critical factors that enables or hinders effective strategy implementation (Metters, 2008). Therefore, the present study tried to integrate organizational change theory and the contingency theory as was reflected in the congruence model as its underpinning theory to examine the moderating role of national culture on the TQM-organizational performance relationship.

The study aims to examine the level to which TQM strategy fits national culture and how it impacts the overall organizational performance of municipalities in five countries namely Jordan, Egypt, Qatar, Saudi Arabia, and Turkey. In sum, this model in conjunction with other theories discussed above proves its strengths to expound the relationships among the study variables.

Three

Theoretical Framework

THEORETICAL FRAMEWORK OF THE STUDY

Following the thorough literature review and the identification of subsequent theoretical gaps, the research framework of the study is designed. The study model is depicted in Figure 3.1 where four latent variables are presented namely Soft Total Quality Management, Hard Total Quality Management, National Culture, and Organizational Performance. Soft TQM is explained by a total of five variables which are management commitment, supplier relationship, employee relations, education and training, strategic planning, customer focus. On the other hand, Hard TQM is explained by process management, quality information and analysis, and strategy planning. Organizational performance is explained by four variables namely financial element, customer, internal process and employee performance (Learning and growth performance) and National Culture is presented by four variables which are Hofstede's (1980) popular cultural dimensions that power distance, individualism, uncertainty avoidance, and masculinity.

There is a call for current researchers to examine the variables that may improve the TQM implementation success.

The framework below is used to test the postulated hypotheses.

HYPOTHESIS DEVELOPMENT

Soft TQM Practices and Organizational Performance

The soft factors are related to performance in a positive way. Flynn *et al.*, (1995) study attempted to investigate the relationship among the eight dimensions of quality management performance through a track analysis. The analysis revealed that soft factors include management support, supplier relationship, customer relationship, and people management. Also, Samson & Terziovski (1999) created six quality factors and regressed

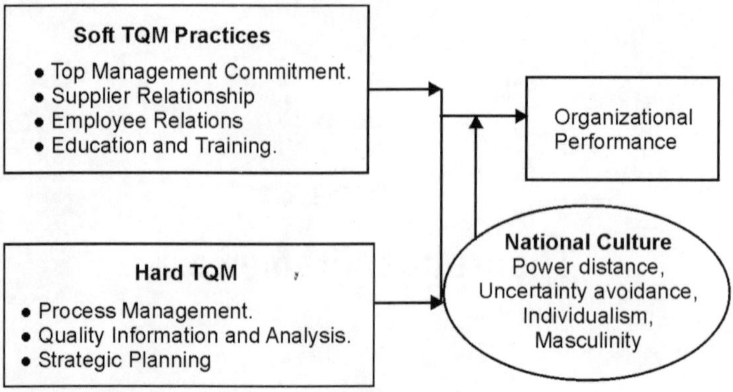

Figure 3.1: Theoretical Framework of the Study

them against organizational performance (through proxies of customer satisfaction, output quality, productivity, employee morale, and delivery performance). The findings showed significant positive links between organizational performance and several soft factors including customer focus, leadership, and people management. Also, Rahman & Bullock (2005) examined manufacturing companies with the help of regression analysis. Their findings showed that quality management comprising of people management, supplier relations, customer focus and shared vision, impact the performance of the firm while several hard quality elements significantly impacts firm performance. They also found that hard elements are reinforced by soft elements of quality management. On the other hand, Powell (1995) showed that three out of his 12 soft TQM factors namely open organization, executive commitment, and employee empowerment were correlated with overall corporate performance in a significant way. Meanwhile Dow *et al.,* (1999) revealed that three out of his nine items of workforce namely shared vision, commitment, and customer focus showed positive connections with quality and performance in a significant way.

Similarly, Ahire *et al.,* (1996) showed consistent findings in their study regarding automobile manufacturing and component companies in the US. They revealed performance in the light of product quality was correlated significantly with the soft TQM elements including employee training, employee empowerment, and employee involvement. The studies however, employed varying sets of indicators as performance measures. For example, Dow *et al.,* (1999) and Ahire *et al.,* (1996) employed a narrow quality focused definition to performance while Powell (1995) made use of a range of specific measures of TQM performance. Soft TQM elements are actually HRM dimensions. The soft TQM coverage in the literature of management is comprehensive and management offered prescriptions are very similar to TQM literature. According to Dean & Bowen (1994), three out of six criteria in Malcolm Bladridge National Quality Award (MBNQA) framework are encompassed in the management literature. They are leadership, HRM and strategic quality planning; all are also soft TQM. Powell (1995) reached the conclusion that organizations obtaining TQM soft elements exhibit superior performance to those who are not following the TQM ideology.

Soft TQM—Top Management Commitment and Organizational Performance

One of the significant factors of TQM strategy which is widely emphasized upon in the literature of TQM is management commitment. In majority of organizations, top management is considered the leader (Deming, 1986), the introducer (Agus, Abdullah, 2000), or the main driver (Ahire, 1996) for the implementation of TQM that creates values, goals and systems for customer satisfaction. Owing to its considerable role, it can be stated that any TQM effort would be useless without the full commitment of top management. In recognition of the significance of management commitment, majority of national quality awards on a global scale have included the leadership criteria as among the core evaluation criteria (Chuan & Soon, 2000). For the well performance of functions, according to Koehler & Pankowski, 1996, TQM organization leadership should be experts in teaching, measurement, communication, team-building, facilitation, decision making, self-management and empowerment. If the entire requirement involves the performance by top management in an effective way, it could be implied that the management's commitment to the TQM implementation would result in superior organizational performance in a general dimensional range such as work process, working environment, cost saving and customer fulfillment. For example, good communication practices may enhance the work process and top management commitment to teambuilding practices would result in an effective working environment. The good practice of measurement may also lead to minimal error and hence, enhance the ability to satisfy the customers' needs. Prior studies have empirically acknowledged the relationship between management commitment and organizational performance (Arawati, 2005; Flynn *et al.*, 1995; Llorens Montes & Verdu Jover, 2004; Powell, 1995; & Yasin *et al.*, 2004). Hence, the following hypothesis is postulated:

H1a: *Soft TQM-Top Management Commitment significantly affects the organizational performance.*

Soft TQM—Supplier Relationship and Organizational Performance

In majority of cases, the price spent for employing a qualified supplier is greater than those paid for other suppliers. Nevertheless, the qualified supplier is more able to offer quality information which would lead to the minimization of the potential of producing products that are defective. In turn, with a minimal work defect, the cost for product quality would also decrease.

Viewed differently, quality material would also result in superior work process which leads to maximized level of employees' satisfaction. In addition, minimal quality cost would enable organizations to produce products at a reasonable cost and to sell products at reasonable prices exceeding customers' expectations. It is evident that long-term relationship with a qualified supplier and a quality based supplier selection would mean superior outcome to organizations. In prior empirical studies, many researchers acknowledged the relationship between supplier relationship and organizational performance (Rahman & Bullock, 2005; Flynn *et al.*, 1995). There are several studies dedicated to this significant factor in the context of non-manufacturing organizations. Khairul Anuar *et al.*, (2001) and Sanchez-Rodriguez & Martinez-Lorente (2004) are among them. Public sector is attributable to many suppliers especially the commercial sectors, government donors, non-governmental organizations, traders and various sectors of different organizations as well as other social organizations. Thus, the following hypothesis is postulated:

H1b: *Supplier relationship significantly affects organizational performance.*

Soft TQM—Employee Relations and Organizational Performance

According to Karuppusami & Gandhinathan (2006), employee relations comprise of employee satisfaction, employee empowerment, employee participation, employee involvement, delegation and empowerment, employee fulfillment, and worker-manager interactions. Similarly, Ahire *et al.*, (1996) claimed the presence of a high correlation between employee involvement and employee empowerment. Literature review concerning quality management confirmed the significant role of employees in successful organizational change initiatives carried out by an organization in an attempt to achieve both sustainability and competitiveness. This is consistent with Akdere's (2006) argument that the TQM practices are related to organizational competitiveness in a positive way through the employee's inputs. A major portion of literature concerning the topic urges that a great deal of attention should be bestowed upon employee practices including employee empowerment, and involvement for the achievement of overall organizational objectives (Kekale & Kekale, 1995).

Employee empowerment in all levels of organization often leads to TQM success but sometimes, it may lead to failure if not carried out according to employees' skills and experience (Gatchalian, 1997). As a result, if employees in the organization are empowered, and provided with quality training, and encouraged to get involved in team work, they are highly expected to play a main role in the success of TQM implementation as TQM successful initiatives call for the members of the organizations' participation.

Similarly, Powell (1995) claimed that employee empowerment is among the TQM values that are significant to organizational performance. Also, Dow *et al.,* (1999) revealed that workforce commitment has a significant positive relation with performance. In addition, Madu *et al.,*'s (1995) survey revealed a significant causal link between employee satisfaction and organizational performance. The stress across the entire stages of TQM implementation is upon the involvement of all the employees in decision-making, problem-solving and organizational success. In other words, TQM emphasizes that employees at all levels should be closely linked to the organizational targets and objectives (Collard, 1989). Every employee is in control of his work and should be capable of participating in the company's business. Involvement calls for employees' empowerment, provision of information, increasing their knowledge, and rewarding quality performance (Oliver, 1998). Empowerment often calls for a change in the organization's infrastructure which involves senior management's giving up of their authority according to a principle requiring the whole organization to establish a quality chain with every part having its own contribution.

It also needs employee involvement to facilitate on-going improvement of quality and maximization of productivity. The philosophy is not only needed in the entire stages but also in every TQM aspect including commitment. Another critical point of employee involvement is that every individual understands their own internal customers receiving their work. Hence, each employee has to discuss internal customers' needs which represent the first step to knowing the requirements of everyone and facilitating customer satisfaction. Besides requesting every staff member to participate in the quality process, an organization should also consider the shared responsibility. In other words, individuals and groups possess common objectives but varying tasks and hence, must work well and comprehend others' works to ensure the effective operation of the whole process.

The study conducted by Khairul Anuar *et al.,* (2001) was conducted in the local government in Malaysia and the findings revealed that among the important factors of quality management is employee focus and it had a positive relationship with organizational performance. Data gathered by the Workplace Employee Relations Survey (WERS, 1990) was utilized by Fernie & Metcalf (1995) and they reported the existence of communication channels, attempts at boosting employee and financial involvement schemes result in enhanced levels of productivity and growth.

In a similar study, Moorhouse (2006) examined the relationship between employee relations practices and enhanced organizational performance and he stated that improved workplace diversity leads to maximized employee commitment and involvement. Other researchers view employee relations as making up only a portion of the process. For example, work intensification is related by some to high performance work practices leading to a possible conflict between practices and policies of work-life balance. There is evidently some debate regarding how far measures to improve work-life balance can be viewed as part of an overreaching method to employee relations and has a hand in the development of high-performing organizations.

According to Ishikawa (1985), employee fulfillment hinges on the way organizations keep satisfying employees' needs i.e. job satisfaction, job commitment, and workmanship pride. In addition, Kerr (1996) examined the Northern Telecom in Canada and claimed that employee fulfillment, commitment and engagement are crucial in the company. Aside from the employee's commitment to his work, sufficient and suitable rewards and recognitions like salary, bonuses and promotions may also add to employee satisfaction. Similarly, Crosby (1989) viewed recognition to be among the most crucial steps in quality improvement process. Several scholars stated that internal customers/employees are the drivers of total quality management movement. When employees acknowledge the value of their work, their performance improves which implies the critical value of employee fulfillment in TQM process.

More importantly, Robbins (2006) stated that employee involvement may be described as a participative process through which employees maximize their commitment to the success of the organization. In other words, participation is important in urging an employee's action on quality management since it often results in changes in his/her working attitude as well as behaviour. TQM involvement indicates an invitation to every firm member to participate in the process of quality improvement (Deming, 1986). The underlying paradigm of the construct is the rationale that worker's involvement would impact their behaviour, maximize their autonomy making them take control of their work depending on the discussion above, the hypothesis is postulated as follows:

H1c: *Soft TQM—Employee relations significantly affects organizational performance.*

Soft TQM—Education and Training and Organizational Performance

Human capital theory generally mentions that the prior acquired knowledge has a key role in intellectual performance and also helps in the integration, gathering of new knowledge, and integration and adaptation to new scenarios (Weick, 1996). More particularly, education may be an indication of ability or other characteristics that employers should consider as it contributes to productivity although it is not easily observable. Hence, schooling is not only accepted for its effect of productivity, but also for its indication of productive ability in labour markets sans the entire information (Spence, 1973; and Riley, 2002). As people accept that without proper education, organizations often fail to achieve goals, universities ask for funds to organize specific courses and workshops. Every project targets different areas including managers, firms, organizations desirous of employing students (Adcroft *et al.*, 2005).

Several authors, managers and entrepreneurs consider entrepreneurial education as the core to organizational performance; in other words, entrepreneurship is the actual difference between success and failure in the context of a global economy in a sense that a connection exists between educational programmes and organizational performance (Cruz *et al.*, 2009). Evidence concerning education and performance outcomes is still limited but empirical studies examining the impact of training in the workplace are innumerable and they report conclusive findings. Some of them are consistent with the view that training positively impact individual or organizational productivity including Holzer *et al.*, (1993); Zwick (2005); Alba-Ramirez (1994) & Conti (2005).

Others state that organizational performance directly links to employee training (Delaney & Huselid, 1996), and suitable training facilitates communication and enhanced work quality (Fussell, Kraut & Siegel, 2000). Suitable training enhances workers' knowledge and skills which in turn, enhance productivity in tasks and the overall organizational productivity. The relationship between training and organizational performance is strong in the context of social organizations (Huang, 2001).

Along the same line of study, Hansson (2007) made use of an international dataset gathered from 26 countries in his attempt to investigate the level to which training investments improve organizational performance. He found that the amount invested in training was the main variable implying that the economic benefits of training are higher than the cost of staff turnover and executive management plays a key role in training. In the context of UAE, Zeffane & Al-Zarooni (2008) investigated the employees' reaction to management training objectives and found that organizational culture impacted job satisfaction which in turn affected organizational commitment. The kind of training planned is extensive and it includes professional training for current skills and knowledge, extensive training for career enhancement that is consistent to organizational goals, lateral training linking to organizational goals, policies and work practices, customer awareness training, and awareness training in the business sector, regulatory change or in the economy. For instance, employee training in change management involves a takeover or merger where organizational goals, policies and practices are convergent. This involves intensive training to incorporate organizational culture and to make sure that employees are aware of the new inclusive organizational purpose.

Nickels (2009) stated that the impact of training upon the performance of employees frequently facilitates growth in the worker and the organization. Training may result to self-fulfilling expectation of improved employee output where employee development corresponds to decreased operational costs and results in greater organization loyalty and improved job satisfaction. He added that the impact of training upon the performance of employee meets and sometimes exceeds expectations, and involves staff cross training, preparing for promotion, maintaining a safe environment and minimization of errors. Moreover, the findings of the Grips & Savermann's (2010) study showed that training of agents significantly impacts the worker's productivity.

H1d: *Soft TQM—Education and training significantly impact the organizational performance.*

Soft TQM—Customer Focus and Organizational Performance

Literature reports that the eventual target of TQM strategy is the satisfaction of customers' needs and the meeting of their changing expectations. If the TQM strategy implementation fails to add value to customers, it is considered a failure (Thiagarajan & Zairi, 1997c). In an attempt to achieve customers' satisfaction, continuous and effective communication between organizations and customers is crucial which lead to high level of customers' involvement in products and service design (Hunt, 1995). For the customers' complete involvement in the entire marketing activities, a long-life relationship strategy is called for through direct interaction. In addition, it is imperative for organizations to develop dependable customer-related databases encapsulating customers' needs and expectations along with on-going monitoring of their degrees of satisfaction.

Additionally, the strategic positioning issue lies in where and how an organization competes. These are significant emerging concepts of the Soft TQM theory that attempts at maintaining a high level of customer satisfaction through high quality and innovative products as well as services. Meanwhile, several researchers revealed that customer satisfaction is very crucial for the organizational performance and that the higher its level, the lower will be the cost spent for operation, the greater will be the profit and the more improved will be the performance of the organization.

Mehra (2001) confirmed the importance of customer-focus for TQM initiatives to succeed by claiming that TQM is a customer-centered strategy. Moreover, on the basis of this emphasis on customer satisfaction and loyalty and its consideration as the core of business success, Mehra (2001) stated that TQM's customer-focus element will gain top importance in future literature dedicated to TQM.

Organization's attempts to produce profits and maximize market share should stem from the development of a loyal customer base through the satisfaction of their expectations. Customer satisfaction has been increasingly becoming important in the scholars and practitioners' circles as they acknowledge that satisfaction and loyalty of customers are the primary profit making generators. Along the same line, Agus *et al.*, (2000) stated that TQM strategy implementation enhances the financial performance of an organization through customer-focus processes. Accordingly, evidenced point to the positive impact of customer focus element of TQM strategy upon organizational performance (Llorens Montes & Verdu Jover, 2004; Yasin *et al.*, 2004). Therefore, the discussion above leads to following hypothesis.

H1e: *Soft TQM—Customer Focus significantly impacts organizational performance.*

Hard TQM and Organizational Performance

The production orientation in TQM is defined by the hard TQM which is related to the systems, tools and methods, thus, putting forth setting of standards of performance and controlling and measuring work conducted in an orderly manner (Wilkinson, *et al.*, 1992).

Based on the research performed by Thiagarajan & Zairi (1997), hard TQM values influence the internal efficiency of the firm while Sitkin *et al.*, (1994) demarcated the common guiding principles of TQM into three features; those that orient towards customer satisfaction, those that elaborate on-going improvement, and lastly, those that take into account the organization as an overall system. Hard TQM is influenced by a vital link with the second and third features. If the soft TQM affect organizational performance, then the question arises; what is the role of the hard TQM elements? Based on research (Powell, 1995; Dow *et al.*, 1999; and Ahire *et al.*, 1996), the degree of Statistical Process Control (SPC), the benchmarking use, and flexible manufacturing systems were not related with performance. Regardless, management literature signifies that hard TQM elements have a major effect on organizational performance. For instance, product and process benchmarking sway to optimal product design and process cost mitigation in DuPont, Ford, Motorola, Xerox, and General Motors (Min, 1992; & McFadden, 1993). In addition, other TQM tools were found to affect performance; six sigma processes in Motorola and in other firms (McFadden, 1993), QFD in Toyota (Sullivan, 1987), seven well known tools in Honda (Maul, 1994), SPC in Motorola (Kumar, 1993) and Taguchi methods in Mazda and Ford (Taguchi & Clausing, 1993).

Hard TQM—Process Management and Organizational Performance

The process management in the government services is more challenging considering the fact that services are more labour-intensive, and they are often produced and consumed at the same time. This makes uniformness and standardization more difficult. Furthermore, the consumer will assess the service by not only considering the result, but also considering the behaviour and even the appearance of the person that is delivering it. Moreover, quality measures for services are rather complex. Quality measures for services include many attributes such as access, competence, courtesy, creativity, dependability, et, Smith, (1993). The Malcolm Baldrige National Quality Improvement Act of 1987 proposed a template for implementing a set of high-performance management practices, including process management (Das *et al.*, 2000). According to Deming, the organizations are composed of interlinked processes and that improvement of these processes is the basis of performance improvements. Baker & Maddux, 2005, stated that there must be continuous evaluation and improvement of the processes to achieve a better performance. They confirmed that the process management demands knowledgeable individuals who are able to appropriately manage in the increasingly complex process-oriented environment. However, process management influence many attributes of organizations' performance (Cotteleer & Bendoly 2006; Davenport 1993).

In any case, the extensive literature on business process management suggests that organizations can enhance the total performance by adopting a process view of business. However, there has not been that much empiric research on the impact of business process management practices and process management on organizational performance.

Zairi (1997) describes Process Management as an organized approach to analyze and constantly improve key activities such as, communications and other major factors of organization's operations. Process Management relies on measuring activity to assess the performance of each and every process, place targets and deliver output levels which can achieve corporate objectives. Lee & Dale (1998) state that Process Management is designated to coordinate the business processes with strategic objectives and customers' demands, but that still requires a change in a company's emphasis from functional orientation to process-wise orientation.

Samson & Terziovski (1999) used process management, and performance as elements of total quality management in their study on the relationship between total quality management practices and performance.

Škrinjar *et al.,* (2008) in his investigation confirms the effect of process management on the organizational performance in a transition economy. The link is even stronger than in the preceding investigation. The results show that business process management leads to a better non-financial performance and—indirectly—to a better financial performance.

Hinterhuber (1995) refers to the following effects (amongst others) of process management: increase in product and service quality; increase of internal and external customer satisfaction. Hirzel (2008) names the following items (amongst others) an organization benefits from process management; improvement of customer satisfaction; improvement of quality.

Tari's (2005) study describes elements that are important for the successful application of TQM from the literature, and he stated that process management (Quality manual, quality system procedures and work Instructions ISO 9001 certificate), is one of the essential factors of them. Hence, the following hypothesis is postulated;

H2 a: *Hard TQM*—Process management *significantly impacts organizational performance.*

Hard TQM—Quality Information and Analysis System and Organizational Performance

Quality management literature has stressed upon effective information system as among the most crucial factors contributing significantly to successful TQM initiatives (Ahire *et al.,* 1996). The significance of information system as the amalgamation of hardware, software, people and processes is the basis behind most national quality awards, including MBNQA. These awards underlie the significance of information systems as one of the major criteria that should be managed and utilized by firms in an effective way (Kartha, 2004). On the basis of Saraph *et al.,*'s (1989) study, the importance of information and analysis systems has been stressed on for the effective performance of the firm particularly in this age of information and communication technology (ICT). They added that only firms having proper and effective information systems can react in a positive way to the dynamic business environment owing to their effective data collection, presentation and dissemination.

Also, several researchers including Flynn *et al.,* (1995) showed a positive relationship between quality information systems and organizational performance. This relationship stems from thorough knowledge and effective use of customer-related information which results in high levels of customer satisfaction and operations efficiency. Hence, the following hypothesis is brought forward for testing:

H2b: *Hard TQM—Quality Information and Analysis System significantly impact organizational performance.*

Hard TQM—Strategic Planning and Organizational Performance

Strategic planning covers activities upon which a firm develops, employs and assesses all other strategies in its attempt to achieve organizational goals (Srinidhi, 1998). In addition, strategic planning is also utilized to keep TQM strategy consistent with the rest of the organizational strategies. In other words, TQM-Strategic planning views the organizational capabilities including sufficient funds, skilled employees and sufficient time to achieve the goals of employed strategies (Black & Porter, 1996).

Researchers stressed on the importance of strategic planning by claiming that the organization's ability to survive in volatile business environment may be gauged through its policies of strategic planning (Chenhall, 2005). Similarly, top management in the TQM context has also been stressed to be involved strategically throughout the strategic planning element of TQM (Krumwiede & Charles, 2006). In an ideal situation, strategic planning views the process through which the organizational vision and mission are transformed into short and long-term plans to be carried out (Tari, 2005). Moreover, strategic planning as a TQM strategy should develop rules of thumb on the way organizations develop its TQM practices in the hopes of achieving its objectives and aligning them with the needs and expectations of customers (Sila & Ebrahimpour, 2002). Literature review of TQM showed that prior studies' findings support the existence of a relationship between strategic planning and organizational performance (Li *et al.*, 2003; Sila & Ebrahimpour, 2005; Sila & Ebrahimpour, 2002; Wu *et al.*, 1997). Hence, the following hypothesis is postulated:

H2 c: *Hard TQM—Strategic Planning significantly impacts organizational performance.*

NATIONAL CULTURE (NC) AS A MODERATING VARIABLE

Culture has been examined in light of organizations by several researchers, e.g. Yusof & Aspinwall, 1999; Chang & Wiebe, 1996; Dellana & Hauser, 1999; Shortell *et al.*, 1995, while others, Denison & Mishra, 1995; and Kotter & Heskett, 1992, added to literature by investigating its impact upon the performance. These studies revealed that cultural strengths are associated with short-term financial performance and that organizations having adaptive values are significantly linked with superior performance in long-term as opposed to short term (Kotter & Heskett, 1992). The inconsistent findings of performance implications of TQM coming from Sila & Ebrahimpour (2002) led several studies (Ehigie & McAndrew, 2005) to suggest the examination of the impact of some organizational variables upon the relationship.

Nevertheless, on the basis of the argument which holds that national culture impacts management practices in organizations as reported by Newman & Nollen (1996), Pagell, Katz & Sheu (2005), it is postulated that various national culture dimensions impact TQM values in different ways. Various values that societies and groups possess, drive their behaviour differently. Hence, the varying stress given to cultural values in society should be reflected in distinct management behaviours (Kelley, Whatley & Worthley, 1987).

Moreover, literature regarding in the field of operations has begun to reveal evidence that specific national culture dimensions also impact TQM implementation. Studies in literature have been invaluable in their contribution to the relationship between national culture and TQM. However, they appear to have an inconsistent theoretical framework that fails to extensively explain the national variations of TQM implementation. For instance, Mathews *et al.*, (2001) investigated the quality systems in the context of three European countries and revealed that differences in the methods do exist and that Hofstede's national culture dimensions of uncertainty avoidance and power distance are both suitable in explaining the variations. On the other hand, Mathews *et al.*, (2001) failed to develop and test the hypotheses regarding the relationships between the two constructs. Similarly, while Sousa-Poza, Nystrom & Wiebe (2001) conducted a comparison of the implementation of TQM values between three countries (US, Switzerland and South Africa) and showed that every region reflected specific relationships between types of organizational culture and TQM values. They stated that specific national cultures call for various methods for the effective implementation of TQM. As with the studies by Mathews *et al.*, (2001), this study also lacked specific hypotheses to test the relationships between the dimensions of national culture and TQM implementation.

Lagrosen (2003) was one of the many researchers who developed hypotheses for this purpose. He gathered data from quality managers in 30 countries who are linked with a large Swedish multinational company. Through Hofstede's framework, Lagrosen (2003) revealed partial support for his hypotheses relating Hofstede's national culture dimensions to TQM values. Moreover, both his analysis and findings were hindered by methodological issues like low number of participants and lack of scale development. Based on the above discussion, the following hypotheses are brought forward:

H3a: *National Culture—Power distance moderates the relationship between Soft TQM and the Municipality's organizational performance.*

H3a1: *National Culture—Power distance moderates the relationship between Soft TQM—Top Management Commitment and the Municipality's organizational performance.*

H3a2: *National Culture—Power distance moderates the relationship between Soft TQM Supplier Relationship and the Municipality's organizational performance.*

H3a3: *National Culture—Power distance moderates the relationship between Soft TQM—Employee Relations and the Municipality's organizational performance.*

H3a4: *National Culture—Power distance moderates the relationship between Soft TQM—Education & Training and the Municipality's organizational performance.*

H3a5: *National Culture—Power distance moderates the relationship between Soft TQM—Top Management Commitment and the Municipality's organizational performance.*

H3b: *National Culture—Uncertainty avoidance moderates the relationship between Soft TQM and the Municipality's organizational performance.*

H3b1: *National Culture—Uncertainty avoidance moderates the relationship between Soft TQM—Top Management Commitment and the Municipality's organizational performance.*

H3b2: *National Culture—Power distance moderates the relationship between Soft TQM—Supplier Relationship and the Municipality's organizational performance.*

H3b3: *National Culture—Uncertainty avoidance moderates the relationship between Soft TQM—Employee Relations and the Municipality's organizational performance.*

H3b4: *National Culture—Uncertainty avoidance moderates the relationship between Soft TQM—Education & Training and the Municipality's organizational performance.*

H3b5: *National Culture—Uncertainty avoidance moderates the relationship between Soft TQM—Top Management Commitment and the Municipality's organizational performance.*

H3c: *National Culture: Individualism moderates the relationship between Soft TQM and the Municipality's organizational performance.*

H3c1: *National Culture—Individualism moderates the relationship between Soft TQM—Top Management Commitment and the Municipality's organizational performance.*

H3c2: *National Culture—Individualism moderates the relationship between Soft TQM—Supplier Relationship and the Municipality's organizational performance.*

H3c3: *National Culture—Individualism moderates the relationship between Soft TQM—Employee Relations and the Municipality's organizational performance.*

H3c4: *National Culture—Individualism moderates the relationship between Soft TQM—Education & Training and the Municipality's organizational performance.*

H3c5: *National Culture—Individualism moderates the relationship between Soft TQM—Top Management Commitment and the Municipality's organizational performance.*

H3d: *National Culture: Masculinity moderates the relationship between Soft TQM and the Municipality's organizational performance.*

H3d1: *National Culture—Masculinity moderates the relationship between Soft TQM—Top Management Commitment and the Municipality's organizational performance.*

H3d2: *National Culture—Masculinity moderates the relationship between Soft TQM—Supplier Relationship and the Municipality's organizational performance.*

H3d3: *National Culture—Masculinity moderates the relationship between Soft TQM—Employee Relations and the Municipality's organizational performance.*

H3d4: *National Culture—Masculinity moderates the relationship between Soft TQM—Education & Training and the Municipality's organizational performance.*

H3d5: *National Culture—Masculinity moderates the relationship between Soft TQM—Top Management Commitment and the Municipality's organizational performance.*

H3e: *National Culture—Power Distance moderates the relationship between Hard TQM and the Municipality's organizational performance.*

H3e1: *National Culture—Power Distance moderates the relationship between Hard TQM Process management and the Municipality's organizational performance.*

H3e2: *National Culture—Power Distance moderates the relationship between Hard TQM Quality Information and Analysis System and Municipality's organizational performance.*

H3e3: *National Culture—Power Distance moderates the relationship between Hard TQM* Strategic Planning *and the Municipality's organizational performance.*

H3f: *National Culture—Uncertainty avoidance moderates the relationship between Hard TQM and the Municipality's organizational performance.*

H3f1: *National Culture: Uncertainty avoidance moderates the relationship between TQM Process management and the Municipality' organizational performance.*

H3f2: *National Culture: Uncertainty avoidance moderates the relationship between Hard TQM Quality Information and Analysis System and the Municipality's organizational performance.*

H3f3: *National Culture: Uncertainty avoidance moderates the relationship between Hard TQM Strategic Planning and the Municipality's organizational performance.*

H3g: *National Culture: Individualism moderates the relationship between Hard TQM and the Municipality's organizational performance.*

H3g1: *National Culture: Individualism moderates the relationship between TQM Process management and the Municipality's organizational performance.*

H3g2: *National Culture: Individualism moderates the relationship between Hard TQM Quality Information and Analysis System and the Municipality's organizational performance.*

H3g3: *National Culture: Individualism moderates the relationship between Hard TQM Strategic Planning and the Municipality's organizational performance.*

H3h: *National Culture: Masculinity moderates the relationship between Hard TQM and the Municipality's organizational performance.*

H3h1: *National Culture: Masculinity moderates the relationship between TQM Process management and the Municipality's organizational performance.*

H3h2: *National Culture: Masculinity moderates the relationship between Hard TQM Quality Information and Analysis System and the Municipality's organizational performance.*

H3h3: *National Culture: Masculinity moderates the relationship between Hard TQM Strategic Planning and the Municipality' organizational performance.*

H4: There are differences in organizational performance mean between these countries.

Four
Research Methodology

In this study, correlation studied using survey method. The survey is utilized to gather information related to the representative sample. This method may be carried out through a survey questionnaire or interview through which data collection is carried out. In addition, through this research method, the respondents were contacted through various means; internet, mail, telephone or in person through self-administered questionnaire.

POPULATION AND SAMPLING DESIGN

The population of the present study helps determine the impact of national culture upon the relationship between Soft and Hard TQM, and performance. A survey based on the Municipality organizations from various countries under study is developed. Hence, the population is confined to the municipalities of these countries.

The determination of sample size played an important role in the research, because a sample that was too small might have provided data that was not necessarily representative. According to Israel, (1992) for population (1000) ±10per cent Precision Levels where Confidence Level Is 95per cent and P =.5. Sample Size = 91. P (a proportion of.5 indicates the maximum variability in a population). Also Kline (2005) further suggested that there are no absolute standards in the literature about the relationship

Table 4.1: Sample of the Study

Country	*Population*	*Sample*	*Percent (%)*
Egypt	393	30	30
Saudi Arabia	235	30	18
Jordan	100	30	8
Turkey	570	30	44
Total	1,298	120	100

Source: Roscoe (1975), Krejcie & Morgan (1970) Tatham, Anderson& Black (1998).

between sample size and path model complexity. Therefore, determining sample size is considered one of the more controversial elements in research design and sampling procedures for the majority of studies. This is because drawing a large sample may waste time, resources and money. On the other hand, a small sample may not give accurate results, which will in turn affect the research validity and reliability. However, Hofstede suggested, that the minimum number of respondents per group or per country in the field of comparison studies between countries to be 20 respondents; below that number, the influence of single individuals becomes too strong (Hofstede, 1994).

A few recommendations have been brought forward by authors regarding the least sample size required for Structural Equation Modelling SEM analysis. According to the rule of thumb, the least sample size of 100 is sufficient for SEM (Medsker, Williams & Holahan, 1994). Many others such as Nunnally (1978) suggested the rule of thumb ratio, by which the number of subjects—to item ratio should be at least 10:1, Ding, *et al.*, (1995) suggested minimum sample size is 100. Also this sample size meets Hair, Tatham, Anderson& Black (1998) suggestion; they suggested that the minimum sample size of 100 to 150 ensures suitable use of likelihood estimation in structural equation modeling. Moreover this sample meets Kline suggestion which was a minimal sample size for path analysis is 100 (Kline 2002).

Therefore, from each country's municipality sector, the sample size is distributed as follows; 30 from Egypt, 30 from Jordan, 30 from Saudi Arabia and 30 from Turkey. In addition to 7 Municipalities (all the population) in Qatar, a total of 127 municipalities in five countries. To select the sample, a cluster sampling will use. This sampling design, which is the most efficient, is a good choice when groups that have heterogeneous members are first identified, and homogeneity inside the groups in the same country so some are chosen at random, in other words the samples will gather in groups or chunks of elements that, ideally, are natural aggregates of elements in the population. In cluster sampling, the target population in first will divide into cluster. Then, a random sample of clusters is drawn and for each selected cluster, either all the elements or sample of elements are included in the sample, whoever, inside every cluster we will chose a random sample 30 municipalities from every four countries. In this method, costs of data collection are low (Sekaran, 2003). Sample size for this study consisted of 120 municipalities, which match of what has been specified by Krejcie & Morgan (1970) that is, 120 for a population of 1,298. Furthermore, the sample size of the present study will comply with the rule of thumb by Roscoe (1975) who stated that in a lot of researches, sample size between 30 and 500 are appropriate. Therefore, 120 are adequate based on the rule of thumb. The selected sample size can be considered reasonable and manageable in terms of cost and time. The sample size of this study is shown in Table 4.1 below: (The study chooses the municipalities that have operation and maintenance managers from these countries). Thus, the sample will be as follows:

In Qatar, either the population (7) Municipalities is too small so it was taking all the population Vocabularies.

Unit of Analysis

In the present study, the unit of analysis comprises of 30 municipalities in Egypt, 30 municipalities in Jodan, 7 municipalities in Qatar, 30 municipalities in Saudi Arabia and 30 municipalities in Turkey represented by operations managers in each municipality. The use of middle managers as target population has been an established practice in studies of cross cultural organization research. For instance, in their examination of organizational practices, Gooderham, Nordhaug & Kristensen (2001) made use of personnel managers in European firms. Similarly, Dellana & Hauser (1999) made use of American managers who are members of the American Society for Quality, in their analysis of the TQM-organizational culture relationship. Additionally, Lagrosen & Lagrosen (2003) selected middle managers who are members of the Swedish Association for Quality, in their study of the way TQM practices relate to organizational structure. In the above studies, manager is the common denominator and in the present study, most of the activities of municipalities are appropriated based on job classification in the civil service system in the context of Saudi Arabia. The study selects managers as they are more familiar with the TQM implementation and quality performance. In other words, managers are chosen as units in the present study as they are the most common unit of analysis in TQM literature. The sample selection is carried out through cluster sampling method.

Whoever, there are differences in managers name in these samples, for example, in Saudi Arabia this name is Director of Operations and Maintenance, or in some municipalities in this country the name is Service Director, in Egypt, Operation Manager, in Turkey, General Director of Operations and Maintenance, in Qatar, Service Director and Jordan, Director of the Operation and Maintenance.

Sampling Procedure

According to literature of research methodology, sampling procedure can be generally categorized into probability sampling and non-probability sampling. There exists four general strategies for the former sampling and they are, systematic sampling, simple random sampling, stratified random sampling, and cluster sampling. This type of sampling uses some type of random sampling in one or more of the steps. Through probability sampling, each subject in the population has an equal opportunity to be chosen as the study sample. On the contrary, non-probability sampling does not make use of random sampling (Kerlinger & Lee, 2000). Probability sampling is used in the present study for the sake of representation as stated by Krosnick (1999). The cluster sampling is used to select the study sample as it encompasses a fairly good cross section of the five developing countries' municipalities. In theory, cluster can be employed for all types of groups, including age, gender, economic status or geographical location (Beins, 2004).

Data Collection Method

Several ways have been suggested to administer questionnaires and these include self-administered questionnaires, postal, telephone, Internet or fax. Every approach possesses its own strengths and weaknesses in a way that no single method is superior to others in every condition. For the administration of questionnaires, several factors have to be kept in mind; giving preference to cost, time constraints, potential response rate and other significant criteria that are important to the study.

Frazer & Lawley (2000) summarized the criteria of questionnaire which highlights the superiority of self-administered questionnaire to all others based on several criteria. Owing to this superiority and the challenges faced in data collection during pilot study, the present study employs the personally administered questionnaire method. Sekaran (2003) recommends that "wherever possible, questionnaires are best administered personally to a group of people."

Personally administered questionnaires have many notable benefits; it provides a high response rate, minimizes interviewer bias, and facilitates mutual personal contact (Oppenheim, 2000). In addition, it provides the required explanation of doubts or to relay additional information to the respondents and to gather completed questionnaires within a short duration (Hayes, 2000& Sekaran, 2003). Non-response test was considered unnecessary as consistent with other prior researches. For instance, Govindarajan & Gupta (1985) did not undergo the test for non-response bias as the response rate is high (82%). The same path was followed by Merchant (1985) as his study's overall response rate was at 85 per cent.

PERFORMANCE AS A DEPENDENT VARIABLE

Over 40 measures were used in the previous studies regarding the subject of performance. In this study four items (financial performance, customer performance, employee performance (learning and growth performance), and internal process performance) comprising of 12 questions were derived from literature to measure the construct. The six point Likert scale is used with 1 strongly Disagree and 6 strongly agree, Hair *et al.*, (2011) in municipalities. The following items are included in the present study's performance scale:

Table 4.2: Organizational Performance Scale

Code	*Item*	*Source*
1.	The municipality has a good budget management.	Chan (2004); Kanji, (2002) Chan (2004); Kanji (2002); Kaplan & Norton (1996); Chan (2004); Kanji (2002); Van de Ven & Ferry (1980) Chan (2004); Kaplan & Norton (1996)
2.	The municipality reduces operating cost.	Chan (2004); Kanji (2002) Kaplan & Norton (1996)
3.	The municipality reduces service delivery cost.	Chan (2004); Kaplan & Norton (1996)
4.	The municipality increases individual satisfaction.	Chan (2004); Fuentes-Fuentes (2004); Kaplan & Norton (1996)
5.	The municipality maintains good reputation.	Chan (2004); Fuentes-Fuentes (2004); Kanji (2002); Van de Ven & Ferry (1980)
6.	The municipality maintains timeliness of service delivered.	Chan (2004)
7.	The municipality maintains motivation of employees.	Van de Ven & Ferry (1980)
8.	The municipality maintains high job satisfaction among employees.	Chan (2004); Fuentes-Fuentes (2004); Kaplan & Norton (1996); Weerakon (1996)
9.	The municipality has employee development programmes.	Chan (2004); Weerakon (1996)
10.	The municipality has successfully identified the emerging needs of the community.	Fuentes-Fuentes (2004); Kaplan & Norton (1996); Kanji (2002)
11.	The municipality has successfully introduced new products and services in a timely manner.	Chan (2004); Kaplan & Norton (1996); Van de Ven & Ferry (1980); Weerakon (1996)
12.	The municipality has successfully developed a procedure to improve quality of service offered in a timely manner.	Kanji (2002)

SOFT TOTAL QUALITY MANAGEMENT AS INDEPENDENT VARIABLE

As previously stated, there have been inconsistent measurements of constructs of TQM strategy. In the current research, the entire questions are measured by a six-point Likert scale from (1) "strongly disagree" to (6) "strongly agree" Hair *et al.*, (2011). An average score is calculated for each construct on the basis of the respective items. The Soft TQM portion of the survey comprises of five items and 44 questions. These Measurements are chosen because it is suitable with research objectives and public organizations. Respondents are requested to indicate their level of agreement with each statement on a 6 point Likert scale. Five critical factors were derived from prior literature regarding Soft TQM (supplier relationship, employee relation, education and training, and customer focus).

Top Management Commitment

The following items are included in the top management commitment scale:

Table 4.3: Management Commitment Scale

Code	*Item*	*Source*
1	In our municipality, top management is committed to quality initiatives.	Ahire *et al.,* 1996; Black & Porter, 1996; Powell, 1995; Saraph *et al.,* 1989; Tamimi, 1995 Chan (2004); Kaplan & Norton (1996); Kanji (2002) Chan (2004); Kanji (2002).
2	In our municipality, top management participates in the quality initiatives.	Black & Porter, 1996; Powell, 1995; Saraph *et al.,* 1989; Tamimi, 1995
3	In our municipality, top management supports quality initiatives.	Anderson *et al.,* 1995; Black & Porter, 1996; Flynn *et al.,* 1994; Li *et al.,* 2003; Powell, 1995; Saraph *et al.,* 1989 Tamimi, 1995
4	In our municipality, top management evaluates the achievement of quality initiatives.	Powell, 1995; Saraph *et al.,* 1989
5	In our municipality, top management reviews quality issues in departmental meetings.	Ahire *et al.,* 1996; Black & Porter, 1996; Li *et al.,* 2003; Saraph *et al.,* 1989
6	In our municipality, top management focuses on service and product quality rather than yields.	Zhang *et al.,* (2000)
7	In our municipality, top management assumes responsibility for systematic and organization-wide improvement activities.	Douglas & Judge (2001)
8	In our municipality, employees have the opportunity to share in and are encouraged to help the organization implement change.	Grandzol & Gershon (1998), Rao & Raghunathan (1999), Wilkinson (1992)

Supplier Relationship

The following items comprise the supplier relationship scale:

Table 4.4: Supplier Relationship Scale

Code	*Item*	*Source*
1.	In our municipality, suppliers are selected based on quality supplier rating systems.	Ahire *et al.*, 1996; Black & Porter, 1996; Li *et al.*, 2003; Powell, 1995; Tamimi, 1995
2.	In our municipality, suppliers are involved in products and associate development.	A hire *et al.*, 1996; Black & Porter, 1996; Flynn *et al.*, 1994; Li *et al.*, 2003; Powell, 1995; Tamimi, 1995
3.	In our municipality, longer term relation-ship is offered to suppliers.	Ahire *et al.*, 1996; Black & Porter, 1996; Li *et al.*, 2003; Tamimi, 1995
4.	In our municipality, specifications provided to supplier are understandable.	Ahire *et al.*, 1996
5.	In our municipality, suppliers have their own quality programmes.	Ahire *et al.*, 1996; Black & Porter, 1996; Flynn *et al.*, 1994
6.	Our municipality always participates in supplier activities related to quality.	Zhang *et al.*, (2000)
7.	Our municipality has detailed information about supplier performance.	Zhang *et al.*, (2000)
8.	Our municipality always gives feedback on the performance of supplier's products and services.	Zhang *et al.*, (2000)

Employee Relations

Employee relations refer to employee participation, satisfaction, empowerment, involvement, fulfillment, and interactions (Karuppusami & Gandhinathan, 2006). The employee relations scale consists of the items below:

Table 4.5: The Employee Relations Scale

Code	*Item*	*Source*
1	In our municipality, we have cross-functional teams.	Zhang *et al.*, (2000)
2	In our municipality, employees are actively involved in quality-related activities.	Zhang *et al.*, (2000)
3	Our municipality implements suggestion activities extensively.	Zhang *et al.*, (2000)
4	Employees are very committed to the success of our municipality.	Zhang *et al.*, (2000)
5	In our municipality, employees are encouraged to fix problems they find.	Zhang *et al.*, (2000)
6	In our municipality, reporting work problems are encouraged.	Zhang *et al.*, (2000)
7	In our municipality, employees are encouraged to provide suggestions for continuous improvement.	Ahire *et al.* (1996), Anderson *et al.* (1995) Black & Porter (1996), Li *et al.* (2003), Powell (1995), Saraph *et al.* (1989), Tamimi (1995)
8	In our municipality, employees are recognized for quality achievement.	Anderson *et al.* (1995), Black & Porter (1996), Saraph *et al.* (1989)
9	Our municipality involves operational workers in quality related decision	Anderson *et al.* (1995), Black & Porter (1996) Saraph *et al.* (1989)

Code	*Item*	*Source*
10	In our municipality, most employees' suggestions are implemented after evaluation.	Grandzol & Gershon (1998), Rao & Raghunathan (1999), Wilkinson (1992)
11	In our municipality, I like my job because I'm doing what I want to do.	Grandzol & Gershon (1998), Rao & Raghunathan (1999), Wilkinson (1992)
12	In our municipality, employees are dedicated to their jobs.	Grandzol & Gershon (1998), Rao & Raghunathan (1999), Wilkinson (1992)
13	Our municipality improves working conditions in order to recognize employees' effort.	Grandzol & Gershon (1998), Rao & Raghunathan (1999), Wilkinson (1992)
14	In our municipality, employees' rewards and penalties are clear.	Grandzol & Gershon (1998), Rao & Raghunathan (1999), Wilkinson (1992)
15	In our municipality, we often work in teams, with members from a variety of departments.	Brah, Wong & Rao (2000)

Education and Training

The following items measure education and training:

Table 4.6: Education and Training Scale

1	In our municipality, managers and supervisors ensure that all employees receive training that helps them understand how and why the organization. does. what it does.	Grandzol & Gershon (1998), Rao & Raghunathan (1999), Wilkinson (1992)
2	In our municipality, employees understand the basic processes used to create our products and services.	Grandzol & Gershon (1998), Rao & Raghunathan (1999), Wilkinson (1992)
3	In our municipality, training in specific work skills (technical and vocational) is given to employees throughout the municipality.	Grandzol & Gershon (1998), Rao & Raghunathan (1999), Wilkinson (1992)
4	In our municipality, resources are available for employee education and training.	Grandzol & Gershon (1998), Rao & Raghunathan (1999), Wilkinson (1992)
5	In our municipality, employees are encouraged to accept education and training.	Grandzol & Gershon (1998), Rao & Raghunathan (1999), Wilkinson (1992)
6	In our municipality, top management has established an environment that encourages continuous education.	Grandzol & Gershon (1998), Rao & Raghunathan (1999), Wilkinson (1992)
7	In our municipality, employees are regarded as valuable, long-term resources worthy of receiving education and training throughout their career.	Grandzol & Gershon (1998), Rao & Raghunathan (1999), Wilkinson (1992)

Customer Focus

The items below measure customer focus:

Table 4.7: Customer Focus Scale

1.	In our municipality, a summary of customer complaints is always given to floor and department. managers.	Brah, Wong, & Rao (2000)
2.	In our municipality, the policy uses the customers' feedback to determine their needs and requirements.	Brah, Wong, & Rao (2000)
3.	In our municipality, customers' requirements and expectations are used as the basis for measuring quality.	Brah, Wong, & Rao (2000)
4.	In our municipality, floor and departments' managers are aware of the level of customer satisfaction.	Brah, Wong, & Rao (2000)
5.	In our municipality, the policy keeps in close contact with our customers.	Brah, Wong, & Rao (2000)
6.	Our municipality collects extensive complaint information from customers.	Zhang *et al.*, (2000)

HARD TOTAL QUALITY MANAGEMENT AS INDEPENDENT VARIABLES

Inconsistencies of the methods of measuring the construct of TQM strategy have been revealed in prior literature. In the present study, the constructs are measured by a six point Likert scale (1) "strongly disagree" to (6) "strongly agree". An average score is calculated for every construct on the basis of the items. The Hard TQM comprises of three items with 24 questions. Respondents are requested to indicate their degree of agreement with each statement through a 6 point Likert scale 1 indicate strongly disagree 6 strongly agree, Hair *et al.*, (2011). Three critical factors of Hard TQM were derived from literature namely, process management, quality information and analysis, and strategic planning.

Process Management

The following items are used to measure process management:

Table 4.8: Process Management Scale

Code	*Item*	
1	Our municipality design processes to be foolproof (preventive-oriented).	Prajogo & Sohal (2006)
2	The municipality has clear, standardized and documented process instructions which are well understood by employees.	Prajogo & Sohal (2006)
3	Our municipality uses an extensive use of statistical techniques to improve the processes and to reduce variation.	Prajogo & Sohal (2006)
4	Our municipality select best technology for facilitate the process.	Prajogo & Sohal (2006)

Table 4.9: Quality Information and Analysis Scale

Code	*Item*	*Source*
1	In our municipality, we have a programme to reduce the time between receiving an order and its satisfaction.	Anderson & Sohal (1999)
2	In our municipality, performance data is collected and analyzed on a regular basis.	Anderson & Sohal (1999)
3	In our municipality, information allows us to control and improve core processes and services.	Anderson & Sohal (1999)
4.	In our municipality, customer and performance data allow us to track performance and the benchmarking data is used.	Anderson & Sohal (1999)
5	In our municipality, everyone has easy access to the needed information.	Anderson & Sohal (1999)
6	In our municipality, we receive timely information and the important data is presented and communicated to employees on a regular basis.	Anderson & Sohal (1999)
7	In our municipality, information systems are always evaluated and improved.	Anderson & Sohal (1999)
8	In our municipality, quality related data is well collected.	Anderson *et al.* (1995), Black & Porter (1996), Li *et al.* (2003), Powell (1995), Saraph *et al.* (1989)
9	In our municipality, quality related data is used to evaluate management performance.	Black & Porter (1996), Li *et al.* (2003), Saraph *et al.* (1989)
10	In our municipality, quality related data is used to manage quality initiatives.	Black & Porter (1996), Saraph *et al.* (1989)
11	In our municipality, timeliness exists in quality related data.	Black & Porter (1996), Saraph *et al.* (1989)

Quality Information and Analysis

The following measures are used for quality information and analysis:

Strategic Planning

The following items measure strategic planning (Table 4.10):

NATIONAL CULTURE DIMENSIONS AS MODERATOR VARIABLES

In this study, the national culture dimensions of power distance, uncertainty avoidance, individualism, masculinity and long term orientation (Hofstede, 2001) are the moderating variables (Table 4.11).

The national culture scores for the countries are based on power distance, uncertainty avoidance, individualism, and masculinity. The previous table presents the countries relevant to the study and the corresponding Hofstede dimensions (Hofstede & Hofstede, 2005). The present study appropriates every participating municipality a country code from 1-5 (i.e. Egypt 1, Jordan 2, Qatar 3, Saudi Arabia 4, and Turkey 5). The

Table 4.10: Strategic Planning Scale

Code	*Item*	*Source*
1.	In our municipality, we have a mission statement which has been effectively communicated to all the employees and gained their support.	Samson & Terziovski (1999)
2.	In our municipality, we have comprehensive planning process which sets and reviews short and long-term goals.	Samson & Terziovski (1999)
3.	In our municipality, plans focus on the achievement of the best practice in the banking industry.	Samson & Terziovski (1999)
4.	In our municipality, when we develop our plans, policies, and objectives, we always incorporate customer requirements and the needs of all stakeholders, including the community.	Samson & Terziovski (1999)
5.	In our municipality, we have a written statement of strategy covering all the operations which is clearly articulated and approved by our senior managers.	Samson & Terziovski (1999)
7.	In our municipality, quality plans is comprehensive.	Black & Porter (1996); Li *et al.* (2003), Saraph *et al.* (1989)
8.	In our municipality, quality plans consider the customer requirements.	Black & Porter (1996), Tamimi (1995)
9.	In our municipality, quality plan is an important agenda.	Black & Porter (1996), Li *et al.* (2003)

Table 4.11: Hofstede's Dimensions in the Selected Five Countries

Code	*Country/region*	*Power distance (PDI)*	*Uncertainty avoidance (UAI)*	*Individualism*	*Masculinity*
1	Arab Countries (Egypt)	80	68	38	53
2	Jordan	–	–	–	–
3	Qatar	–	–	–	–
4	Saudi Arabia	80	68	38	53
5	Turkey	66	37	45	85

main aim behind the present study is to examine the relationship between Soft TQM, Hard TQM as independent variables, and performance as dependent variable with national culture as the moderator. The variables comprise of the dimensions of national culture, the dimensions of soft and hard TQM and the performance dimensions.

The dimensions of national culture are measured through the use of the Values Survey Module 1994 (VSM, 94). VSM 94 was the latest version of the questionnaire developed by Hofstede (2003) while Hofstede (1980) presented the pioneering VSM 80 in his book entitled, *Culture's Consequences*. Hofstede recommended the use of VSM 80 for the future 74 cross-cultural studies. The survey comprises of 27 content questions along with six demographic questions which were selected from 1966-1973 Hermes' (IBM) attitude survey questionnaires for the global comparisons of work-related values with a few questions adopted from other sources.

Table 4.12: VSM 94 Questions

Dimensions	*Items*
Power Distance (PDI)	Have a good working relationship with your direct superior.
	Be consulted by your direct superior in his/her decisions.
	How frequently, in your experience, are subordinates afraid to express disagreement with their superiors?
	Municipality structure in which certain subordinates have two bosses should be avoided at all costs.
Individualism (IDV)	Have sufficient time for your personal or family life.
	Have good physical working conditions (good ventilation and lighting, adequate work space, etc.).
	Have security of employment.
	Have an element of variety and adventure in the job
Masculinity (MAS)	Work with people who cooperate well with one another.
	Have an opportunity for advancement to higher-level jobs.
	Most people can be trusted.
	When people have failed in life it is often their fault.
Uncertainty Avoidance (UAI)	How often do you feel nervous or tense at work?
	One can be a good manager without having precise answers to most questions that subordinates may raise about their work.
	Competition between employees usually does more harm than good
	Municipality's rules should not be broken—not even when the employee thinks it is in the municipality's best interest.

By 1981, an experimental extended version of VSM called the VSM 81 was introduced. The following year heralded the introduction of VSM 82 containing 47 content questions along with six demographic questions. 13 out of the 47 questions were required to calculate the scores while the rest are for experimental use.

VSM 94 was introduced in 1994 having 26 items with an attempt to compare the culturally determined values of people from two or more countries or regions. It comprises of 20 content questions, four questions for every one of the five cultural dimensions. Responses were scored on a six point Likert scale with 1=strongly disagree and 6=strongly agree, Hair *et al.,* (2011). The five dimensions of national culture included power distance, individualism, masculinity, uncertainty avoidance, and long-term orientation.

According to Hofstede (2003), the replies to the 20 content questions of VSM 94 are impacted by the respondents' nationality as there are systematic differences between the average answer from samples with varying nationalities. Hofstede (2003) added that the same dimensions will not exist if samples come from similar nationality, with different occupations and different employers.

Hofstede (2008) introduced the VSM 08 in January 2008; it comprises of 34 item questionnaire with 28 content questions for the seven dimensions of national culture (four questions for every dimension) and six demographic questions. The dimensions of Indulgence versus Restraint and Monumentalism versus Self-Effacement were added based on the study by Michael Minkov (2007). Indulgence is referred to as society's facilitation of relatively free gratification of some desires and feelings in leisure, merry-making with friends, spending consumption and sex while restraint refers to society's control over gratification and where people living therein are less able to partake of life's enjoyments. Monumentalism refers to society's reward for people who are proud and resilient while self-effacement refers to society's reward for humility and flexibility. This version is considered quite new and as such, no empirical work has utilized it in literature. In the present research, the VSM 94 is utilized which was copyrighted in February 2004 by the Institute for Research on Intercultural Cooperation (IRIC). IRIC was a non-profit organization established by Hofstede in December 1980 under the Dutch law for the purpose of research. Owing to financial considerations, the Institute was closed on April 1, 2004.

PILOT OF THE STUDY

The first draft of the questionnaire has undergone significant phases of revisions to correct the problems and crystalize any arising uncertainty. Leading to that, it was a critical step to perform the pilot test using the data gathered from a sub-set of the participants to test for the credibility of the measure (Sproull, 2004). While pretest evaluation of the questionnaire considered two academicians and professionals, the pilot test considered respondent from the similar pool of respondents of the research from which the real data were gathered (Bradburn *et al.*, 2004). Albeit, the proto test was performed to modify the measure before being distributed to gather the original data of the study, to modify the indecisive questions, to conclude the time needed to respond to the questionnaire, and at last to measure the credibility of the measure used. Further below are the steps performed for the proto test and the source of the data gathered.

To gather the data for the proto research, the head of 30 Director of operation and maintenance in Municipalities from AL-Qassem Region in KSA have been requested to respond to the questionnaire. In addition, they were asked to give a view on the questions asked and also on the feedback if they were vividly understood to mitigate the possibility of misunderstanding. As such, few of the questions were modified to remove the uncertainty and enhance the quality of the data of the research. Depending on the gathered data, the credibility of the instrument were conducted.

Measuring the Reliability and Validity of the Measure

Reliability is the estimation of the degree of consistency among numerous measurements of a construct (Hair *et al.,* 2010). As such, to gauge the consistency of items used to measure a construct, the reliability analysis of the instrument was performed. The reliability of the instrument signifies that the measure will payback similar outcome if used repetitively. As highlighted by Sekaran (2003), there are four methods that have been routinely used to make sure regarding the credibility of their measuring instruments. These methods are: test-retest methods, alternative form methods, split half method and most commonly Cronbach's alpha coefficient method.

Alternatively, based on Davis (2000), the first three methods have been criticized to have practical weaknesses. More specifically, test retest reliability measure may render lower scores due to the possible subject changes. On similar lines, using different form may invoke more expenses since the researchers are needed to enhance two different but equivalent forms of the same measure. The split half method, alternatively, may produce different reliability coefficients depending on the manner in which the items are divided.

Alternatively, Cronbach's alpha method which test for measure reliability can have its own power to supersede above mentioned concerns related to other methods. Because of its pragmatic nature, Cronbach's alpha method has been the predominant reliability testing method used, specifically, among the social science researchers.

Aligning to the critical path of social science research, this study used the Cronbach's alpha method to test the credibility of the measurements. The Cronbach's alpha coefficient mentions the consistency of the items that measure the same construct. Giving an alternate view, a high Cronbach's alpha coefficient mentions that the items of the construct indicates high consistency and share high inclination to measure the meant construct. In establishing the acceptable and threshold cut point of the Cronbach's alpha coefficient, Nunnally (1978) indicated some minimum standards for Cronbach's alpha. For instance, Cronbach's alphas 0.7, 0.8 and 0.9 for exploratory, basic and critical issue-based research respectively. As showcased in Table 4.2, it can be seen that the Cronbach's alpha coefficients for all the constructs under research were at the acceptable degree of internal consistency. Vividly, significant of the calculated values of the coefficient alpha surpassed the concurred lower degree for alpha (that is 0.7) (Nunnally & Beinstein, 1994). Factually, it was debated by Hair *et al.,* (2010) that 0.6 is the lowest acceptable degree of Cronbach's alpha for any construct to acquire an acceptable reliability. As such, albeit the coefficient alpha for Service Design and Risk taking constructs are lower than 0.7, they are still acceptable by researchers for exploratory research

(Hair *et al.*, 2010). It can also be observed that there were no items removed to enhance the internal consistency of the constructs. Overall, all the items considered in the research have signified to showcase a sound degree of internal consistency when measuring their respective desired measures.

Table 4.13: Reliability Analysis of Pilot Study

Constructs	*No. of original items*	*Cronbach's Alpha*	*Item deleted*	*Cronbach's Alpha if item deleted*
Performance	12	0.913	Nil	0.913
Soft TQM	44	0.947	Nil	0.947
Hard TQM	24	0.923	Nil	0.923
National Culture	16	0.746	Nil	0.746

Since the measurement can be of a good level of reliability but is devoid of the validity, the reliability can be a pre-requisite of sound measurement but does not specify the soundness of the measurement (Churchill, 1979; Sekaran, 2003). Albeit, this research tried to test for the validity of the measure before moving over to the data collection stage. As established by Nunnally & Bernstein (1994), validity specifies to the degree to which the measurement measures what it is desired to measure. In the literature of research methodology, there have been various types of validity measures. To the point, the literature of research methodology, specifically in the behavioural science, exposed that details and construct validity are the most commonly used validity measures (Kerlinger & Lee, 2000; Leary, 2004; Nunnally & Bernstein, 1994).

Overall, content validity is the measure that signifies to what degree the measure appears to measure what it is desired to measure. Therefore, the content validity is keenly dependant on the judgmental evaluation by subject matter experts to assure that the measurement items consist of the construct measure of all the parameters of the construct. To assure the content validity of the measurements, the development of items covers overall the measurements of this research depending on a comprehensive review of the literature. Moreover, thorough discussions with various academicians and practitioners were performed to build the items of construct. Moreover, the questionnaire was given away to few of the key respondents to be reviewed, assessed for understandability and criticized.

Five

Results and Discussion of the Study

OVERVIEW OF DATA COLLECTED

The approval was obtained of the research and the support from His Royal Highness Prince, the Minister of Municipal and Rural Affairs in KSA through the orientation of the rest of the Ministry's sectors and obtaining of permission from the authorities from other countries' municipalities.

Additionally, the Saudi cultural attaché in Malaysia provided his support to the research by providing official letters addressed to the Saudi cultural attachés in other countries in the sample study requesting the cooperation and assistance of the municipalities.

The research procedures of developing the research questionnaires were conducted in a diplomatic manner throughout the five developing countries.

For the above reasons, and in addition to the fact that the respondents comprise of responsible leaders in the municipalities of the study sample, the international cooperation with the countries are strengthened and through this, the response may be considered an official as opposed to an academic response. This is the reason behind the 100 per cent response rate which is an exceptional case in this study.

A sample questionnaire is provided in Appendix 1 (?????) of this study. The study sample can be considered as an appropriate representation of the population having the right number of respondents from the five countries. Consistent with the small study sample are those found in studies by Talib *et al.,* (2012) who obtained a sample of 172 out of 600 and Claver *et al.,* (2002) who obtained a sample of 106 out of 175. A total of 127 questionnaires were distributed for the purpose of data collection to municipalities across four countries in the Middle East and Turkey. The study obtained 100 per cent rate of return and therefore, 127 questionnaires were deemed usable.

Data Screening and Cleaning

Data screening and cleaning is an initial step taken prior to data analysis. Several authors like Pallant (2005) and Hair *et al.,* (2006) contended that this step is essential as it clarifies data entry and gets rid of mistakes that may adversely affect the analysis. The screening process entails steps like checking for out of range scores or those out of range of possible scores. Missing values have also been mentioned by the above authors.

The study collected data through a six-point Likert scale with 1 depicting strongly disagree, 2 depicting disagree, 3 depicting somewhat disagree, 4 somewhat disagree, 5 agree and 6 strongly agree. Data was screened through frequency tables to identify whether or not the responses are within the range of 1-6 for all the respondents. The procedure was performed for the categorical demographic data and all entries were revealed to be in order as no missing values stood out in the dataset. There were however type errors in one of the demographic variables and they were rectified by turning to the questionnaires and correcting the error in the SPSS data sheet. Finally, missing values were detected in the dataset. The dataset was pronounced ready for the next test.

Normality Test

Normality is the primary assumption in data analysis and it describes the shape of data distribution for an individual metric variable that corresponds to the general delivery. Hair *et al.,* (2006) considers it as the benchmark for statistical methods because it requires the use of f and t-statistics for the purpose of hypothesis testing where the variation from the normal distribution should be small. Otherwise, large variations render the invalidity of all statistical hypothesis testing. There are various ways where a distribution can be distinguished from a normal one. Two shape descriptors namely skewness and kurtosis are the most common ways used to provide a description of the dataset shape or distribution.

Skewness is a method that identifies whether or not the distribution was centered (symmetric) or it is shifted to either side (left or right). In other words, skewness refers to a measure of symmetry/distribution, the skewness values that falls out of the range of –1 to +1 reveals a significantly skewed distribution (Hair *et al.,* 2006). According to Kline (1998), a higher threshold of 3 is recommended. Kurtosis, on the other hand assesses the flatness or peakness of the distribution in comparison to normal distribution. The recommended kurtosis distribution ranges from –2.0 to +2.0 as recommended by Coakes & Steed (2003). Kline (1998) recommended a higher threshold of +/–10. The measurement is such that the higher the positive kurtosis value, the higher will be the peak and this goes both ways.

The first step in data cleaning is the elimination of the issues that may appear which range from missing values to out of range values. The skewness and kurtosis is, therefore, checked for the data collected to determine no extreme values. In the present study, the skewness values ranged from –0.140 to –0.880 and no values were revealed to be outside the range of –1 to +1. Along the same line, most of the kurtosis values fell within the limits of +/–1 with values ranging from –0.752 to +0.119. The results revealed that the cleaned dataset has no significant violation against the assumption of normality and hence, data is assumed to be within the normally distribution limitations.

Demographic Profile of the Respondents

The respondents' demographic profile is illustrated in Table 5.1. The sample comprises of majority of male respondents (76.4%) while the rest (23.6%) constitute of female respondents from the municipalities of the countries selected. This distribution is normal as majority of governmental positions in the Middle East are occupied by men. The distribution of respondents consisted of 30 (23.6%) for each country with the exception of Qatar who had only 7 (5.5%) respondents. Most of the respondents had engineering degrees (48%), followed by a general college degree (23.6%), master and doctorate degrees (22%), and high school certificate (6.3%). Majority of the respondents majored in engineering (47.2%), followed by those who majored in business (32.2%) and others who majored in other fields represent 20.5 per cent. The respondents' educational background

Table 5.1: Demographic Profile of the Respondents

Demographic	*Categories*	*Frequency*	*%*
Gender	Male	97	76.4
	Female	30	23.6
Countries	Saudi Arabia	30	23.6
	Egypt	30	23.6
	Turkey	30	23.6
	Jordan	30	23.6
	Qatar	7	5.5
Educational background	High School	8	6.3
	Degree in engineering	61	48.0
	College Degree	30	23.6
	Master/Doctorate	18	22
Education major	Engineering	60	47.2
	Business	41	32.3
	Others	26	20.5
Religion	Islam	113	89.0
	Christianity	10	7.9
	Others	4	3.1

and their major shows that most of the sample study comprises of those with engineering background instead of management/business background. Finally, majority of them were Muslims (89%) while the rest were Christians (7.9%) and others (3.1%).

Descriptive Analysis

Descriptive analysis indicates the actual conditions, populations, and phenomena and it provides a summary of the set of quantitative data. Researchers make use of statistics to provide a description of the population/sample under study. Descriptive statistics analysis refers primarily to means, ranges, and numbers of valid cases of a variable. The descriptive statistics of the study's principal constructs are listed in Table 5.2.

Table 5.2: Descriptive Statistics of All Principal Constructs

Variable	*Construct*	*Mean*	*Std Deviation*	*Skewness*	*Kurtosis*
Soft TQM practices	Top Management Commitment	4.06	1.07	–0.756	0.275
	Supplier Relationship	4.01	0.96	–0.855	0.571
	Employee Relations	4.12	0.993	–0.829	0.14
	Education and Training	3.94	1.11	–0.645	–0.152
	Customer Focus	4.03	1.04	–0.994	0.926
Hard TQM practices	Process Management	4.06	1.03	–0.381	–0.148
	Quality Information and Analysis	4.06	1.06	–0.484	–0.201
	Strategic Planning	4.05	1.09	–0.82	0.536
Culture	Power Distance	4.19	0.981	–0.539	–0.35
	Uncertainty Avoidance	4.22	0.883	–0.448	–0.217
	Individualism	4.04	0.99	–0.841	0.576
	Masculinity	4.03	0.957	–0.454	–0.045
Organizational performance	Organizational Performance	4.11	0.959	–0.657	0.224

Table 5.2 presents the mean and standard deviation of the soft TQM practices. The table shows that the means range from 3.94 to 4.12 while the standard deviation range from 1.07 to 1.11. Specifically, the mean of hard TQM practices range from 4.05 to 4.06 with standard deviation range from 1.03 to 1.06. The means for the four dimension of culture range from 4.03 to 4.22 with a standard deviation range of 0.88 to 0.98. Finally, the performance measure's mean is 4.11 with a standard deviation of 0.96. All the variables' means were moderately high with no low level mean scores indicating that respondents were of a consensus that all variables impact

the effectiveness of the organization. Employee relations gained the highest mean among all the independent variables while the education and training gained the lowest mean. Culture, the moderator variable, reveals the highest mean to be revealed by uncertainty avoidance whereas masculinity reveals the lowest. Although the remaining TQM practices did not obtain as high as employee relation in terms of mean scores—this does not imply that the activities can be taken lightly.

All variables standard deviations range from 0.88 to 1.11 which shows the presence of significant acceptable variability among the data set. The variation value shows that the study variables answers were significantly different from each other which indicates the presence of tolerable variances among them. All the 13 constructs showed normality of skewness and kurtosis with values ranging from -1 to +1 indicating the absence of outlier or extreme values that may adversely affect the analysis validity. The 13 constructs are, therefore, ready for the next analysis.

Group Comparison of Responses

Among the issues that researchers may face is the heterogeneity of responses. In other words, the study may find a separate set of responses to the same questions owing to demographics. This may result in a separate kind of analysis to be conducted for every group. For instance, if the responses differ between the genders, the study should refrain from using just one analysis for both as this may result in generalization which could lead to erroneous findings. Therefore, this section provides the comparison of responses between different respondent categories with gender as the category used for comparison. In order to achieve the comparison process, both Pallant (2005) and Hair *et al.,* (2006) recommended that t-test and the analysis of variance (ANOVA) should be used. The former test was employed for independent samples when there is a need to compare the mean scores of two differing respondent groups or conditions to determine if the present characteristics or conditions of the groups impact the responses. The test is an assessment of the significance of the statistical different between two distinct samples means for one variable. It is described as the ratio of the difference between the sample means to their standard error. The t-statistics is then compared to the critical dependent value on the significant value with alpha at 0.05 and t critical at 1.96.

This study conducted the t-test to determine the differences in means of all the study items between the genders (male and female). The findings show no significant difference in the respondents' means for all the items under study indicating that gender has no influence upon the responses provided and that responses are individual invariant. In other words, there is homogeneity in responses and hence, there is no need to divide the dataset.

Correlations and Linearity

All 13 constructs were exposed to correlation analysis to shed a light on the relationship between the constructs. The correlation analysis has two objectives: it tests the correlation between the dependent variable and the independent variable; and it tests the convergent validity of the constructs. Table 5.3 contains the correlation analysis results. They indicate the presence of relationship between dependent and independent variables. It is evident from the table (Table 5.3) that correlation coefficients are both significant and positive. The least correlation is between culture construct of masculinity, and quality information & analysis at 0.34 while the highest one is between employee relations and customer focus at 0.90. On the basis of Cohen's Guidelines of correlation strength, any absolute correlation coefficient values that fall between 0.3-0.49 is deemed to have moderate strength and those that fall above 0.5 is deemed of great strength.

In this study, the significant correlations fall in the range between 0.340 and 0.896. The results show that correlation between dependent and moderating variable is positive and significant with organizational performance positively and significantly linked to the entire constructs ranging from as low as 0.37 (masculinity) to as high as 0.88 (employee relations).

Table 5.3: Correlation coefficient

Construct	*TM*	*SR*	*ER*	*E&T*	*CF*	*PM*	*QI*	*SP*	*PD*	*UA*	*IND*	*MAS*	*OP*
TM	1												
SR	.81*	1											
ER	.84*	.79*	1										
E&T	.73*	.70*	.84*	1									
CF	.81*	.73*	.90*	.81*	1								
PM	.70*	.68*	.77*	.68*	.75*	1							
QI	.76*	.70*	.83*	.69*	.85*	.77*	1						
SP	.78*	.66*	.85*	.72*	.88*	.78*	.91*	1					
PD	.64*	.60*	.68*	.59*	.67*	.69*	.55*	.62*	1				
UA	.49*	.47*	.63*	.59*	.55*	.58*	.47*	.53*	.67*	1			
IND	.69*	.69*	.80*	.73*	.74*	.66*	.73*	.73*	.62*	.63*	1		
MAS	.42*	.44*	.45*	.52*	.45*	.38*	.34*	.38*	.56*	.53*	.51*	1	
OP	.86*	.73*	.88*	.76*	.87*	.75*	.82*	.84*	.64*	.53*	.72*	.37*	1

*significant at 1 per cent level of significance

TM = Top Management, SR = Supplier Relationships, ER = Employee Relations, E&T = Education and Training, PM = Process Management, QI = Quality Information and Analysis, SP = Strategic Planning, PD = Power Distance, UA = Uncertainty Avoidance, IND = Individualism, MAS = Masculinity, and OP = Organizational Performance

Additionally, the tests of correlation coefficients examine the convergent validity. Badri *et al.,* (1995) contended that convergent validity checks the level to which the instruments explain or predict the value of its counterpart independent instrument. Convergent validity is also referred to as external/predictive validity and it serves to observe the relationship strength between the constructs through Pearson's Correlation Coefficients. Hence, convergent validity is tested for all the constructs. From the above table, the correlation between the soft TQM practices fall between 0.70 and 0.90 while the relationship between hard TQM practices fall between 0.77 and 0.91. Finally, national culture constructs relationship fall between 0.51 and 0.67. As all the relationships are high, this indicates that they support the presence of convergent validity among the constructs.

With regards to linearity/linear relationship among the variables, Hair *et al.,* (2006) & Pallant (2005) recommended the utilization of P-P plots to determine the relationship in a way that if the plots reveal a diagonal line pattern, it is deemed to have linear relationship. Accordingly, a visual inspection of the P-P plots show that all the constructs that measure independent, dependent and moderator variables are linear.

RELIABILITY

The reliability test is primarily conducted to determine the constructs' internal consistency and the alpha construct plays a key role in such determination. Alpha value falling lower than the minimum value is deemed to have adequate reliability after which the factor is dropped for the confirmatory factor analysis with the help of structural equation modelling. According to Pallant (2005), reliability or internal consistency can be defined as the level to which items that form the scale, measure the same underlying attribute. Additionally, reliability can be gauged through various ways with the most widely used method as the Cronbach's alpha coefficient. Similarly, Hair *et al.,* (2006) defined reliability as the level to which the observed variable measures the actual value and is free of error. Table 5.4 presents the result of the reliability test of this study.

Talib *et al.,* (2012) contended that top management commitment has a good internal consistency with Cronbach alpha coefficient at 0.932 and in this study, the Cronbach alpha coefficient is at 0.938. As for supplier relationship, the alpha coefficient is at 0.919 which is consistent with Talib *et al.,*'s (2012) coefficient of 0.910 while employee relations is 0.952 as presented in the table; a figure which is higher than 0.842 found by Yunis *et al.,* (2013). In addition, education and training reliability is at 0.925 which is higher compared to the figure (0.902) reported by Talib *et al.,* (2012). The other constructs display similar trends where the reliability of the constructs appears to be either equal to or over the reliability of the studies in the field of TQM practices. However, national culture shows only an

Table 5.4: Cronbach's Coefficient Alpha for the Study Constructs

Variable	*Construct*	*Items*	*Cronbach's Alpha*
Organizational Performance	Organizational performance	12	0.933
Soft TQM Practices	Top Management	8	0.938
	Supplier Relationship	8	0.919
	Employee Relations	15	0.952
	Education and training	7	0.925
	Customer focus	6	0.906
Hard TQM Practices	Process Management	4	0.856
	Quality information and analysis	11	0.96
	Strategic Planning	9	0.945
National Culture	Power Distance	4	0.757
	Uncertainty Avoidance	4	0.723
	Individualism	4	0.822
	Masculinity	4	0.718

acceptable level of reliability compared to all the constructs which displayed reliability of above 0.7 as suggested by Nunally & Bernstein (1994).

EXPLORATORY FACTOR ANALYSIS (EFA)

The EFA is conducted prior to the regression analysis. In the prior section, it was stated that the constructs of each variable are significantly related to the constructs of the same variable and those from different variables. Nevertheless, a simpler structure that can be obtained can provide more clarified results. For instance, are the five constructs that represent soft TQM practices separate from the three constructs of hard TQM practices? This is the case in theory but in practice, an inter-link among them is realistic. Hence, in order to answer the question of the inter-linkage among constructs, a statistical tool is needed.

Another question to be addressed is whether or not the questions used in data collection could help shed a light on the relationship between each construct and the variable they are under, or a smaller number of items are appropriate in explaining such a relationship. Hence, a method of data reduction is called for to answer the questions. Spicer (2005) stated that there are three major kinds of situations where in data reduction are called for. First, when a bigger number of variables need to be replaced by smaller numbers. Second, when there is a need to examine whether or not the questions addressing few constructs can be combined to explain their theoretical representation. Third, when the stress is theoretically motivated and a set of questions are required for theory confirmation. Among the techniques utilized is factor analysis.

Specifically, factor analysis is an interdependence method that needs to be conducted in several phases of development and assessment of measures. The premise behind factor analysis is the parsimony of data and data interpretations in which items are combined into common interlinked and meaningful dimensions. The factor analysis is primarily utilized to define the structure of variables in the analysis (Hair *et al.*, 2006). Prior to conducting the factor analysis, several criteria must be fulfilled to confirm the suitability of the study. Two main issues arise in determining whether or not the data set is appropriate for factor analysis (Pallant, 2005).

The first criterion is the sample size as contended by Tabchnick & Fidell (2001) where at least 300 cases are needed for factor analysis although smaller sample size (e.g. 100 cases) are deemed sufficient if solutions have high loading market variables (over 0.80). According to Hair *et al.,* (2006), generally, a sample fewer than 50 observations would not be factor analyzed and those of 100 or over are more preferable.

Table 5.5 presents the total number of items (96) measuring all the study variables. The soft TQM practices constructs comprise of top management with 8 items, supplier relationship with 8 items, employee relations with 15 items, education and training with 7 items and customer focus with 6 items. Meanwhile, the hard TQM practices constructs comprise of process management with 4 items, quality information and analysis with 11 items and strategic planning with 9 items. The moderator namely the national culture comprise of power distance with 4 items, uncertainty avoidance with 4 items, individualism with 4 items and masculinity with 4 items. Finally, the dependent variable namely the organizational performance comprise of 12 items.

The second criterion is the strength of the inter-correlation of the items (Pallant, 2005). Tabachnick & Fidell (2001) proposed an examination of the correlation matrix to identify coefficients higher than 0.30. If only a few correlations are present at this level, then factor analysis is deemed inappropriate. On the basis of the correlation matrix, most of the correlation coefficient is over 0.30 with the exception of a few cases and hence, factor analysis is appropriate to be conducted in the present study.

Two statistical measures that can assist in the assessment of the performing factor analysis are the Bartlett's test of Sphericity (Bartlett, 1954) and Kaiser-Meyer-Olkin (KMO) measure of sampling adequacy (Kaiser, 1974). The former should be significant at ($p<0.05$) to be suitable for factor analysis while the latter ranges from 0 to 1 with a recommended value of 0.6 minimum. Hair *et al.,* (2006) explained that the index can be interpreted in the following way; 0.8 or above are meritorious, 0.7 or above is middling, 0.6 or above is mediocre, 0.5 or above is miserable, whereas below 0.5 is unacceptable. In the present study, KMO is reported between 0.787 and

0.953 as listed in Table 5.5. Moreover, the Varimax rotation is widely suggested by researchers in the clarification of factors (Loehlin, 1998). It is advocated to minimize correlation throughout factors and maximize within them in order to result in clear factors (Nunnally, 1978). Only those items with loading over 0.50 on one factor and low cross-loadings are kept for the next analysis (Nunnally, 1978).

Additionally, factor loading is used to determine the convergent and discriminant validity of the measures (Hurley & Hult, 1998) and to specify the strength of the relationship among items and the latent construct. Hair *et al.*, (2006) stated that factors loadings ±0.5 or higher are deemed to be practically significantly. In this study, the items are dropped if they show the following tendencies; failed to load into any factor with a value of 0.50 or higher, they are free standing items (in one factor one item exists with high factor loading), and had cross loading on two factors.

The results are presented through the following way; KMO results, the scree plot results, the variance explained result, and the rotated matrix with factor loadings result. As for the number of factors to include, this is decided through the scree plot and Eigen value of more than 1. Utilizing only one of the two may result in the inclusion of erroneous factors.

It is evident from the above table (Table 5.5) that the factor analysis was conducted on three primary variables; the independent variables comprising soft and hard TQM which are formed through 5 and 3 constructs respectively, the moderating variable namely the national culture formed by 4 constructs, and finally, the dependent variable formed by one construct. The analysis was carried out separately for the three mentioned variables. The number of factors extracted, the KMO, the Bartlett's test of Sphericity and the variance extracted are all presented in Table 5.5.

Beginning with the independent variables, the soft and hard TQM practices were examined together and the result showed that KMO and Bartlett's test of Sphericity supported factor analysis. The soft TQM revealed that 5 factors explained 69 per cent of the variance. Nevertheless, some items from customer focus loaded on the top management factor, while one factor from supplier relations loading on another factor. The second stage of the factor analysis involved 41 items and resulted identical results to the first stage. Education and training item 5 cross loaded and was therefore eliminated. On the third stage of the analysis, 5 factors were extracted and a slight increase in variance explained was noted although KMO and Bartlett's test were above 9.90 and significant. In addition, the items 3, 5 and 6 of customer focus loaded on top management factor and were deleted along with item two of the same construct and supplier relations item 1. The next stage of the factor analysis revealed the number of factors to decrease to 4 but KMO and Bartlett's test were revealed to be high and significant and the variance explained decreased to 68 per cent. Consequently, the following items were dropped; employee relations items

Table 5.5: Exploratory Factor Analysis Process for Study Variables

Number of Extracted Factors	*KMO*	*Bartlett's Test of Sphericity*	*Variance Extracted (%)*	*Remarks*
Independent Variables Soft TQM practices				
5	0.941	5254	69	Customer focus 1 and 4 and supplier relations 4 dropped-loaded in the wrong factor
5	0.939	4813	69	Education and training 5 dropped-cross loaded,
5	0.942	4675	69.6	Customer focus 3, 2, 5 and 6 dropped-loaded in the wrong factor
4	0.942	4219	68	Employee relations 15 dropped-loaded in the wrong factor
4	0.942	4083	68	Employee relations 5 dropped-cross loaded, 2, 10, dropped, Top Management 7 dropped supplier relations 1 dropped
4	0.941	3937	68	Final set. 30 items
Independent Variables Hard TQM practices				
3	0.953	2991	72.5	Quality information and analysis item 1, 2, 9, 10 and 11 and strategic planning 2, 7 and 8 dropped-cross loading
3	0.942	1922	72	Strategic planning item 1 and 4 dropped-cross loading
3	0.937	1625	73	Strategic planning item 5 and 1 quality information and analysis dropped-wrong factor loading and cross loading
3	0.927	1250	75	Final set. 13 items
Moderating Variable (National Culture)				
4	0.870	979*	66	Uncertainty avoidance 1, 3 and 4 dropped-cross loaded and low item loaded.
4	0.852	774*	71	Individualism 2 and power 3 dropped-cross loading and wrong facto loading
3	0.787	498*	68	Uncertainty 2 and masculinity 4 dropped-cross loading and wrong factor loading.
3	0.750	421*	70	Final set. 9 items
Dependent Variable (the adoption of Programming and performance budgeting)				
1	0.919	1009*	58	Total number of items with loading more than 0.5 is 12 items

**significant at 1 per cent.

15, 5, 2, 10, education and training item 5 and top management 7 owing to erroneous factor loading and cross loading. Finally, the final stage had 4 cleanly loaded factors with KMO and Bartlett's test high and significant and variance explained at 68 per cent. The final set of items comprise of soft TQM practices (30 out of 44 items). As for hard TQM practices, the first stage of the analysis generated 3 factors with variance explained at 72.5 per cent and KMO higher than 0.9, and significant Bartlett's test of Sphericity. Some items were however highly loaded in two factors namely quality information and analysis items 2, 9, 10, and 11 and strategic planning items 2, 7, and 8—they were all removed. The second stage was run and the results obtained were similar to that of the first stage. Two items namely strategic planning items 1 and 4 cross loaded on two factors and was thus removed. The next stage provided the same result with slightly higher variance explained of 73 per cent. In this stage, another two items namely strategic planning items 5 and 1, and quality information and analysis were wrongly loaded and cross loaded and were hence, dropped. Finally, the variance explained increased to 75 per cent in the last stage and there were no cross loadings. A highly significant Bartlett's test of Sphericity was noted and a high (over 0.90) KMO value. There were a final total of 13 items of hard TQM practices out of the original 24.

The moderating variable was exposed to the same process as the first two variables above. In the first stage, factor analysis had 4 factors, with KMO above 0.85, significant Bartlett's test, and variance explained at 66 per cent. Nevertheless, uncertainty avoidance items 1, 3 and 4 highly cross loaded in two factors with low item loading in one factor, and were eventually dropped. In the second stage, the results were identical to the first one although variance explained decreased to 71 per cent. In this stage, individualism item 2 and power distance item 3 cross loaded and loaded in the wrong factor and were removed. In the third stage, three factors were extracted and KMO decreased to lower than 0.80 but higher than 0.75 which is still acceptable. Bartlett's test was noted to be significant whereas variance explained decreased to 68 per cent. Uncertainty avoidance item 2 and masculinity item 4 were removed because of cross loading and wrong factor loading. In the final stage, 3 factors remained with an acceptable KMO at 0.750, and a significant test of Sphericity but the variance explained showed an increase to 70 per cent. Finally, the remaining items included 9 out of the original 16 items.

Moreover, Table 5.5 also presents the dependent variable namely organizational performance which originally comprised of 12 times. The items were retained following the factor analysis. Based on the table (Table 5.5), 1 factor was extracted with KMO higher than 0.9, significant Bartlett's test and variance explained at 58 per cent.

Prior to the final stage of hypothesis testing, the reliability of the extracted items needs to be examined to make sure that the items removed do not impact the new factors reliability. Reliability is defined by Hair *et al.*, (2006) as the level to which a variable or set of variables is consistent to what it is expected to measure. Thus, reliability analysis was conducted through Cronbach's Alpha to identify and ensure internal consistency reliability among the times of each factors extracted from the exploratory factor analysis. Nunnally & Bernstein (1994) claimed that alpha value higher than 0.5 are deemed to have adequate reliability and if the factors revealed low reliability in the later scale, they will be dropped from the next analysis.

Tables 5.6a, 5.6b, and 5.6c present the new structure of factors and their reliability. The items included in these tables are the final items that are used for hypotheses testing. The scree plot is another way to confirm the number of factors. It entails examining the graph of the Eigen value and detecting the point with the graph bends or breaks thereafter the curve will flatten out (Castello *et al.*, 2005). Points greater than the break point are often the correct number of factors. On the basis of Figure 5.1, although the break happens after one factor, the soft TQM factors are 4 as presented in Table 5.5. The fact that 5 constructs composed the original variable cannot be overlooked when looking at the scree plot. Hence, according to the Eigen values and the theoretical knowledge of the 5 constructs, 4 factors were retained following the filtering process.

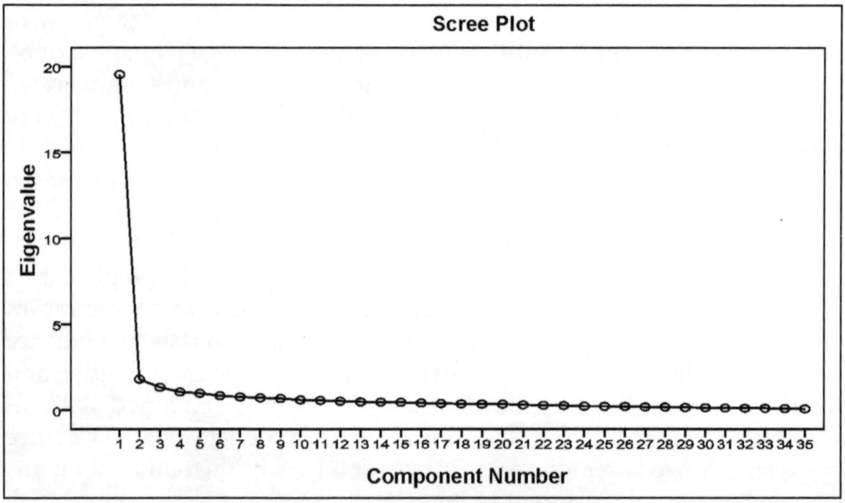

Figure 5.1: Scree Plot of soft TQM practices

Along the same line, Figure 5.2 presents the scree plot for hard TQM practices. The graph reveals that only a single factor should be retained as the line breaks at factor 2 and proceeds to flatten out. On the basis of the theoretical model, the hard TQM practices have three primary constructs and the Eigen value reveals that 3 factors are suitable. With regards to the moderator variable namely national culture, Figure 5.3 shows its scree plot.

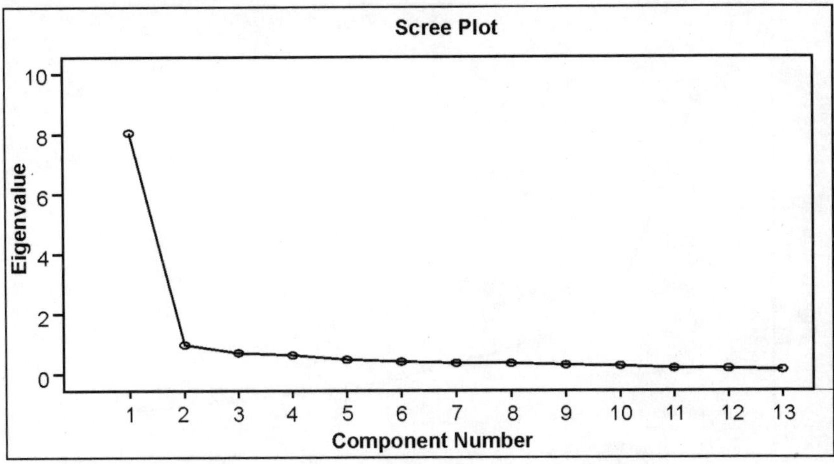

Figure 5.2: Scree Plot of hard TQM practices

In theory, 4 constructs composed national culture but on the basis of filtering, 3 factors were retained. According to the scree plot in Figure 5.3, the line flattens out after 3 factors which is consistent with the results found in Table 5.5. Finally, the dependent variable (organizational performance) scree plot is shown in Figure 5.4. One factor is used based either on the screen plot or Eigen value.

The final set of items for soft TQM practices is presented in Table 5.6. From the table, it is evident that top management construct comprising of 7 items is included in the hypothesis testing. Item 7 was dropped on account

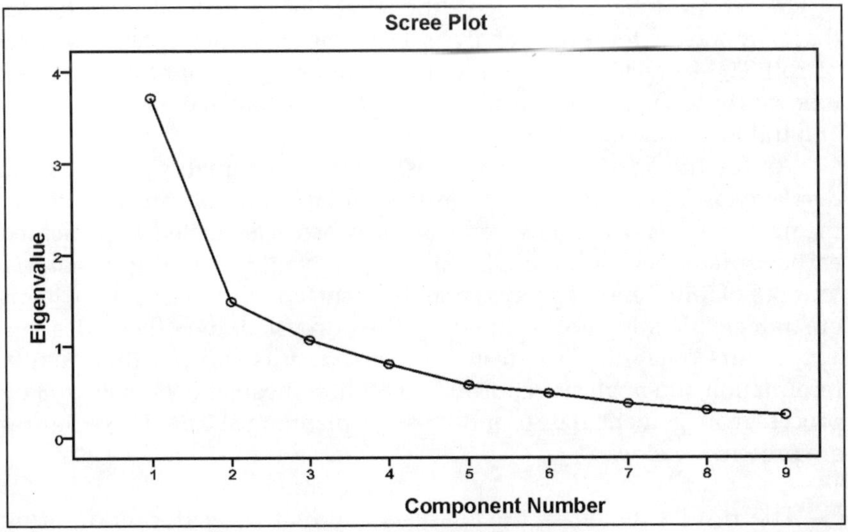

Figure 5.3: Scree Plot of National Culture

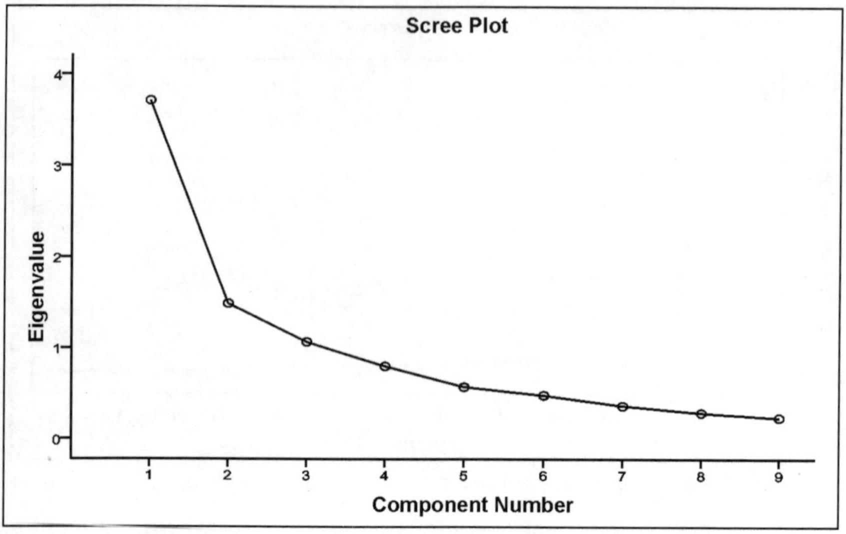

Figure 5.4: Scree Plot of Organizational Performance

of loading lower than 0.5. On the other hand, employee relationship construct comprise of 11 out of 15 items for hypothesis testing.

Meanwhile, employee relationship items 1, 3, 4, 6, 7, 8, 9, 11, and 14 are included with 2, 5, 10 and 15 excluded for factors loading of less than 0.5. As for education and training, 6 out of 7 items were retained and for supplier relations 6 (items 2, 3, 5, 6, 7, 8) out of 8 items were retained for further analysis.

Moreover, Table 5.6a presents the reliability of the final set of factors that continues on for further analysis. From the table, the Cronbach's alpha of soft TQM practices for employee relations is the highest with 0.95, followed by top management at 0.94, supplier relations at 0.9 and education and training at 0.89.

As for the hard TQM practices, their factor analysis results are displayed in Table 5.6b. All the constructs of this variable are included in the next analysis with a few items of the constructs deleted as presented earlier in Table 5.5. Six out of 11 items of quality information and analysis, four out of four items of process management, and three out of nine items of strategic planning are retained for the purpose of hypotheses testing. The factors reliability was tested and the results showed that quality information and analysis reported the highest mean at 0.93, followed by process management at 0.86, and strategic planning at 0.84. These figures are presented below.

The results of the factor analysis conducted on the moderating variable's (national culture) 16 items are presented in Table 5.6c. It is evident

Table 5.6a: Factor Loading and Reliability Test for Soft TQM Practices

	Final Factors				
Items	*Top management*	*Employee relations*	*Education and training*	*Supplier relationship*	*Cronbach's Alpha*
TOP_MANG_1	0.786				0.94
TOP_MANG_2	0.736				
TOP_MANG_3	0.713				
TOP_MANG_4	0.709				
TOP_MANG_5	0.575				
TOP_MANG_6	0.709				
TOP_MANG_8	0.556				
EMP_1		0.670			
EMP_3		0.569			0.95
EMP_4		0.614			
EMP_6		0.608			
EMP_7		0.651			
EMP_8		0.530			
EMP_10		0.524			
EMP_11		0.615			
EMP_12		0.593			
EMP_13		0.606			
EMP_14		0.546			
EDU_1			0.770		
EDU_2			0.674		
EDU_3			0.665		
EDU_4			0.717		0.89
EDU_6			0.772		
EDU_7			0.598		
SUPP_2				0.653	
SUPP_3				0.666	
SUPP_5				0.647	
SUPP_6				0.697	
SUPP_7				0.706	0.90
SUPP_8				0.673	

Table 5.6b: Factor Loading and Reliability Test for Hard TQM Practices

	Factors			*Reliability*
Item	*Quality Information and Analysis*	*Process Management*	*Strategic Planning*	*Cronbach's Alpha*
QUAL_3	0.653			0.93
QUAL_4	0.678			
QUAL_5	0.755			
QUAL_6	0.860			
QUAL_7	0.763			
QUAL_8	0.701			
PROC_1		0.723		0.86
PROC_2		0.704		
PROC_3		0.790		
PROC_4		0.676		
PLAN_3			0.701	0.843
PLAN_6			0.816	
PLAN_9			0.639	

from Table 5.5 that national culture's uncertainty avoidance was dropped following filtering and only 9 items were retained after the analysis. As for factor reliability of national culture, the Cronbach's alpha reliability for masculinity is 0.722, power distance is 0.758 and individualism is 0.80.

Table 5.6c: Factor Loading and Reliability Test for National Culture

	Component			*Reliability*
Item	*Individualism*	*Masculinity*	*Power distance*	*Cronbach's Alpha*
INDIVI_1	0.779			0.80
INDIVI_3	0.854			
INDIVI_4	0.746			
MASC_1		0.828		0.722
MASC_2		0.707		
MASC_3		0.781		
POWER_1			0.892	0.758
POWER_2			0.821	
POWER_4			0.556	

In addition, the dependent variable's (organizational performance) factor analysis results are presented in Table 5.6d along with its reliability. Organizational performance reliability remained at 9.933 as no item was eliminated following the factor analysis.

Table 5.6d: Factor Loading and Reliability Test for Organizational Performance

	Component	*Reliability*
Item	*Organizational Performance*	*Cronbach's Alpha*
OP_1	0.637	0.933
OP_2	0.759	
OP_3	0.762	
OP_4	0.793	
OP_5	0.710	
OP_6	0.772	
OP_7	0.821	
OP_8	0.769	
OP_9	0.763	
OP_10	0.763	
OP_11	0.769	
OP_12	0.795	

From the above results, it is clear that the study variables are ready for the next stage of analysis namely the regression analysis for hypotheses testing.

REGRESSION ANALYSIS

The regression analysis of the proposed framework and hypotheses testing is discussed in the present section. Prior to regression analysis, several critical issues have to be addressed.

Multi-collinearity

Multi-collinearity arises when two or more independent variables are significantly correlated (Hair *et al.*, 2006). A severe multi-collinearity leads to impossible mathematical operations and unstable results as the influence on the dependent variable are indiscernible (Kline, 1998). A possible severe multi-collinearity's arises in a model when separate variables actually measure the same thing. It is said deemed to be severe when the value of correlation is high at 0.9 according to some researchers (Hair *et al.*, 2006; Kline, 1998; & Pallant, 2005).

The assessment of multi-collinearity in the multivariate level is not as simple and easy compared to the bivariate level (Kline, 1998; Hair *et al.*, 2006). Tolerance is one of the ways that detects multi-collinearity and it is referred to as the amount of variability of the selected independent variable not explained by its counterparts (Hair *et al.*, 2006). Tolerance values of lower than 0.1 depict a severe case of multi-collinearity (Kline, 1998).

The variance inflation factor (VIF) is another way to detect multi-collinearity. The lower the VIF value, the greater will be the multi-collinearity (Hair *et al.*, 2006). According to Myers (1990) and Kline (1998), if the VIF value is over 10, this shows a multi-collinearity problem. In the present study, the tolerance and the VIF values are utilized to detect the presence of multi-collinearity of all items and variables. The result of the multi-collinearity test for both items and variables are depicted in Table 5.7. The table shows that each independent variable has been utilized as a dependent variable to examine the multi-collinearity between each independent variable and its counterparts. The tolerance values are all higher than 0.1 and the VIFs are lower than 10 for all the variables which indicate no multi-collinearity problem.

HYPOTHESIS TESTING

Relationship between Independent and Dependent Variables

The hypothesis testing is conducted through the regression analysis. The first stage of hypothesis testing addresses the direct relationships between the independent and dependent variables. Following the examination of the direct relationships, the moderating effect is tested. The first model tests the relationship between the independent variables while the second

Table 5.7: Tolerance and VIF for all independent variables

Dependent variable														
TM			*ER*			*E&T*			*SR*			*QI*		
IV	*Tol*	*VIF*	*IV*	*Tol*	*VIF*	*IV*	*Tol*	*VIF*	*IV*	*Tol*	*VIF*	*IV*	*Tol*	*VIF*
ER	.77	1.30	E& T	.90	1.11	SR	.71	1.40	QI	.61	1.64	PM	.82	1.22
E&T	.92	1.09	SR	.77	1.29	QI	.57	1.77	PM	.66	1.52	SP	.74	1.35
SR	.90	1.11	QI	.78	1.28	PM	.63	1.59	SP	.73	1.36	IND	.65	1.53
QI	.67	1.49	PM	.87	1.15	SP	.73	1.38	IND	.62	1.63	MAS	.79	1.27
PM	.78	1.28	SP	.76	1.32	IND	.61	1.63	MAS	.78	1.28	PD	.64	1.55
SP	.76	1.33	IND	.63	1.59	MAS	.82	1.23	PD	.59	1.71	TM	.65	1.55
IND	.63	1.59	MAS	.79	1.27	PD	.58	1.74	TM	.70	1.43	ER	.74	1.36
MAS	.79	1.28	PD	.58	1.71	TM	.55	1.82	ER	.59	1.69	EDU	.92	1.09
PD	.58	1.72	TM	.78	1.28	ER	.53	1.89	EDU	.93	1.07	SR	.76	1.32

Dependent variable														
PM			*SP*			*IND*			*MAS*			*PD*		
IV	*Tol*	*VIF*	*IV*	*Tol*	*VIF*	*IV*	*Tol*	*VIF*	*IV*	*Tol*	*VIF*	*IV*	*Tol*	*VIF*
SP	.76	1.32	IND	.66	1.53	MAS	.82	1.22	PD	.61	1.65	TM	.54	1.86
IND	.62	1.62	MAS	.79	1.27	PD	.70	1.44	TM	.53	1.88	ER	.53	1.88
MAS	.78	1.28	PD	.59	1.69	TM	.55	1.83	EMP	.52	1.91	E&T	.89	1.12
PD	.58	1.74	TM	.55	1.81	ER	.54	1.86	EDU	.93	1.08	SR	.70	1.44
TM	.66	1.51	ER	.55	1.83	E&T	.90	1.12	SUPP	.68	1.46	QI	.62	1.62
ER	.72	1.38	E&T	.89	1.12	SR	.69	1.45	QUAL	.55	1.81	PM	.63	1.59
E&T	.90	1.11	SR	.69	1.45	QI	.59	1.70	PM	.63	1.59	SP	.75	1.34
SR	.72	1.40	QI	.57	1.77	PM	.64	1.57	SP	.73	1.37	IND	.74	1.35
QI	.72	1.38	PM	.66	1.52	SP	.78	1.29	IND	.64	1.56	MAS	.83	1.21

Note: TM= Top Management, SR=Supplier Relationships, ER=Employee Relations, E&T=Education and Training, PM= Process Management, QI=Quality Information and Analysis, SP=Strategic Planning, PD=Power Distance, UA=Uncertainty Avoidance, IND=Individualism, and MAS= Masculinity

one tests the soft and hard TQM variables and the moderating variable as independent variables to test whether they are moderators. According to Barron and Kenny (1986), in order to test whether or not the variable should be considered as a moderator, it must be included in the equation as an independent variable and its direct effect on the dependent variable should be determined. In case the variable is found to be significant, then it is tested for its indirect effect. Hence, the first model tests the direct relationship between soft and hard TQM practices, and organizational performance as presented by the following equation:

$$\mathrm{OP} = a_i + b_1TM + b_2ER + b_3E\&T + b_4SR + b_5PM + b_6QI + b_7SP + \varepsilon \quad (1)$$

Where TM represents top management, ER represents employee relations, E&T represents education and training, SR represents supplier relationships, PM represents process management, QI represents quality information and analysis and finally, SP represents strategic planning.

Table 5.8: Regression Result for Model 1

Variable	*Unstandardized Coefficients*	*Standardized Coefficients*	*T-value*	*Tolerance*	*VIF*
Constant	3.285		17.753	0.549	1.820
TM	0.850*	0.457*	4.620	0.541	1.847
ER	0.949*	0.433*	4.348	0.930	1.075
E&T	0.247**	0.162**	2.134	0.699	1.430
SR	0.472*	0.287*	3.279	0.630	1.587
PM	0.442*	0.278*	3.016	0.638	1.568
QI	0.543*	0.333*	3.632	0.881	1.135
SP	0.220*	0.378*	4.836	0.549	1.820

Note: R^2 = 36%
Adj. R^2 = 32%
F-value = 9.56*
*, ** significant at 1 per cent and 5 per cent respectively.
Dependent variable: organizational performance TM = Top Management, SR = Supplier Relationships, ER = Employee Relations, E&T = Education and Training, PM = Process Management, QI = Quality Information and Analysis, and SP = Strategic Planning.

The regression results of the first model are shown in Table 5.8. According to the results, the soft and hard TQM practices are significantly and positively associated with organizational performance. The standardized beta reveals the direction and the strength of the partial correlation between each independent variable and organizational performance. The table shows that standardized beta for soft TQM practices and it is clear that top management has the highest influence on organizational performance, followed by employee relations, supplier relationship, and finally education and training. On the same line, hard TQM practices standardized beta shows that strategic planning has the highest influence followed by quality information and analysis. The weakest influence is reported from process management.

The tolerance and VIF tests of multicollinearity reveal values that are greater than 0.2 and less than 10 respectively which indicate that the model is free from severe multicollinearity. The goodness of the model R^2 and the adjusted R^2 are reported to be 36 per cent and 32 per cent respectively of the variation in the performance of the municipalities as clarified by the independent variables. Additionally, the f-value shows the goodness of fit is significant at 1 per cent indicating good model fit. Moreover, in order to confirm the two important classical assumptions of normality and homoscedasticity, the three graphs provided below attest to the model's non-violation of the classical assumptions. The histogram in Figure 5.5 reveals the residual fall in +/– 3 standard deviations. It indicates that the residual model is normally distributed and based on the P-P plot of the same histogram, the observation lies on the line in the plot reflecting no major deviations of the residual of normality (as recommended by Pallant, 2011).

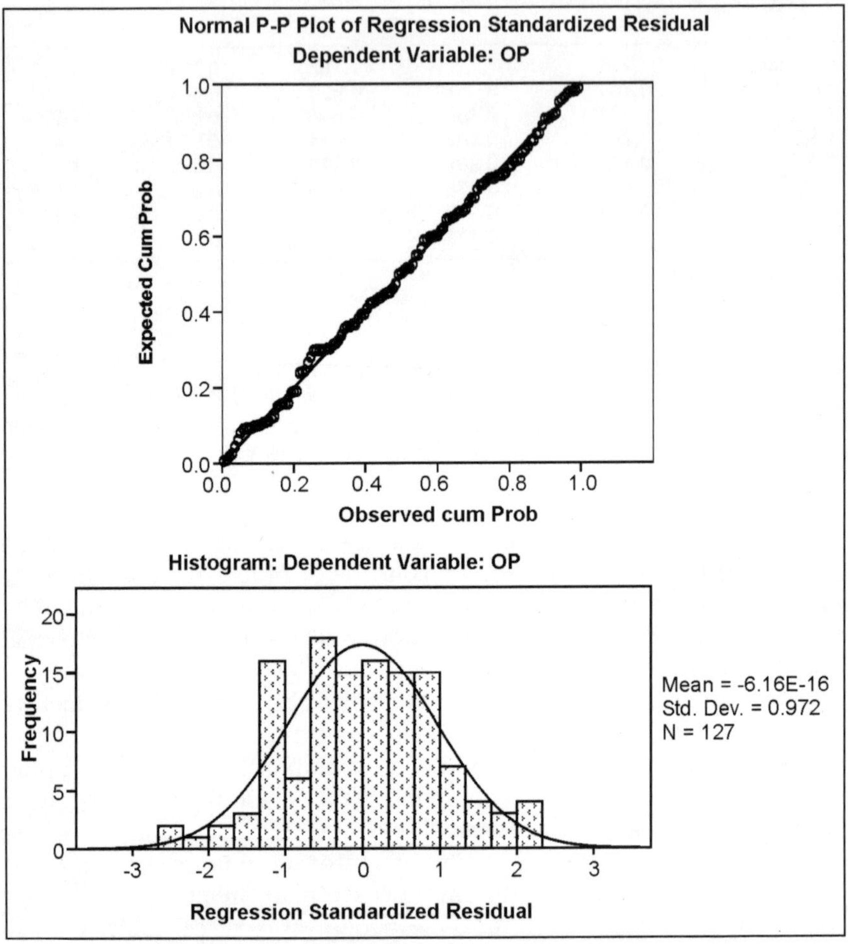

Figure 5.5: Model One Residual Distribution

Regarding the classical assumption of homoscedasticity, it stresses that the variance of the error term should be constant in different observations. The scatter plot displays that the residual appears to be gathered around zero with no pattern of outliers (see Figure 5.6).

The next discussion will revolve around model two which is

$$OP = a_i + b_1\, TM + b_2\, ER + b_3\, E\&T + b_4\, SR + b_5\, PM + b_6\, QI + b_7\, SP + b_8\, IND + b_9\, PD + b_{10}\, MAS \qquad (2)$$

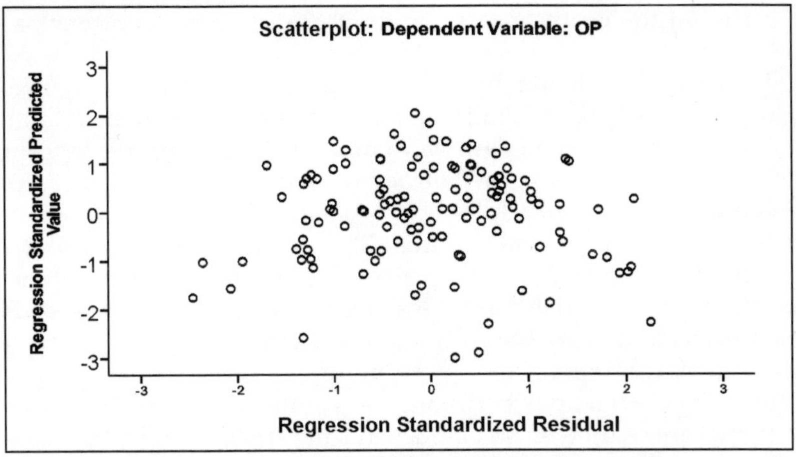

Figure 5.6: Scatter Plot for Residual for Model One

Where TM, ER, E&T, SR, PM, QI and SP represent the same whereas IND represents individualism, PD represents power distance and MAS represents masculinity.

Model two is conducted in three phases with initial stage including the first moderator construct (individualism), the second adding the construct of national culture (masculinity), and third adding the construct of national culture (power distance). In doing this, the changes in R^2, R^2

Table 5.9: Regression Result for Model 2

Variable	*B*	*Beta*	*B*	*Beta*	*b*	*Beta*	*Tolerance*	*VIF*
C	1.376*		1.298		0.844*			
TM	1.082*	0.582*	1.083*	0.583*	1.002*	0.539*	.531	1.882
ER	1.202*	0.548*	1.203*	0.549*	1.087*	0.496*	.893	1.120
E&T	0.246*	0.162*	0.237*	0.156*	0.253*	0.166*	.523	1.913
SR	0.473*	0.288*	0.469*	0.286*	0.389*	0.237*	.683	1.464
PM	0.611*	0.385*	0.609*	0.384*	0.402*	0.254*	.552	1.813
QI	0.697*	0.428*	0.698*	0.428*	0.673*	0.413*	.628	1.594
SP	0.057***	0.098***	0.058***	0.100***	0.022	0.037	.725	1.379
IND	0.637*	0.682*	0.626*	0.670*	0.478*	0.512*	.611	1.637
MAS			0.030	0.032	-0.042	-0.044	.783	1.277
PD					0.344*	0.389*	.574	1.741
R^2	0.755		0.755		0.842			
Adj. R^2	0.738		0.737		0.829			
F-value	45.35*		40.15*		62.03*			

* and *** significant at 1 per cent and 10 per cent respectively.

Dependent variable: organizational performance TM = Top Management, SR = Supplier Relationships, ER = Employee Relations, E&T= Education and Training, PM = Process Management, QI = Quality Information and Analysis, SP = Strategic Planning, PD = Power Distance, UA = Uncertainty Avoidance, IND = Individualism, and MAS = Masculinity.

adjusted and the coefficients show the three components strengths as moderators.

The result of the hierarchical regression for model two is contained in Table 5.9. The results are similar to that of those of model one as all the variables significantly and positively impact organizational performance. Additionally, the first construct of the moderator, individualism significantly and positively affects organizational performance. The goodness of model fit improved from R^2 36 per cent and Adjusted R^2 32 per cent to 76 per cent and 74 per cent respectively. The addition of masculinity in the model showed insignificant result in R^2 or adjusted R^2 which indicate that masculinity, as a moderator, does not influence organizational performance.

In the final stage, power distance was added and showed a positive and significant result with other independent variables with the exception of strategic planning which has an insignificant result. A marked improvement of R^2 and adjusted R^2 was noted at 84 per cent and 83 per cent respectively. The three stages confirmed the model's goodness of fit. As for the strength of the influence of each independent variable, the beta shows similar results to that of model one where among the soft TQM practices top management came first, followed by employee relations, supplier relationship and education and training. Contrastingly, in hard TQM practices, quality information and analysis has the strongest influence followed by process management and strategic planning with the latter having no significant influence. As for national culture construct, individualism led the list as it has the highest influence on organizational performance. This is followed by power distance and masculinity with the latter being insignificant.

Finally, with regards to diagnostics, the tolerance and VIF fall below the limit of severe multicollinearity of 0.2 and 10 respectively. Figure 5.7 and 5.8 presents the normality and homoscedasticity of the residuals. Moreover, the histogram, P-P plot and scatter plot reveal the non-violation of the assumptions of normality and homoscedasticity.

The fundamental idea behind a moderator is the understanding of the way a third variable can modify an established relationship's direction/strength (Rose *et al.*, 2004). The moderating effect is tested following the establishment of the relationship between one or more independent variable and dependent variable. This section deals with testing the moderating effect of national culture on the soft and hard TQM practices-organizational performance relationship. Earlier analysis revealed that the components of soft and hard TQM practice are all significantly and positively impacts organizational performance. Additionally when the proposed moderators were added as independent variables, individualism and power distance turned out to be statistically significant and positively associated with performance but masculinity was not. In this stage, each

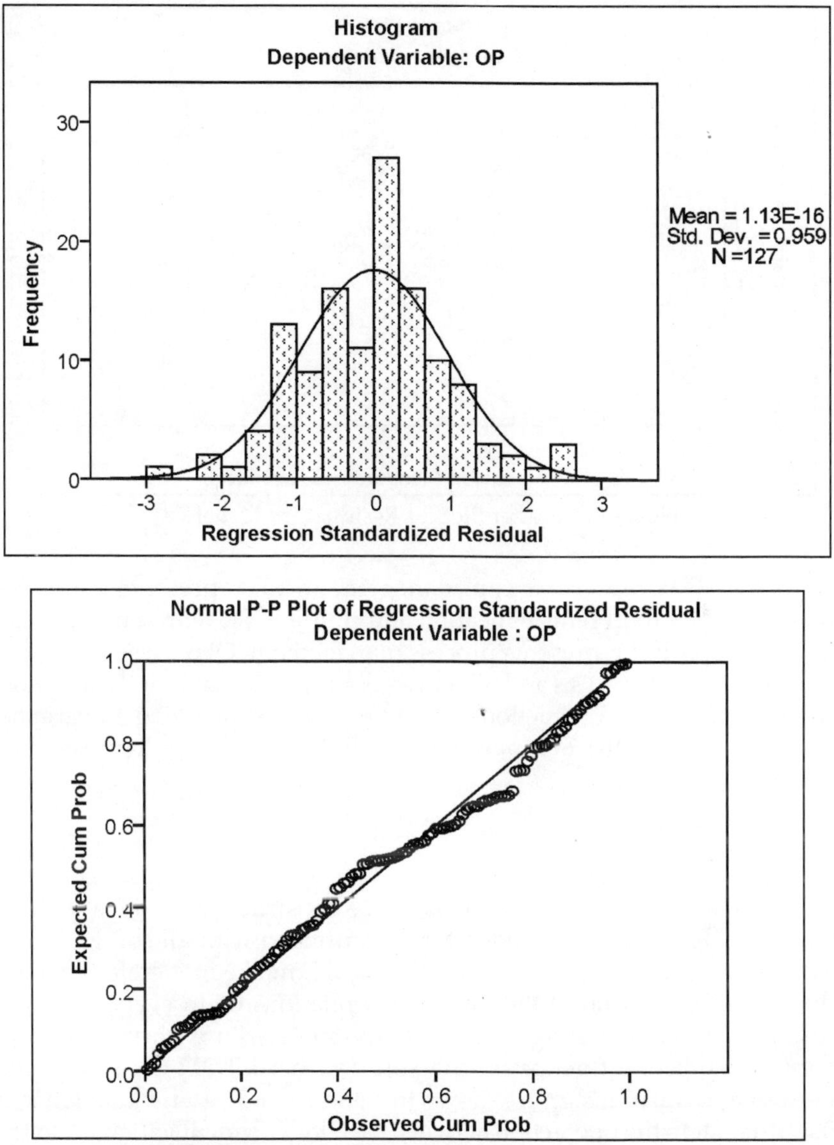

Figure 5.7: Model Two Residual Distributions

of these moderators are tested for their impact on the established soft and hard TQM practices-organizational performance relationship.

The model of moderating effect tested in this study is represented by the following equation:

$$OP = a_i + b_1 TM + b_2 ER + b_3\, E\&T + b_4\, SR + b_5 PM + b_6\, QI + b_7 SP + b_8\, X^*M \quad (3)$$

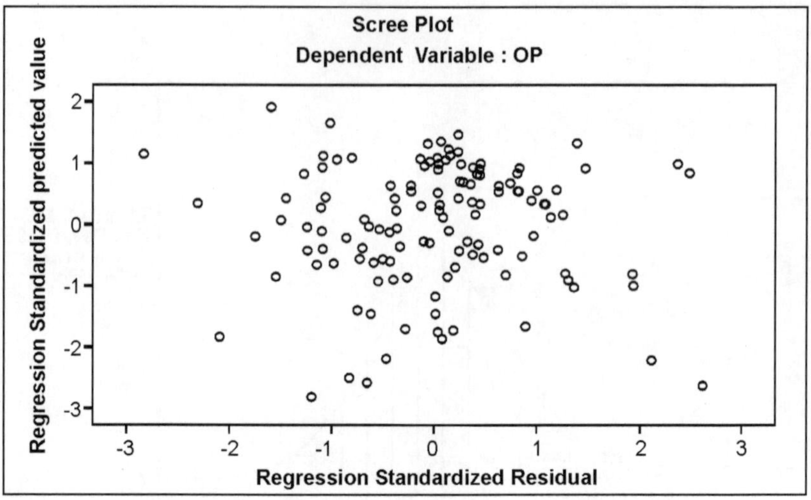

Figure 5.8: Scatter Plot for Residual for Model Two

Where TM represents top management, ER represents employee relations, E&T represents education and training, SR represents supplier relationships, PM represents process management, QI represents quality information and analysis and SP represents strategic planning. In addition, X*M represents the interaction effect with X as the independent variable, M as one of the constructs of national culture and b_1, b_2, b_3 represent the coefficients.

Individualism

Individualism makes up one of the three constructs of national culture that is being tested as a moderator. It is utilized with all soft and hard TQM practices in sequential order to reveal how the moderator changes the strength/direction of the established relationship in every case. The results of the moderating variable individuals with each independent variable and its influence on the soft and hard TQM-organizational performance relationship are shown in Table 5.10a. The term interaction is used to refer to the interaction between each independent variable and the moderator.

The interaction with the moderator is significant in three cases; with top management, with employee relationship and with education and training. The first one proved to be negative and significant while the second one is positive and significant. The results suggest that top management positively and significantly relates with organizational performance but the relation turns negative when individualism is added as a moderator. This indicates that individualism reverses the top management-organizational performance relationship which results in weaker and negative relationship.

Meanwhile, employee relationship significantly and positively relates to organizational performance and this relationship becomes more significant with the addition of individualism. The total effect is the aggregate of the coefficients of the independent variable in the interaction. Hence, the first relationship (top management-organizational performance) lessens upon the introduction of individualism from 1.46 to 1.35 while the second relationship (employee relationship-organizational performance) slightly increases from 0.37 to 0.60 when moderated with individualism.

Moreover, education and training appears to lessen in its direct relationship significance with organizational performance with the addition of individualism. Specifically, upon the introduction of individualism, education and training-organizational performance significant relationship disappears and is replaced by the interaction effect of 0.16. As for the other models, with the introduction of individualism as a moderator, the R^2 and the adjusted R^2 fall in the range of 75 per cent and 76 per cent, and 73 per cent and 74 per cent respectively. The entire models reveal a high and significant f-value indicating the goodness of models.

Table 5.10a: The Interaction Effect of Individualism

	*TM *INDI*	*ER*INDI*	*E&T*INDI*	*SR*INDI*	*PM*INDI*	*QI*INDI*	*SP*INDI*
Variable				*Coefficient*			
Constant	1.44*	1.38*	1.37*	1.36*	1.33*	1.37*	1.01*
	(7.72)	(7.99)	(7.61)	(7.22)	(6.56)	(7.10)	(3.00)
TM	1.46*	1.07*	1.11*	1.06*	1.10*	1.08*	1.05*
	(5.39)	(7.95)	(7.74)	(7.25)	(7.63)	(7.73)	(7.19)
ER	1.21*	0.37	1.24	1.20*	1.20*	1.20*	1.19*
	(6.31)	(0.44)	(0.59)	(6.00)	(6.19)	(6.20)	(6.08)
E&T	0.24*	0.23*	-0.38	0.24*	0.24*	0.25*	0.24**
	(3.06)	(2.27)	(-0.98)	(2.93)	(3.02)	(3.04)	(2.96)
SR	0.48*	0.26*	0.48*	0.13	0.47*	0.47*	0.46*
	(4.57)	(3.39)	(4.43)	(0.32)	(4.45)	(4.54)	(4.45)
PM	0.62*	0.63*	0.63*	0.62*	0.93*	0.61*	0.62*
	(6.10)	(6.17)	(6.37)	(5.54)	(2.68)	(5.79)	(5.81)
QI	0.68*	0.69*	0.71*	0.70*	0.70*	0.76	0.69*
	(6.08)	(6.42)	(6.50)	(5.67)	(5.64)	(1.36)	(5.93)
SP	0.01**	0.48*	0.06**	0.058**	0.06**	0.06***	0.19
	(2.00)	(4.69)	(2.16)	(2.07)	(2.17)	(2.03)	(1.59)
X*M	−0.11***	0.23*	0.16***	0.09	−0.08	−0.02	−0.03
	(−1.71)	(2.14)	(1.66)	(0.97)	(−1.03)	(−0.13)	(−1.15)
INDI	0.62*	0.64*	0.63*	0.64*	0.65*	0.64*	0.73*
	(12.9)	(14.3)	(13.2)	(13.4)	(13.05)	(12.76)	(9.11)
R2	76%	76%	76%	76%	76%	75%	76%
Adj. R2	74%	74%	74%	74%	74%	73%	74%
F-value	36*	43*	33*	30*	30*	29*	35*

*, ** and *** significant at 1 per cent, 5 per cent and 10 per cent respectively.

Dependent variable is organizational performance, TM*INDI the model for the interaction effect between Top management and individualism. Same thing applied for the other interaction terms.
T-value in the parentheses

Power Distance

The result of the moderating effect of power distance in each soft and hard TQM practices and organizational performance relationship is presented in Table 5.10. The interaction effect of power distance is insignificant in all independent variables. In other words, power distance does not moderate the relationship between the relationship of these variables and organizational performance. The result also reveals no interaction between power distance and organizational performance. The independent variables' significance differs on the basis of the model with the exception of process management which seems to be insignificant throughout the models. In soft TQM practices, employee relationship proved to be the strongest variable on average and this is followed by top management, supplier relations, and education and training.

In hard TQM practices, quality information and analysis is the strongest variable followed by process management (insignificant) and strategic planning. All the models showed positive and significant with power distance with the exception of top management where the relationship is negative and insignificant. In addition, power distance is significant in the entire models with the exception of the first one. The R^2 and adjusted R^2 and the f-test revealed that the model is good with R^2ranging from 68 per cent to 69 per cent and the adjusted R^2 ranging from 66 per cent to 67 per cent. The f-value is revealed to be significant in the models which show all the models goodness of fit.

Masculinity

The results of the masculinity effect on each of the soft and hard TQM practices and the way it influences organizational performance are detailed in Table 5.10c. In Table 5.9, when moderators are tested as independent variables, it was revealed that masculinity had no significant relationship with organizational performance. Despite the insignificance of the relationship, masculinity may still have a significant relationship through other variables.

Masculinity may moderate between the two variables rather than be an independent variable. It is evident from Table 5.10c that there are only two particular cases where hard TQM practices interact with masculinity to relate with organizational performance. Masculinity however appears to weaken the positive and significant relationship between process

Table 5.10b: The Interaction Effect of Power Distance

	*TM *PD*	*ER*PD*	*E&T*PD*	*SR*PD*	*PM*PD*	*QI*PD*	*SP*PD*
Variable	*Coefficients*						
C	1.41*	1.36*	1.43*	1.40*	1.42*	1.37*	1.58**
	(5.01)	(5.12)	(4.98)	(4.56)	(4.66)	(4.78)	(2.16)
TM	1.07*	0.82*	0.84*	0.85*	0.83*	0.81*	0.83*
	(2.90)	(5.85)	(5.72)	(5.73)	(5.77)	(5.54)	(5.87)
ER	0.88*	0.34	0.89*	0.88*	0.89*	0.90*	0.88*
	(4.00)	(0.85)	(4.05)	(4.27)	(4.05)	(3.99)	(4.01)
E&T	0.23*	0.25*	-0.11	0.22*	0.24*	0.24*	0.24**
	(2.54)	(2.68)	(-0.3)	(2.58)	(2.63)	(2.69)	(2.53)
SR	0.34*	0.33*	0.34*	0.8603	0.33*	0.32*	0.33*
	(2.72)	(2.74)	(2.88)	(1.35)	(2.66)	(2.68)	(2.82)
PM	0.17	0.16	0.16	0.16	0.23	0.17	0.17
	(0.96)	(0.93)	(0.92)	(0.88)	(0.49)	(0.92)	(0.95)
QI	0.56*	0.55*	0.56*	0.57*	0.58*	0.80**	0.58*
	(3.99)	(4.28)	(4.18)	(4.19)	(4.00)	(1.99)	(4.08)
SP	0.09***	0.09***	0.09**	0.08**	0.09***	0.09***	0.03
	(1.96)	(1.88)	(1.99)	(1.78)	(1.94)	(1.87)	(0.15)
X*M	0.58	0.14	0.08	-0.13	-0.02	-0.05	0.01
	(8.99)	(1.16)	(0.87)	(-0.9)	(-0.16)	(-0.52)	(0.32)
PD	-0.06	0.57*	0.55*	0.57*	0.55*	0.57*	0.52*
	(-0.63)	(9.97)	(8.46)	(8.65)	(8.27)	(8.11)	(3.23)
R2	68%	69%	68%	69%	68%	68%	68%
Adj. R2	66%	67%	66%	67%	66%	66%	66%
F-value	24*	23*	24*	24*	25*	24*	26*

*, ** and *** significant at 1 per cent, 5 per cent and 10 per cent respectively. Dependent variable is organizational performance, TM*PD the model for the interaction effect between Top management and Power Distance. Same thing applied for the other interaction terms. T-value in the parentheses

management and strategic planning and while masculinity increases, the relationship decreases in strength. The process management impact falls from 0.172 to 1.41 following the introduction of masculinity. Strategic coefficient also falls from 0.62 to 0.52. This indicates that masculinity adversely impacts the relationship between hard TQM constructs of process management and strategic planning, and organizational performance.

The independent variables are significant in most models with the exception of education and training which seems to be significant in only two models. As for the variables strengths, the strongest of soft TQM constructs is employee relationship, followed by top management, supplier relations and education and training which has the weakest strength. Masculinity on the other hand, appears to be significant in the models with the R^2 and adjusted R^2 values ranging from 42 per cent-46 per cent and 38 per cent-42 per cent respectively. Meanwhile, the goodness of fit as presented by the F-value depicts a high and significant value indicating the goodness of the models.

Table 5.10c: The Interaction Effect of Masculinity

Variable	TM *MAS	ER*MAS	E&T*MAS	SR*MAS	PM*MAS	QI*MAS	SP*MAS
	Coefficients						
C	2.39*	2.35*	2.38*	2.39*	2.38*	2.42*	0.99
	(7.68)	(7.69)	(7.68)	(7.77)	(7.94)	(7.86)	(1.65)
TM	0.82	0.85*	0.89*	0.89*	0.91*	0.92*	0.85*
	(1.48)	(4.81)	(5.02)	(5.03)	(5.26)	(5.16)	(4.96)
ER	0.995*	0.04	0.99*	0.99*	1.08*	1.01*	0.96*
	(4.74)	(0.06)	(4.75)	(4.74)	(5.23)	(4.81)	(4.73)
E&T	0.17	0.17	0.03	0.17	0.19***	0.16	0.24**
	(1.49)	(1.56)	(0.06)	(1.49)	(1.77)	(1.48)	(2.10)
SR	0.44*	0.40*	0.44*	0.49	0.41*	0.45*	0.43*
	(3.19)	(2.85)	(3.21)	(1.06)	(3.06)	(3.26)	(3.21)
PM	0.46*	0.41*	0.45*	0.45*	1.72*	0.48*	0.46*
	(3.25)	(2.92)	(3.24)	(3.21)	(3.35)	(3.39)	(3.36)
QI	0.58*	0.53*	0.57*	0.58*	0.59*	0.12	0.54*
	(3.99)	(3.65)	(3.94)	(4.00)	(4.19)	(0.25)	(3.87)
SP	0.20*	0.20*	0.20*	0.20*	0.20*	0.20*	0.62*
	(4.64)	(4.68)	(4.54)	(4.62)	(4.77)	(4.66)	(3.90)
X*M	0.02	0.24	0.04	-0.01	-0.31**	0.13	-0.10*
	(0.14)	(1.56)	(0.35)	(-0.11)	(-2.56)	(0.97)	(-2.71)
MAS	0.24*	0.25*	0.25*	0.24*	0.24*	0.23*	0.58*
	(3.52)	(3.73)	(3.56)	(3.55)	(3.68)	(3.40)	(4.10)
R2	42%	44%	42%	42%	45%	43%	46%
Adj. R2	38%	40%	38%	38%	41%	39%	42%
F-value	9.5*	10*	9.5*	9.5*	11*	10*	11*

*, ** and *** significant at 1 per cent, 5 per cent and 10 per cent respectively. Dependent variable is organizational performance, TM*MAS the model for the interaction effect between Top management and Masculinity. Same thing applied for the other interaction terms. T-value in the parentheses

Uncertainty Avoidance

The details of the uncertainty avoidance interaction effect with soft and hard TQM practices and the way it influences organizational performance is summarized in Table 5.10d. It is evident from the table that there is only one instance where hard TQM practices interact with uncertainty avoidance and relate to organizational performance. Uncertainty avoidance appears to lessen the positive and significant relations between process management and organizational performance. In other words, the relationship between process management and organizational performance is decreased upon the introduction of uncertainty avoidance. The impact decreases from 1.40 to 1.16.

Almost all the independent variables showed significance in most models with the exception of education and training which is insignificant in all models. As for the strength of variables, the variable of soft TQM with the highest strength is top management followed by employee relationship, supplier relations and education and training (the weakest).

As for the hard TQM practices, the strongest variable is quality information and analysis. This is followed by process management and finally strategic planning. Uncertainty avoidance is significant in the entire models with R^2 an adjusted R^2 ranging between 55 per cent to 57 per cent, and 52 per cent to 54 per cent respectively. The F-value's measurement of goodness of fit reveals a high and significant value indicating the goodness of models.

Table 5.10d: The Interaction Effect of Uncertainty Avoidance

	*TM *UA*	*ER*UA*	*E&T*UA*	*SR*UA*	*PM*UA*	*QI*UA*	*SP*UA*
Variable	*Coefficients*						
Constant	1.40*	1.43*	1.41*	1.44*	1.48*	1.42*	1.50**
	4.50	4.55	4.54	4.54	4.80	4.56	2.15
TM	0.58	0.92*	0.98*	0.96*	0.94*	0.94*	0.94*
	1.22	5.90	6.22	5.99	6.12	6.04	5.87
ER	0.79*	1.33**	0.86*	0.83*	0.80*	0.77*	0.79*
	4.23	2.07	4.51	4.22	4.35	4.16	4.13
E&T	0.14	0.12	–0.72	0.14	0.13	0.13	0.13
	1.39	1.19	–1.34	1.43	1.37	1.28	1.35
SR	0.44*	0.45*	0.45*	0.79***	0.46*	0.44*	0.44*
	3.62	3.67	3.76	1.68	3.83	3.63	3.60
PM	0.31**	0.30**	0.34*	0.33**	1.40*	0.34*	0.31**
	2.47	2.37	2.70	2.55	2.79	2.64	2.40
QI	0.57*	0.56*	0.56*	0.58*	0.50*	0.05	0.56*
	4.43	4.43	4.45	4.43	3.99	0.09	4.25
SP	0.15*	0.15*	0.15*	0.15*	0.14*	0.15*	0.11
	3.70	3.79	3.76	3.66	3.58	3.82	0.58
X*M	0.09	–0.14	0.21	–0.08	–0.24*	0.12	0.01
	0.78	–0.89	1.61	–0.76	–2.25	1.05	0.17
UA	0.51*	0.51*	0.51*	0.50*	0.50*	0.50*	0.49*
	7.01	6.89	6.98	6.82	7.01	6.87	3.07
R2	55%	55%	56%	55%	57%	55%	55%
Adj. R2	52%	52%	53%	52%	54%	52%	52%
F-value	16*	16*	16*	16*	17*	16*	16*

*, ** and *** significant at 1 per cent, 5 per cent and 10 per cent respectively. Dependent variable is organizational performance, TM*MAS the model for the interaction effect between Top management and Masculinity. Same thing applied for the other interaction terms. T-value in the parentheses

Difference in Organizational Performance

This section discusses the hypothesis of whether or not the mean performances across countries are similar. ANOVA is utilized for the testing of mean differences between the countries. It is a one way analysis of variance and the results of the testing are displayed in Table 5.11. The results indicate a significance difference between the countries with regards to their organizational performance. Nevertheless, the test does not reveal which countries are different and by how many degrees. Table 5.11 also presents the significant mean differences between the countries. From the table, it is evident that highest significant mean was higher compared to

Egypt, Jordan. While Egypt shows a significantly higher mean compared to Turkey, its mean is significantly lower than Qatar. Meanwhile, Turkey's organizational performance is significantly higher in comparison to Jordan's.

Table 5.11: Organizational Performance Mean Difference

Variable	*F-value*		*Mean difference*				
			Saudi Arabia	*Egypt*	*Turkey*	*Jordan*	*Qatar*
Organizational performance	22.4*	Saudi Arabia	—				
		Egypt	1.07*	—			
		Turkey	–0.03	1.11*	—		
		Jordan	1.36*	0.29	1.39*	—	
		Qatar	0.01	–1.1*	0.05	–1.34	—

* Significant at 1 per cent.

SUMMARY OF RESEARCH ACHIEVEMENTS

This section discusses the achievements of the study based on the research questions. As stated in Chapter one these research questions are as follows:

What is the Relationship between Soft TQM practices and Municipalities performance?

What is the Relationship between Hard TQM practices and Municipalities performance?

What is the moderating effect of National Culture on improving the relationship between Soft-Hard TQM and performance?

Are there any differences in performances between these five countries?

This section summarizes the results and findings related to each of these four research questions of this study, and the outcome of the hypothesis testing that were undertaken. The selections of these hypotheses reflect the need for the relationships between the Soft-Hard TQM, Performance, and the Effect of national Culture in these relationships.

Research Question One

The first research question concerned whether what is the Relationship between Soft TQM practices and Municipalities performance in five Developing Countries (Egypt, Jordan, Qatar, Turkey, Kingdom of Saudi Arabia)? And the objective was to determine the nature of any such relationship. The hypothesis developed for the research Literature regarding quality management, that revealed soft factors are related to performance in a positive way. Flynn *et al.,* (1995), Samson & Terziovski

(1999). Other findings showed significant positive links between organizational performance and several soft factors including leadership, people management and customer focus. Also, Rahman & Bullock (2005); Powell (1995), Dow *et al.;* (1999); Ahire *et al.,* (1996) & Powell (1995) reached the conclusion that organizations obtaining TQM soft elements exhibit superior performance. The Five hypotheses that were devised for each of the Soft TQM aspects were listed in section 5.6.1. Addressing this, research question was involved using regression analysis. Section 2.2.6 show us the literature review the relationship between Soft TQM and Performance. Table 5.12 below summarize the hypothesis proposed earlier in chapter three and whether these hypotheses are supported or not. All hypotheses were formulated in the alternative form. The table indicate that all four factors have a direct positive and significant relationship with the organizational performance. All the variables are significant at 1 per cent level of significance except employee relationship which is significant at 5 per cent level of significance. The possible relationship between Soft TQM factors and Performance was tested using standardized beta correlation coefficient. A summary of the results are to be found in Table 5.12.

Table 5.12: Results of Hypothesis Testing for Direct Relationships

Hypothesis	*Coefficient*	*Remarks*
H1a Soft TQM—Top Management Commitment significantly affects the organizational performance.	0.850*	Supported
H1b: Soft TQM—Supplier relationship significantly affects organizational performance.	0.472*	Supported
H1c: Soft TQM—Education and training significantly impact the organizational performance.	0.247**	Supported
H1d: Soft TQM—Employee relations significantly affects organizational performance.	0.949*	Supported

* and **Significant at 1 per cent and 5 per cent respectively.

On other words, that all of the Four Soft TQM aspects were significantly related with organizational Performance. However, with regard critical Factor of Soft TQM Top Management Commitments (TM), in general Developing Countries, in particular and countries throughout the search, the public and employee look to the actions and commitments of Top management of governmental organization. Managers, as a guide for any success in these organizations, this factor is most directed to the governmental organization and its progress towards commitment to total quality management. The successful implementation of Soft-Hard TQM depends on a strong commitment from the management. This finding is in line with the TQM literature that strongly emphasizes the commitment of management as one of the determinants for Soft TQM and Hard TQM to be successful. However, for The Municipalities in these five Developing countries, the role of management is more towards the leader or the main driver of Soft and Hard TQM implementation. The introduction point of TQM implementation in these five developing countries.

This finding is in line with the TQM literature that strongly emphasizes the commitment of management as one of the determinants for TQM to be successful. In most organizations, the management of an organization acts as the introducer of TQM implementation (Arawati & Abdullah, 2000). However, this result is in line with the previous results as (Arawati, 2005; Flynn *et al.,* 1995; Llorens Montes & Verdu Jover, 2004; Powell, 1995; and Yasin *et al.,* 2004).

With respect to critical Factor of Soft TQM Employee Relations (ER), the detail discussion on this definitions was presented in Chapter two of this thesis. As discussed earlier, this study defined Employee Relations (ER) strategy as being consisted of employee relations comprise of employee participation, employee satisfaction, employee empowerment, employee involvement, employee fulfillment, delegation and empowerment and worker-manager interactions, Karuppusami & Gandhinathan (2006). In any organization, Employee relations is critical factor to achieve both sustainability and competitiveness (Ehigie & Mc Andrew, 2005; Ooi, Bakar, Arumugam, Vellapan & Loke, 2007; Palo & Padhi, 2005; Sila, 2005) to achieve organizational competitiveness Akdere's (2006). In these five developing countries, the wide consensus and agreement in the literature regarding the positive effect of these practices on the organizational performance. However, this result is in line with the previous results as (Powell (1995); Dow *et al.,* (1999); Madu *et al.,*'s (1995); Khairul Anuar *et al.,* (2001); Moorhouse (2006)). However, in general, in most of developing countries and especially in Arab countries, the achievement of organizations' goals depend on partially employee relations.

With regard to the critical factor of Soft TQM Education & Training (E&T), according to Shiryan *et al.,* (2012), employee training is an issue in Saudi Arabia's organizations as other Arab countries need to be significant with organizational performance. So, these developing countries have not had sufficient training to acquire the requisite skills and follow traditional control practices (Aladwani 2001; Forstenlechner & Rutledge, 2010; Mimouni & Metcalfe, 2012). This result is in line with the previous results as (Cruz *et al.,* (2009); Holzer *et al.,* (1993); Zwick (2005); Alba-Ramirez (1994); Conti (2005); Delaney & Huselid, (1996); Fussell, Kraut & Siegel, (2000); and Huang, (2001). As a result, the interaction between National Culture—Individualism and process management is natural, result to difference between employees.

With respect to critical factor of Soft TQM Supplier Relationships (SR), in the Municipalities as other Public sector is characterized by many suppliers particularly the commercial sector including government, donors, non-governmental organizations, traders and other sectors of different organizations and other social organizations, the Municipalities also work with their suppliers to develop a relationship to optimize supplied resources. The finding of this study also reported that the factor of supplier relationship was significantly related to organizational performance in these municipalities. However, municipalities are service governmental organizations that have multiple relations with many kinds of suppliers; therefore the relations with these organizations have relationship with Municipalities performance. This result in line with some previous results as Rahman & Bullock, (2005); Flynn *et al.,* (1995) stated. Because municipalities are governed by the rules and regulations in dealing with suppliers, it is natural that national culture is not significant in the relationship. The spirits supplier relationship and organizational performance in these Municipalities, has no moderating effect.

At the end, customer focus, Fifth hypothesis is dropped and not included because that is not load in the exploratory factor analysis process for study variables which means fully ignored because it has not any effect in Municipalities' performance in this study, this result in contrasts perfectly with some previous studies as done by Llorens Montes & Verdu Jover, 2004; Yasin *et al.,* 2004; Agus *et al.,* 2000. Because this study in public sector is the opposite of previous studies that is in private sector, in the developing countries. This confirms that in the developing countries in general and in these five countries in particular, employee in government sectors do not care to focus on customers, but are interested in following the procedures and laws that govern their work unlike the private sector, which has first goal for the costumer, this is due to the nature of competition in the private sector.

Research Question Two

The second research question concerned whether what is the Relationship between Hard TQM practices and Municipalities performance in five Developing Countries (?) And the objective was to determine the nature of any such relationship. The hypothesis developed for the research literature regarding quality management, literature reveals that hard TQM elements have a significant impact on organizational performance in a positive way. For example, product and process benchmarking lead to optimal product design and process cost reduction in DuPont, Ford, Motorola, Xerox, and General Motors (Min, 1992; & McFadden, 1993). Moreover, other TQM tools were found to achieve performance; six sigma processes in Motorola and in other companies (McFadden, 1993), QFD in Toyota (Sullivan, 1987), seven simple tools in Honda (Maul, 1994), SPC in Motorola (Kumar, 1993) and Taguchi methods in Mazda and Ford (Taguchi & Clausing, 1993).

The three hypotheses that were devised for each of the Hard TQM aspects were listed in section 5.6.1. Addressing this research question involved doing using regression analysis. Section 2.2.6 show us the literature review the relationship between Hard TQM and Performance. Table 5.13 below summarize the hypothesis proposed earlier in Chapter 3 and whether these hypotheses are supported or not. All hypotheses were formulated in the alternative form.

Table 5.13: Results of Hypothesis Testing for Direct Relationships

Hypothesis	*Coefficient*	*Remarks*
H2 a: Hard TQM—Process management significantly impacts organizational performance.	0.442*	Supported
H2b: Hard TQM—Quality Information and Analysis System significantly impact organizational performance.	0.543*	Supported
H2 c: Hard TQM—Strategic Planning significantly impacts organizational performance.	0.220*	Supported

* and ** Significant at 1 per cent and 5 per cent respectively.

The Table 5.13 indicate that all the practices have a direct positive and significant relationship with the organizational performance. All the variables are significant at 1 per cent level of significance. With respect to critical factor of Hard TQM, Process Management (PM), perhaps one of the most studied elements of TQM by researchers is Critical success factors of TQM studied by different authors is strategic planning, Masood *et al.*, (2012). The finding of this study, this factor of process management (PM) was significantly related to organizational performance. As mentioned, in most cases, the municipalities in these countries provide services to citizens and residents therefore, it cannot delay or store these services, so the importance of Process Management (PM) in the municipalities can be seen. This result in line with some previous results as (Li *et al.*, 2003; Sila & Ebrahimpour, 2005; Sila & Ebrahimpour, 2002; Wu *et al.*, 1997, Škrinjar, *et al.*, (2008) Hinterhuber, 1995). Also, the result of the interaction between Masculinity and process management is a natural result of work in those municipalities.

With respect to critical factor of Hard TQM, information and analysis (QI) was found to be a significant predictor of organizational performance. In the literature of TQM, the information and analysis system (QI) has been recognized to have a significant role in organizations' overall performance in municipalities in these countries. It has been widely known that the information system allows the operational cost reduction, increases the productivity, improves the service quality, reduces the risk and uncertainty in the decision making processes and optimizes the use of the workforces (Bilich & Neto, 2000). This result in line with some previous results as Flynn *et al.* (1995) Saraph *et al.*'s (1989).

With regard to the critical factor of Hard TQM, Strategic Planning (SP) was significantly related to organizational performance in the municipalities in these five countries. This result is in line with the previous results as (Li *et al.*, 2003; Sila & Ebrahimpour, 2005; Sila & Ebrahimpour, 2002; Wu *et al.*, 1997). However, Municipalities in these countries are moving to implement strategic planning according to the perspective of the private sector to achieve better performance.

Research Question Three (Moderating effect)

As stated in chapter two, various studies have been dedicated to the study of national culture. In order to comprehend cultural dimensions, prior studies have put forward several models although only a few of them are currently used in an extensive manner. However, non-studies dealt with the relation between Soft TQM, Hard TQM, Performance, National culture. As a moderator between Soft TQM, Hard TQM and Performance, most of study instead dealt with organizational culture and its effect in performance. As stated in chapter two, following four Dimensions of Hofested Culture Dimensions are chosen in this study:

Individualism

Table 5.14 below summarize the hypothesis proposed earlier in chapter 3 about whether individualism moderates the relationship between soft and hard TQM practices and organizational performance. The result shows that there were only three hypotheses that were supported in the soft TQM practices, namely top management, employee relationship, and supplier relations. For hard TQM practices, none of the hypotheses were supported. As have been explained earlier, the individualism has an adverse influence in moderating the relationship between top management and organizational performance.

With respect to the result of National Culture—individualism, it is surprising negatively as moderator the relationship between Soft TQM and the Municipality's organizational performance. The result of that fits perfectly with the results of Hofestede (1980) in his studies on those countries where the individualism is low. Moreover, according the national culture for those countries, The Citizens Direction are defined by directions of their leaders.

With Respect to National Culture—individualism as a moderator between Soft TQM—Employee Relationship and the Municipality's performance, this moderate effect is positive, it may, because it is dependent on the individual differences in their attributes, accepting the responsibilities and powers and other employee relationships that are affected by individual differences.

Table 5.14: Results of Hypothesis testing for moderating Relationship of individualism

Hypothesis	*Coefficient*	*Remarks*
H4a: National Culture—individualism moderates the relationship between Soft TQM Top Management and the Municipality's organizational performance.	–0.11***	Supported
H4b: National Culture—individualism moderates the relationship between Soft TQM Employee Relationship and the Municipality's organizational performance.	0.23*	Supported
H4c: National Culture—individualism moderates the relationship between Soft TQM Education & Training and the Municipality's organizational performance.	0.16***	Supported
H4d: National Culture—individualism moderates the relationship between Soft TQM Supplier relationship and the Municipality's organizational performance.	0.09	Not Supported
H3e: National Culture—individualism moderates the relationship between hard TQM Process Management and the Municipality's organizational performance.	–0.08	Not Supported
H4f: National Culture—individualism moderates the relationship between hard TQM Quality information & analysis and the Municipality's organizational performance.	–0.02	Not Supported
H4g: National Culture—individualism moderates the relationship between hard TQM strategic planning and the Municipality's organizational performance.	–0.03	Not Supported

* and *** Significant at 1 per cent and 10 per cent respectively.

With regard National Culture—individualism as a moderator between Soft TQM—Supplier relationship, and the Municipality's performance, there is no moderate effect, because this relationship in public sector governor by roles and system, However, with regard to National Culture—individualism as a moderator between all Hard TQM factors, and the Municipality's performance not supported, all of factors of Hard TQM, and the Municipality's performance, this moderate effect is not supported, that means there is no moderate effect between individualism as a moderator with these factors relations with Municipality's performance, this is due to the nature of the work of the government sectors in those countries whoever, this result is logical result because there are many differences between the role of competition in those sectors and private sectors.

Power Distance

Table 5.15 below summarize the hypothesis proposed earlier in chapter 3 and whether these hypotheses are supported or not. The hypothesis proposed as whether the national culture constructs moderate the relationship between soft and hard TQM practices. All hypotheses were formulated in the alternative form. In this section, the hypotheses of power distance as a moderator is summarized. The table indicate that power distance does not moderate the relationship between soft and hard TQM practices and organizational performance.

Table 5.15: Results of Hypothesis testing for moderating Relationship of power distance

Hypothesis	*Coefficient*	*Remarks*
H3a: National Culture—Power distance moderates the relationship between Soft TQM Top Management and the Municipality's organizational performance.	0.58	Not Supported
H3b: National Culture—Power distance moderates the relationship between Soft TQM Employee Relationship and the Municipality's organizational performance.	0.14	Not Supported
H3c: National Culture—Power distance moderates the relationship between Soft TQM Education & Training and the Municipality's organizational performance.	0.08	Not Supported
H3d: National Culture—Power distance moderates the relationship between Soft TQM Supplier relationship and the Municipality's organizational performance.	–0.13	Not Supported
H3e: National Culture—Power distance moderates the relationship between hard TQM Process Management and the Municipality's organizational performance.	–0.02	Not Supported
H3f: National Culture—Power distance moderates the relationship between hard TQM Quality information & analysis and the Municipality's organizational performance.	0.05	Not Supported
H3g: National Culture—Power distance moderates the relationship between hard TQM strategic planning and the Municipality's organizational performance.	0.01	Not Supported

* Significant at 1 per cent.

With respect to the result of National Culture—Power distance does not moderate the relationship between soft and hard TQM practices and the Municipality's organizational performance because the nature of public sector, the works in those sectors are in according to a certain routine and specific procedures.

Masculinity

Table 5.16 below summarize the hypothesis proposed earlier in chapter 3 about whether national culture construct masculinity moderates the relationship between soft and hard TQM practices and organizational performance. The result shows that there were only 2 hypotheses that were supported in the hard TQM practices, namely process management and strategic planning. However the moderating effect has an adverse effect of the relationship between those two hard TQM practices and the organizational performance.

Table 5.16: Results of Hypothesis testing for moderating Relationship of Masculinity

Hypothesis	Coefficient	Remarks
H5a: National Culture—Masculinity moderates the relationship between Soft TQM Top Management and the Municipality's organizational performance.	0.02	Not Supported
H5b: National Culture—Masculinity moderates the relationship between Soft TQM Employee Relationship and the Municipality's organizational performance.	0.24	Not Supported
H5c: National Culture—Masculinity moderates the relationship between Soft TQM Education & Training and the Municipality's organizational performance.	0.04	Not Supported
H5d: National Culture—Masculinity moderates the relationship between Soft TQM Supplier relationship and the Municipality's organizational performance.	–0.01	Not Supported
H5e: National Culture—Masculinity moderates the relationship between hard TQM Process Management and the Municipality's organizational performance.	–0.31*	Supported
H5f: National Culture—Masculinity moderates the relationship between hard TQM Quality information & analysis and the Municipality's organizational performance.	0.13	Not Supported
H5g: National Culture—Masculinity moderates the relationship between hard TQM strategic planning and the Municipality's organizational performance.	–0.10*	Supported

* Significant at 1 per cent.

With respect to the result of National Culture –Masculinity, it is clear that this dimension of the national culture does not have any moderate effect on overall soft TQM and Hard TQM components except on two factors of Hard TQM namely Process Management., This is due to the nature of this factor it fits with Masculinity that Hofested (1980) found in high level in these countries, with regard, strategic planning. This is due to the nature of these five societies in which they were searched, according to Hofstede (1980).

Uncertainty avoidance

Table 5.17 below summarize the hypothesis proposed earlier in chapter 3 about whether national culture construct uncertainty avoidance moderates the relationship between soft and hard TQM practices and organizational performance. The result shows that there was only 1 hypothesis that was supported in the hard TQM practices, namely process management. However the moderating effect has an adverse effect of the relationship between that hard TQM practices and the organizational performance.

With respect to the result of National Culture –Uncertainty Avoidance, although this factor did not loaded in the Exploratory Factor Analysis (EFA) but the study tries to know effect of this factor as a moderator to the relationship between Soft-Hard TQM and Performance, for comparison

Table 5.17: Results of Hypothesis Testing for Moderating Relationship of Uncertainty Avoidance

Hypothesis	*Coefficient*	*Remarks*
H6a: National Culture—uncertainty avoidance moderates the relationship between Soft TQM Top Management and the Municipality's organizational performance.	0.09	Not Supported
H6b: National Culture—uncertainty avoidance moderates the relationship between Soft TQM Employee Relationship and the Municipality's organizational performance.	–0.14	Not Supported
H6c: National Culture—uncertainty avoidance moderates the relationship between Soft TQM Education & Training and the Municipality's organizational performance.	0.21	Not Supported
H6d: National Culture—uncertainty avoidance moderates the relationship between Soft TQM Supplier relationship and the Municipality's organizational performance.	–0.08	Not Supported
H6e: National Culture—uncertainty avoidance moderates the relationship between hard TQM Process Management and the Municipality's organizational performance.	–0.24*	Supported
H6f: National Culture—uncertainty avoidance moderates the relationship between hard TQM Quality information & analysis and the Municipality's organizational performance.	0.12	Not Supported
H6g: National Culture—uncertainty avoidance moderates the relationship between hard TQM strategic planning and the Municipality's organizational performance.	–0.01	Not Supported

* Significant at 1 per cent.

only, since this factor depicts the society's tolerance of uncertainty and unexpected situations, it is logical that this dimension of the national culture does not have moderate effect between any of the dimensions of the overall Soft TQM and Hard TQM except Process Management as factor from Hard TQM, because Process Management regarding the way organizations design and produce products and services. In the government sector, they work according to specific mechanisms of action.

As regard fourth Questions in Research Questions that is inclined with the difference in organizational performance between these five developing countries:

Table 5.18 that is extracted from the previous Table 5.11, summarizes the difference in mean hypothesis. The hypothesis proposed to investigate whether there is a significant difference in organizational performance mean among the five countries studied. The results suggest that there is evidence of difference in mean between the countries studied, this is partially depended on national culture.

Table 5.19 below shows the significant difference between the five countries in term of national culture constructs. In general, in all the four cases, there is a significant difference between the five countries in term of national culture constructs. In terms of difference between courtiers, the

Table 5.18: Results of Hypothesis Testing for Moderating Relationship of Masculinity

Hypothesis	*F-value*	*Remarks*
H7: there a significant difference in organizational performance mean between all countries	22.4*	Supported

* Significant at 1 per cent.

results show that the difference exists between Saudi Arabia with Egypt and Jordan in individualism. In addition, there was a difference between Egypt with turkey and Jordan. Similarly, there was a difference between Turkey and Jordan as well as between Jordan in Qatar. Same results apply for power distance. The third construct was masculinity shows that Saudi Arabia and Egypt differ significantly from Turkey and Jordan, while Turkey differs from Jordan, and lastly Jordan differs from Qatar. The last construct which was uncertainty avoidance in Jordan differs significantly from Saudi Arabia, Egypt, Turkey and Qatar. In summary, Saudi Arabia has a higher mean than Egypt and Jordan in individualism and power distance as well as higher than Jordan in masculinity and uncertainty avoidance. On the other hand, Turkey has a higher mean than Saudi in term of Masculinity. Egypt display a lower mean in Individualism, power distance and Masculinity than Turkey but higher mean in all culture constructs compared to Jordan. Moreover, Turkey scores higher means than Jordan in all culture constructs.

Table 5.19: National Culture Mean Difference

Variable	*F-value*		*Mean difference*			
			SA	*Egypt*	*Turkey*	*Jordan*
Individualism	21*	Egypt	0.68*	–		
		Turkey	–0.36	–1.03*	–	
		Jordan	1.3*	0.63*	1.66*	–
		Qatar	–0.12	–0.79	0.24	–1.42*
Power Distance	26*	Egypt	0.76*			
		Turkey	0.08	–0.68*		
		Jordan	1.68*	0.93*	1.62*	
		Qatar	0.42	–0.34	0.34	–1.27*
Masculinity	11*	Egypt	0.05			
		Turkey	–0.60*	–0.65*		
		Jordan	0.77*	0.72*	1.37*	
		Qatar	–0.49	–0.54	0.11	–1.25*
Uncertainty Avoidance	18*	Egypt	0.08			
		Turkey	–0.20	–0.28		
		Jordan	1.11*	1.03*	1.31*	
		Qatar	–0.69	–0.78	–0.49	–1.80*

Six
Research Conclusion

SUMMARY

The study's primary objective was to examine the moderating impact of National Culture (NC) on the two inter-dependent TQM categories namely Soft-Hard TQM and Organizational performance in the context of the Municipalities of Five developing countries viz. Egypt, Jordan, Qatar, Saudi Arabia and Turkey. The hard TQM comprises of system, tools, and techniques whereas the soft TQM are those dealing with long-term nature and is described as the humanistic intangible elements that are challenging to directly measure; for instance, top management commitment, customer focus, teamwork, training and empowerment and effective communications.

The study was basically motivated by the inconsistent findings in literature with regards to the relationship between soft TQM-hard TQM and the Organizational performance. Moreover, the inconsistent findings of the relationships between these factors have been considered as an unresolved top issue that requires further investment. Additionally, there are several organizational variables that have to be considered in the relationship. Owing to the oversight of the prior studies in examining the impact of culture in the above mentioned relationship, this study attempts to do so.

On a universal level, TQM is a concept that includes soft and hard elements which have been acknowledged in the last few decades as the most popular and widely practiced management premise employed by organizations to develop competitive advantage and improve their performance. A comprehensive research work has been carried out by researchers to study the effect of both soft and hard TQM practices on both organizational performance and competitive advantage. These researches form a part of the extant studies dedicated to studying the TQM impact in the context of different types of organizations including manufacturing, service, SMEs, higher educational institutions and public sector organizations.

Nevertheless, a thorough review of the current quality management literature highlighted the inconclusive findings concerning the relationship between soft-hard TQM practices and organizational performance as mentioned by Kaynak (2003). Many of the studies dedicated to determining the soft-hard TQM and performance relationship revealed a positive result. Despite the evidence to the fact that the implementation of TQM—an overall concept—enhances organizational performance, some studies showed the failure of some TQM implementation initiatives. Owing to the above inconclusive findings, a new group of research arose where in some researchers like Ehigie & McAndrew (2005) contended that the relationship should be changed in terms of some influencing variables. It has however been widely accepted in the literature of quality management that the failure of some TQM initiatives were attributed to the absence of a supportive ambiance in the company.

The considerable role of culture generally stems from the belief that an organization would fail in implementing its strategy without taking its culture into consideration. Culture, therefore, can be considered as among the basic determinants of the establishment of the fit between the adoption of strategy i.e. between TQM and the environment.

The study is conducted to achieve the objectives as follows:

To determine the relationship between Soft TQM practices and the municipalities' performance.

To determine the relationship between Hard TQM practices and municipalities' performance.

To examine the effect of national culture on the improvement of the relationship between Soft-Hard TQM and performance.

To determine whether there are differences in performance among the five selected countries.

For the purpose of achieving these objectives, a thorough review of the literature was conducted and reported mainly in Chapter Two. The prior literature concerning soft-hard TQM showed that the two elements of TQM have not been extensively researched in the government sector and in municipalities, despite the fact that they are widely acknowledged in manufacturing and service organizations. Additionally, as previously mentioned, most of the prior studies regarding soft-hard TQM advocated their positive impact on organizational performance. However, not all the cases of both soft and hard TQM implementation practices were successfully conducted. As such, some researchers have focused on exploring the reasons behind some cases of TQM and initiative project failure. In an attempt to clarify this issue, some scholars recommended that the impact of some influential variables upon these relationships may shed light on the findings. Generally, the controversial relationships call for further examination into the topic.

It has also been widely acknowledged in the literature of contingency theory that the failure of organizational strategy implementation may be related to the absence of fit between the strategy and the culture in the organization. In this context, many researchers have overlooked the issue of supportive culture and according to Reed *et al.,* (2000), some studies used organizational culture rather than national culture. However, the developing countries' culture may be one of the primary factors that could shed light on the findings and hence, they need further investigation. In essence, the study reacts to the call of further investigation, employs the fit concept of the contingency theory and examines the role of national culture upon the relationship.

On the basis of literature review conducted and discussed in Chapters One and Two, there are five critical factors of soft TQM and three of hard TQM. This study considers some soft TQM factors and some hard ones that have been widely examined in quality management literature in the context of service and public organizations. The soft factors are—Top Management Commitment, Supplier Relationships, Employee Relations, Education and Training, Customer Focus, and the hard factors are—Process Management, Quality Information, and Strategic Planning. In addition, the four national culture dimensions are Power Distance, Uncertainty Avoidance, Individualism and Masculinity.

Several issues were highlighted in Chapter Two which indicated the presence of opportunities for future research. First, the direct impact of TQM strategy on the organizational performance has been widely contended by researchers and it lays down the innovation-oriented environment which has a positive relation with innovation and performance while some others claimed that the employment of TQM principals may disrupt innovation in the organization. This calls for further examination in different contexts.

Second, according to Sila & Ebrahimpour (2005), on the basis of the comprehensive review of TQM literature, the number of articles that empirically evidenced the positive relationship was more compared to those supporting a negative relationship. The inconsistent findings concerning TQM dimensions and organizational performance relationship require further investigation in order to provide conclusive evidence.

Third, as many scholars recommended, the failure of several strategy implementation initiatives may be related to the absence of fit between the organizational culture and the intended strategy. This stems from the fact that the role of culture in organizational strategy implementation processes is largely unexplored. According to the contingency theory, organizational change theory and the congruence model, this research area is open to countless of research opportunities.

On the basis of the study objectives and the discussions in Chapters One and Two, the study variables were extracted and the study framework formulated in Chapter Three. The framework may be theoretically based on theories including the resource-based view of the organization, the contingency theory and the organizational change theory. Nevertheless, owing to the focus on the fit between organizational variables, this study selected the congruence model for suitable theoretical guidance. In the context of the countries selected, the TQM initiatives implementation is embarked upon to facilitate organizational change process in order to obtain superior position and achieve competitiveness. This study views national culture as one of the factors attributed to these initiatives failure or success.

The present study employed a quantitative research methodology to test the developed research framework and methodology was addressed and justified in Chapter Five. Consistent with the selected research design, a survey questionnaire that reflected the study constructs was utilized for data collection. The questions used in the questionnaire were adapted and adopted from several resources for their face and content validity. In addition, a six-point Likert scale was adopted for the measurement of the items. The average of the items used to represent the overall constructs is obtained to get the final score of each construct. A high mean value reflects high level of TQM, NC and a superior organizational performance.

In order to guarantee valid and authentic study results, the measure utilized was run through a robust validation process. Before the actual data was collected, the measurable items for every construct were revised with the help of academicians and practitioners to confirm their face and content validity and a pilot study was carried out involving a total of 30 respondents (Al-Qasseem Municipalities, KSA). It was only after the results of the pilot study indicated satisfactory goodness of measure that the questionnaire was distributed for data collection.

By Diplomatic path, the returned questionnaires were 127 in number and therefore, a response rate of 100 per cent was achieved. Following the collection of actual data, the construct validity and reliability of measure were confirmed. The EFA in SPSS was run to confirm both convergent and discriminate validity. At every phase of measure development and validation, several recommended modifications were conducted. Consequently, this study established the construct validity to ensure that the gathered results are valid and reliable and they explain the phenomenon under study in an efficient way.

After the confirmation of the construct validity and reliability, the respondents' demographic profiles were noted. Male respondents constituted 76 per cent while the rest of the respondents (23%) were female. Each of the four countries had the same percentage of respondents (23.6%) with the exception of Qatar that had only 5.5 per cent of the total respondents. As for the educational background of the respondents, they were distributed as follows: 48 per cent had engineering degrees, 23.6 per cent had college degrees, 22 per cent had master/doctorate degrees, and 6.3 per cent had high school degrees. As for their area of study, 47.2 per cent had an education degree majoring in engineering, 32.3 per cent had business degrees, while the remaining respondents (20.5%) had other degrees. The respondents' religions were divided as follows: 89 per cent were Muslims, 7.9 per cent were Christians while the rest (3.1%) had other religions.

The study hypotheses were tested through the use of hierarchical regression analysis with the help of the SPSS software. The analysis was utilized to investigate the explanatory power of soft and hard TQM, and their dimensions towards organizational performance. The analysis was also used to determine the moderating impact of NC and its dimensions on the mentioned relationship. The study findings were discussed in Chapter Five and further discussions are provided in the next sub-sections. This study concludes with recommendations and suggestions for future studies.

IMPLICATIONS FOR RESEARCH

This study aims to contribute to organizational performance in the context of the five developing countries' (Egypt, Jordan, Qatar, Saudi Arabia, and Turkey) municipalities and its relevant factors. It also attempts to enlighten relevant individuals on the practical results of strategic applications of organizational performance in these municipalities. This study should be the few of its kind to be conducted in the contest of the developing countries' public sector environment in an attempt to examine the relationship between Soft-Hard TQM and organizational performance. The present study's theoretical and practical implications are discussed in this section and the other following sections.

Moreover, hardly any study has been done to investigate the relationship between soft-hard TQM and organizational performance with the moderating effect of national culture in municipalities. This study also attempts to extend extant literature in its attempt to highlight the last hypothesized portion of the relationship (moderating impact of NC) using the hierarchical regression method. A detailed evaluation of this study's contributions is provided in the following sub-sections.

Theoretical Implications

This study conducted an analysis on the basis of theoretical as well as practical frameworks as this is viewed as an ideal and invaluable step in the management of present issues and in tackling matters that relate to the relationship between soft and hard TQM and organizational performance in varying cultures. The various phases of this study was developed in a manner that considers the outcomes and patterns of previous research and issues related to the association of national culture, soft and hard TQM practices and organizational performance.

A thorough review of literature revealed that the studies dedicated to the topic have investigated several researchers point of view concerning the way TQM variables relate with organizational performance (variables such as people, customer management, supplier partnerships, communication of improved information, customer satisfaction orientation, external interface management, strategic quality management, teamwork structures for improvement, operational quality planning, quality improvement measurement systems and corporate quality culture, zero-defects mentality, flexible manufacturing, process improvement, measurement, management support, suggestions, data use, supervision, suppliers, ongoing improvement and customer orientation).

Only a few studies have tackled some of the critical TQM factors in the context of both soft and hard TQM practices in various cultures and in the evaluation of the relationship between specific soft TQM practices namely top management commitment, supplier relationship, employee relations, education and training, customer focus and hard factors of process management, quality information and analysis, strategic planning, with organizational performance in various cultures. From this, the theoretical implications of the present research can be stated as follows:

First, theoretically, this study shed a light on the crucial element of soft-hard TQM practices in the public sector, in the context of their municipalities. The study also contributed to TQM literature by reconfirming the unresolved issue of the relationship between soft-hard TQM, and organizational performance. The literature reviewed regarding this relationship highlighted inconsistent results, despite the extensive research work dedicated to the examination of TQM and organizational relationship, findings have been inconsistent. Owing to these inconsistent findings, further investigation and discussion is warranted. This study therefore significantly contributed to literature by examining the relationship between soft-hard TQM and performance in various cultures as an innovative strategy to develop a model that better explains various organizational performances. As previously mentioned, the findings of the direct association between some TQM factors and organizational performance reported by prior authors were inconclusive (Prajogo & McDermott, 2005). In addition, the failure of some TQM initiatives in literature has been widely attributed to the absence of a conducive culture. Generally, this study's findings confirmed and supported the presence of a positive effect of soft-hard TQM on organizational performance.

Second, this study shed a light on the role that societies and national culture plays in the performance of the organization. The study findings showed that the relevancy of supportive culture in any strategic organizational change. The lack of such a national culture may result in the wastage of organizational resource through the failure of strategy employment. These findings are consistent with the organizational change theory as both hard and soft TQM practices were viewed as change initiatives that are targeted to modify organizational process and managerial practices. Additionally, the findings also revealed the significance of establishing a good fit between NC and the soft-hard TQM practices to guarantee a successful implementation as postulated by both the contingency theory and the congruence model.

Third, in contrast to many of the prior studies that were conducted in the context of the manufacturing sector, this study extended literature by examining the municipalities of five developing countries. As previously argued, although the public sector's importance is evident, in any economic development plan, majority of studies conducted concerning TQM in the public sector were confined to conceptual, descriptive and observational studies. This study attempts to contribute to empirical insights into the municipalities of five developing countries namely Egypt, Jordan, Qatar, Saudi Arabia and Turkey.

Fourth, this study's research framework was empirically examined in terms of TQM practices in the municipalities' system in various cultures. The findings support the validity and reliability of the study framework and therefore, the determinant factors implications can be contributed to management literature. In addition, the research framework can be used as a research tool to examine the determinant factors in determining whether or not to employ other factors of soft-hard TQM.

Fifth, along with testing the developed hypotheses, this study carried out a robust goodness of measure analysis for the validation of the research instrument and the establishment of both construct validity and reliability. This study went beyond the traditional testing procedures such as Cronbach's alpha coefficient and the exploratory factor analysis—it carried out confirmatory factor analysis. As such, this study conducted a rigorous validation of the research instrument to guarantee that the findings are valid and reliable because ineffectively validated measures often result in erroneous conclusions.

Managerial Implications

As for the managerial implications of the study, the findings contribute to the knowledge of practitioners and policy-makers in the five-developing countries. Based on the study findings, soft and hard TQM practices are related with organizational performance. They also indicated the presence of differences in the organizational performance mean among the countries. Stated differently, this study highlighted the way soft TQM and hard TQM and NC improve the overall performance of the organization. The results are expected as municipalities offer services to citizens and the absence of TQM principles will naturally negatively impact the municipalities' performance. Some managerial implications are discussed as follows;

First, the application of soft and hard TQM practices were revealed to have a positive effect on the organizational performance and this indicates the inter-correlation among the TQM practices and hence, an interactive on organizational performance. On the basis of this scenario, the selected soft and hard TQM practices facilitate the effect on organizational performance. Organizations, therefore, will be able to increase their performance by enhancing these soft and hard TQM practices. In these municipalities of the five developing countries, soft and hard TQM practices were revealed to contribute to organizational performance and therefore employing these factors will lead to the superior performance of the municipalities.

Second, the present study's findings can promote the awareness among municipalities' administrators of the importance of the ongoing employment of soft and hard TQM in their organizations. The findings also revealed that soft and hard TQM should be considered as one of the main characteristics of the organization, whether public or private, to perpetuate its survival and achieve strategic competitive edge among its rivals.

Third, soft and hard TQM strategies have been viewed as organizational change initiatives and therefore extensive efforts should be expended to facilitate a supportive culture for them. Consistent with the organizational change theory, the study findings indicated that national culture can facilitate or hinder the implementation of soft and hard TQM initiatives. Hence, the administration of municipalities can guarantee successful implementation of such strategies through the provision of a supportive national culture (NC).

Fourth, the study findings revealed that NC negatively moderates some of the selected soft and hard TQM strategies and the organizational performance relationship. Hence, the TQM effectiveness is linked to the considerations of cultural forces (Al-Zamany *et al.,* 2002). This may also indicate that since these strategies are geared towards western practices, they may not be welcomed in high cultural driven countries such as Arab countries. This obstacle may hinder the successful TQM processes implementation (Al-Zamany *et al.,* 2002).

Fifth, the study findings are invaluable for the municipalities that provide consultation in terms of soft and hard TQM strategies implementation. The municipalities should refrain from insisting on these strategies' implementation and assessment, and they should first facilitate their alignment with their national culture.

On a final note, this study revealed differences in organizational performance among the municipalities of the five developing countries. The next section provides the study limitations.

LIMITATIONS

Despite the study's many contributions, it is important that future studies and relevant individuals who avail from its findings keep the study limitations into consideration when using the results as they are, and when generalizing them to a larger sample. Every research work is characterized by limitations and for the present study's limitations, they are provided as follows:

This study employed the survey questionnaire design and a cross-sectional data which collects data at a specific point in time for hypotheses testing. In case of survey research design, information obtained is often confined to the level of association between variables. Hence, even though causal relationships can be inferred from the results, they cannot be determined.

A thorough review of literature revealed that soft TQM are long-term strategies while hard TQM are short-term strategies in nature. Based on this, the investigation of the relationship between soft and hard TQM and organizational performance at a specific point in time will not be as accurate as the results will depend on the implementation period. This indicates that to be able to examine the strategies impact on the organizational performance, it should be kept in mind that longitudinal studies should be carried out.

Some factors that couldn't be controlled in the study lead to study limitations in terms of generalizability of results.

The study's results and its conclusion are drawn from the collected data in the form of representatives of municipalities' perceptions concerning the hard and soft TQM strategies at one time. The study failed to consider the ongoing changes in the psychological human aspects that could have occurred in the representatives owing to their ongoing exposure as well as their increasing experience. This stems from the cross-sectional method approached and the absence of follow-up data.

Owing to the time and cost limitations, the research throughout the five countries were only confined to 30 municipalities which may impact the results accuracy.

The questionnaires employed the six-point Likert scale upon which the respondents measured their level of agreement towards statements regarding soft TQM, hard TQM, national culture, and organizational performance of the municipalities. This measure may have caused patterned response—which is referred to the respondent's tendency to answer the questions in an automatic manner without reading the statements. This issue takes place as different individuals have different takes on the numbers utilized to measure their perceptions. Nevertheless, it is challenging to assume that all the questions have been completely comprehended and they have accordingly provided high quality data.

As with most cases of quantitative research design, the limitations can be related to the fact that respondents are asked to interpret their perception of the statements into numbers of the Likert scale. The answers may, therefore, be influenced by biased perceptions in that specific situation (Macinati, 2008). Therefore, there may be a presence of bias in the collected data.

Viewed through the methodological perspective, this study made use of perceptual measures to gauge the construct of organizational performance. Even though measure has been run through rigorous validity and reliability tests while it was developed and pre-tested through the pilot study or through prior testing on the basis of actual data collected, it is still questionable in comparison to the objective measures outcomes. Hence, future studies could take help from using perceptual as well as objective measures in order to draw accurate conclusions concerning organizational performance.

The study findings have their basis on data gathered from the operational director of the municipalities in the five countries. The directors were considered to be the best authoritative representatives who are most capable of describing soft and hard TQM practices and the level of organizational performance of their municipalities. These constructs may be evaluated by future studies through other stakeholders like employees and citizens.

A final limitation of this study is the general.lack of accurate data in developing countries. In other words, the lack of public databases confines to the ability to compare findings with other sources. In addition, in the selected countries, no other studies have tackled the impact of this study's constructs and therefore, the research was conducted without the benefit of other findings for explanations and benchmarking.

On the basis of the above enumerated limitations, it can be stated that the study conclusions could have been different if the research design employed is longitudinal as opposed to cross-sectional. In addition, the generalization of these results on other public sectors and for that matter, other sectors of the economy would be difficult. This is because the results reached concerning the negative impact of information and analysis system on the organizational performance may turn out differently in other sectors.

RECOMMENDATIONS FOR FUTURE RESEARCH

This study has some recommendations for future studies concerning organizational performance in the hopes of enriching literature on the subject. Some of these recommendations are listed below:

Future studies can replicate the present one in the context of many other developing countries and conduct a comparison among them. They can also increase the investigation and access to extensive findings in the prediction of organizational performance in other countries, and the variables affecting them, specifically when moderated by culture.

The current study succeeded in examining the relationship between soft TQM, hard TQM, national culture and organizational performance in the municipalities of five developing countries. Future studies could examine the same variables under different contexts to determine their impact and to examine if the findings are consistent with this current study's findings. This may be interesting to determine as other studies have highlighted the differences in the organizations according to their culture and according to different sample studies—this is a viable direction for future studies to undertake.

It is suggested that further studies to examine other variables' prediction of organizational performance. These variables could include role of the quality department, zero-defects mentality, flexible manufacturing measurement, management support, suggestions, supervision, and ongoing improvement concerning organizational performance. While the present study employed national culture as the moderating variable, it is hoped that future studies examine other moderator variables such as quality culture. This may result in further insight into the variables' impact on the prediction of organizational performance. Future studies are also recommended to undertake a different method of study, i.e. the qualitative method which could be employed effectively in municipalities as interviews conducted with respondents may provide superior results, especially concerning the cultural context. Finally, future studies may be conducted on the staff members to examine their perception of organizational performance.

References

Ababaneh, R.I. (2010). The role of organizational culture on practising quality improvement in Jordanian public hospitals. *Leadership in Health Services, 23*(3), 244-259.

Abas, Z., and Yaacob, Z. (2006). Exploring the relationships between total quality management (TQM), strategic control systems (SCS) and organizational performance (OP) using a SEM framework. *Journal of American Academy of Business*, Cambridge, 9, 161-170. Retrieved October 5, 2006, from ProQuest Database.

Abdelmoula, Elhaj *et al*. The Impact of Implementation of Total Quality Management on Plants Productivity: Evidence from Poultry Processing Plants-Saudi Arabia-*central Region International Journal of Engineering Science and Technology*, Vol. 3, No. 5 May 2011.

Abdelsalam, H.M., Reddick, C.G., ElKadi, H.A., and Gama, S. (2012). Factors Affecting Perceived Effectiveness of Local E-Government in Egypt. *International Journal of Information Communication Technologies and Human Development (IJICTHD)*, 4(1), 24-38.

Abdul Karim, M.R. (1999). *Reengineering the public service: Leadership and change in an electronic age*. Subang Jaya: Pelanduk Publications.

Abdullah, M., Ahmad, Z., and Ismail, A. (2008). The importance of soft TQM factors for quality improvement: Case study of electrical and electronics firms in Malaysia. *International Journal of Business and Management*, 3(12), 60-69.

Aboyassin, N.A., Alnsour, M., and Alkloub, M. (2011). Achieving total quality management using knowledge management practices: A field study at the Jordanian insurance sector. *International Journal of Commerce and Management, 21*(4), 394-409.

Abrahamson, E. (1996). Management Fashion. *Academy of Management Review 21*/ 1, 254-285.

Abu-Jarad, Ismael Younis, Nor'Aini Yusof, Davoud Nikbin (2010). "A Review Paper on Organizational Culture and Organizational Performance", *International Journal of Business and Social Science*, Vol. 1, No. 3, pp. 26-46.

Adcroft, A., Dhaliwal, S., and Willis, R. (2005). Insatiable demand or academic supply: the intellectual context of entrepreneurship education. *European Business Review, 17*(6), 518-531

Adler, N.J. (1997). International dimensions of organizational behavior. 3rd ed. Cincinnati, OH: Shout-Western College Publishing Lundberg, J. (2007). *Lifting the crown— citation z-score. Journal of Informatics, 1*(2), 145-154.

Agus, A., and Abdullah, M. (2000). The mediating effect of customer satisfaction on TQM practices and financial performance. Singaporean Management Review, 22, 55-73.

— — and Hassan, Z. (2000). Exploring the relationship between the length of total quality management adoption and financial performance: An empirical study in Malaysia. *International Journal of Management, 17*(3), 323-333.

Ahire, S.L., Landeros, R., and Golhar, D.Y. (1995). Total quality management: A literature review and an agenda for future research. *Production and Operation Management, 4* (3), 227-306.

— — and Dreyfus, P. (2000). The impact of design management and process management on quality: an empirical examination. *Journal of Operations Management, 18*, 549-575.

— — and O'Shaughness, K.C. (1998). The role of top management commitment in quality management: an empirical analysis of the auto parts industry. *International Journal of Quality Science 3*(1), 5-37.

— — Golhar, D.Y., and Waller, M.A. (1996). Development and validation of TQM implementation constructs. *Decision Sciences, 27*(1), 23-56.

— — Landeros, R., and Golhar, D.Y. (1995). Total quality management: A literature review and an agenda for future research. *Production and Operations Management, 4* (3), pp. 277-306.

Akdere, M. (2006). Quality management through human resources: An integrated approach to performance improvement. *The Business Review*, Cambridge, 5, 233-239. Retrieved December 20, 2006, from ProQuest database.

Aladwani, A.M. (2001). Change management strategies for successful ERP implementation. *Business Process Management Journal*, Vol. 7, p. 266.

Al ajmi, S., Dennis, C. and Altayab, Y., (2011). The effect of national culture on service provision within Takaful industry: A comparative study in Kuwait and Egypt, *Journal of Islamic Marketing*, Vol. 2 Issue 3, pp. 225-245.

Alba-Ramírez, Alfonso (1994). Formal Training, Temporary Contracts, Productivity and Wages in Spain. *Oxford Bulletin of Economics and Statistics 56*(2):151-70.

Al-Fakhri, M.O., Cropf, R.A., Higgs, G. and Kelly, P. (2008). e-Government in Saudi Arabia: between promise and reality. *International Journal of Electronic Government Research, 4* (2) 59-85.

Al-Fawwaz, T.M., and Badah, A. (2012). Using Six Sigma to Evaluate the Administrative Performance of Vocational and Technical Training Institutions in Jordan. *International Journal of Business and Management, 7*(20), p. 90.

Al-Habeese, M., Al-bourini, F., and Abou-Moghli, A. (2012). Atitudes of Municipalities Managers toward the effect of information technology (IT) on Administrative decision-making effectiveness: A case study in valley Area. *European Scientific Journal, 8*(5).

Alhyari, S., Alazab, M., Venkatraman, S., Alazab, M., and Alazab, A. (2012). Six sigma approach to improve quality in E-services: An empirical study in Jordan. *International Journal of Electronic Government Research (IJEGR), 8*(2), 57-74.

Al-Mansour, A.H. (2007). Application of TQM to financial services. Retrieved December 19, 2010, from, http://faculty.kfupm.edu.sa/CEM/bushait/cem515/term-papers/TQM Finance.pdf.

Al-Marri, K., Ahmed, A.M.M.B., and Zairi, M. (2007). Excellence in service: an empirical study of the UAE banking sector. *International Journal of Quality and Reliability Management, 24*(2), 164-176.

Al-Momani, Mohammad Faleh (2002), "Reformation of the Local Regime in Jordan: State of the Greater Municipalities in the North Region". Unpublished MA Thesis, Aal Al-Bait University, Mafrqa, Jordan.

Al-Musleh, A.M. (2011). *Development of a framework for total quality management principles in the construction companies with special reference to the construction companies in the state of Qatar* (Doctoral dissertation).*t, 20*(4), 296-307.

Al-Omari, H. (2006). E-government architecture in Jordan: a comparative analysis. *Journal of computer science,* 2(11), 846-852.

Al-Obeidat, R.A., and Abu-Shanab, E.A. (2010). Drivers of E-government and E-business in Jordan. *Journal of Emerging Technologies in Web Intelligence,* 2(3), 204-211.

Al-Qahtani, Salem S., and Moaddi M. Al-Methheb. "Implementation of Total Quality n Management in Some Saudi Public Sector Organizations." *JKA: Econ & Adm* 13.2 (1999): 23-38.

AlSaleh, N.A. (2007). 'Application of quality tools by the Saudi food industry', *The TQM Magazine, Vol. 19,* No. 2, pp. 150-161. Web sit: http://www.kaqa.org.sa.

AlShaya, A. (2002). "A study of the use of information sources, with special emphasis on CD-ROMs and the internet, by Saudi physicians in major government hospitals in Riyadh, Saudi Arabia", unpublished PhD thesis, University of Wales, Aberystwyth.

Alshehri, Mohammed, *et al*. "The Effects of Website Quality on Adoption of E-Government Service: AnEmpirical Study Applying UTAUT Model Using SEM." *arXiv preprint arXiv:1211.2410* (2012).

Al-Shobaki, S.D., Fouad, R.H. and Al-Bashirb, A. (2010). The implementation of total quality management (TQM) for the banking sector in Jordan. *JJMIE, 4*(2).

Al-Tarawneh, H.A., and Mubaslat, M. (2011). The Implementation of Total Quality Management (TQM) On the Higher Educational Sector in Jordan. *International Journal of Industrial Marketing, 1*(1), p. 1.

AL-Trawneh, Ahmed (2010). "Total quality Management and leadership An Experimental Investigation of ISO Cetificated Companies in Gordan. Interdisciplinary, *Journal of Contemporary Research in Business,* Vol. 2, No. 1, pp. 382-398.

Al-Zamany, Y., Hoddell, S.E.F., and Savage, B.M. (2002). Understanding the difficulties of Implementing quality management in Yemen. *The TQM Magazine, 14*(4), 240-247.

Al-Zu'bi, Hasan Ali, and Mahfuz Judeh (2011). Measuring the Implementation of Total Quality Management: Ibn Al-Haytham Hospital Case Study. *International Journal of Business and Management* 6.5. p. 114.

Amaratunga, D., Baldry, D. and Sarshar, M. (2001). Process Improvement through Performance Measurement: The Balanced Scorecard Methodology. *Work Stud,* 50(5), 179-188.

Ammons, D.N. (1985). Common barriers to productivity Improvement in local government. *Public Productivity Review.* 9. pp. 187-202.

Anderson, J., Rungtusanatham, M., Schroeder, R., and Devaraj, S. (1995). A path analytic model of a theory of quality management underlying the Deming management method: Preliminary empirical findings. *Decision Sciences,* 26: 637-658.

Anderson, J.C., Rungtusanatham, M. and Schroeder, R.G. (1994). A theory of quality management underlying the deming management method, *Academy of Management Review, Vol. 19* No. 3, pp. 472-509.

Anderson, M., and Sohal, A.S. (1999). A study of the relationship between quality management practices and performance in small businesses. *International Journal of Quality & Reliability Management,* 16(9), 859-877.

Andrews, R., Boyne, G.A., Law, J., and Walker, R.M. (2005). External Constraints on Local Service Standards: The Case of Comprehensive Performance Assessment in English Local Government. *Public Administration,* 83(3), 639.

Anschutz, E.E. (1995). *TQM America: How America's Most Successful Companies Profit from Total Quality Management.* McGuinn & McGuire.

Antony, J., Leung, K., Knowles, G. and Gosh, S. (2002). Critical success factors of TQM implementation in Hong Kong industries. *International Journal of Quality and Reliability Management, Vol. 19* No. 5, pp. 551-66.

Antony, J.P., and Bhattacharyya, S. (2010). Measuring organizational performance and organizational excellence of SMEs – Part 2: an empirical study on SMEs in India. *Measuring Business Excellence,* 14(3), 42-52.

Anwar, S.A.; Jabnoun, N. (2006). The development of a contingency model relating national culture to total quality management. *International Journal of Management, 23*(2), pp. 272-280.

Appelbaum and P. Bcrg, (2001). High performance work systems and tabor market stmcliires, in I Ber and A L Kalleberjf (eds.), *Some book of Labor Markets.* New York: Kluwer Academic/Plenum Publishers.

Appelbaum, S., Steed, A. (2005). Critical success factors in the client: Consulting relationship. *Journal of Management Development.* Vol. 24, Issue: 1, pp. 68-93.

Arasli, H., and Ahmadeva, L., (2004). "No more tears!" A local TQM formula for health promotion", *International Journal of Health Care Quality Assurance,* Vol. 17(3), pp. 135-145.

Arawati, A. (2005). The structural linkages between TQM, product quality performance, and business performance: Preliminary empirical study in electronics companies. *Singapore Management Review,* 27(1), 87-105.

Armstrong-Stassen, G., Reavley, M., and Ghanam, D. (2005). Organizational downsizing and its perceived impact on quality practices, *International Journal of Quality & Reliability Management, Vol. 22* No. 9, pp. 950-976.

Arslan, A. (2007). Turkish Local e-Governments: A Longitudinal Study. *The Electronic Journal of e Government,* Vol. 5 Issue 2, pp. 95-106, available online at www.ejeg.com.

— — (2009). "A Strategic Orientation Model for the Turkish Local e-Governments."*1st International Conference on eGovernment and eGovernance" of TURKSAT (Turksat Satellite Communication Cable TV and Operation Inc.), Social Sciences Research Society (SoSReS), Ankara, Turkey..*

— — Innovative Management Practices and Their Impact on the Local E-Government Performance: The Turkish Provincial Municipalities. *African Journal of Business Management* 5.24 (2011).

Arumugam V.C., Mojtahedzadeh Rouhollah and Malarvizhi C.A. (2011). Critical Success Factors of Total Quality Management, *European Journal of Economics, Finance and Administrative Sciences,* Issue 33, pp. 25 42.

Avelé Donatien and Fillion Gérard, (2011). Contingency and Management Control Tools for Municipal Public Services of Cameroonian Cities Interpretation of Practices: *Journal*, Vol. 6 No. 2 March, 11, pp. 4-35.

Azhar, K. (2003). *Business Policy and Strategic Management*, New Delhi, Tata McGraw-Hill.

Azzone, G., Masella, C. and BerteleÁ, U. (1991). Design of performance measures for time-based companies. *International Journal of Operations & Production Management, Vol. 11* No. 3, pp. 77-85.

Badri, M.A., Davis, D. and Davis, D. (1995). A study of measuring the critical factors of quality management, *International Journal of Quality & Reliability Management, Vol. 12* No. 2, pp. 36-53.

Baidoun, S. and Zairi, M. (2003). A proposed model of TQM implementation in the Palestinian context, *TQM and Business Excellence*, Vol. 14 No. 10, pp. 1193-211.

Baker, B.L. (2003). *TQM practice and theory: A meta-analysis of empirical studies.* Colorado Technical University.

Baker, G., and Maddux, H. (2005). Enhancing organizational performance: Facilitating the critical transition to a process view of management. *SAM Advanced Management Journal, 70*(4), 43.

Bal'arabi, Abdel Karim (2002). The Relation between the determinants of the organizational Hierarchy and the Local Administration Performance; unpublished MA Thesis, Al-Yarmouk University-Irbid.

Ballantine, J., Brignall, S. and Modell, S. (1998). Performance measurement and management in public health services: A comparison of U.K. and Swedish practice. *Management Accounting Research, 9*, 71-94.

Barley, S.R. (1995). Culture In N. Nicholson (Ed.), *The Blackwell encyclopedic dictionary of organizational behavior*. Cambridge, MA: Blackwell.

Bartlett, M.S. (1954). A note on the multiplying factors for various chi square approximations. *Journal of the Royal Statistical Society, 16*(Series B), pp. 296-298.

Bate, M. (1995). Ph.D. Thesis, University of Cambridge.

Behery, M.H. and Paton, R.A. (2008). Performance appraisal-cultural fit: Performances outcomes within the UAE, *Education, Business and Society: Contemporary Middle Eastern Issues*, Vol. 1, No. 1, pp. 34-49.

Behn, R.D. (2003). Why measure performance? Different purposes require different measures. *Public Administration Review, 63*(5), 586-606.

Bennis, W.G. (1996). Becoming a leader of leaders. In *Rethinking the Future*, ed. R. Gibson, pp. 148-162. London: Brealey.

Bevanda, V., Sinkovic, G., and Currie, D., (2011). Implementing a Performance Measurement System in Croatia, *Measuring Business Excellence*, Vol. 15 (4), pp. 50-61.

Bititci, U.S., Carrie, A.S. and McDevitt, L. (1997). Integrated performance measurement systems: an audit and development guide, *TQM Magazine*, Vol. 9 No. 1.

— —, Carrie, A.S. (1998). Integrated performance measurement systems: Structures and relationships, EPSRC final research report, grant no. GR/K 48174

Black, S.A. and Poter, L.J. (1996). "Identification of the critical factors of TQM", *Decision Sciences*, Vol. 27 No. 1, pp. 1-21.

Bond, M.H. *et al.*, (2004). "Culture-level dimensions of social axioms and their correlates across 41 cultures", *Journal of Cross-cultural Psychology*, Vol. 35 No. 5, pp. 548-70.

Boyne, G.A. (2004). Explaining public service performance: Does management matter? *Public Policy and Administration, 19*(4), 100-117.

Brah, S.A., Tee, S.S.L., and Rao, B.M. (2002). Relationship between TQM and performance of Singaporean companies. *International Journal of Quality & Reliability, 19*(4), 356 379.

— —, Wong, J.L., and Rao, B.M. (2000). TQM and business performance in the service sector: A Singapore study. *International Journal of Operations and Production Management, 20*(11), 1293-1312.

— and Lim, H.Y. (2005). The effects of technology and TQM on the performance of logistics companies. *International Journal of Physical Distribution & Logistics Management, 36*(3), 192-209.

Brewer, G.A. and S. Selden (2000). "Why Elephants Gallop: Assessing and Predicting Organizational Performance in Federal Agencies", *Journal of Public Administration Research and Theory, 10*, pp. 685-711.

Brown, M. (1996). Keeping Score: Using the Right Metrics to Drive World Class Performance, Quality Resources, New York, NY.

Budhwar, P.S., and Sparrow, P.R. (2002). An integrative framework for understanding crossnational human resource management practices. *Human Resource Management Review, 12*, 377-403.

Burgess, K. (1995). Prospering in a global economy. *Journal of the Operational Research Society*, Vol. 46, No. 5, pp. 553-61.

Burlton, R. (2001). *Business process management: profiting from process*. Que Publishing.

Cagliano, A.C., (2010). Understanding Supply Chain Complexity. An Approach Integrating Performance Measurement and System Dynamics. VDM Verlag Dr. Muller. Cambridge, MA: Harvard University Press.

Cameron, K.S. and Quinn, R.E. (1999). Diagnosing and changing organizational culture: Based on the competing values framework. Reading, M.A.: Addison-Wesley.

Casadesu's, M. and de Castro, R. (2005). *How improving quality improves supply chain.*

Chakravarthy, B.S. (1986). Measuring strategic performance. *Strategic management journal, 7*(5), 437-458.

Chaker, M.N. and Jabnoun, N. (2010). Barriers to service quality in Islamic banks in Qatar. *International Journal of Commerce and Management.*

Chan, Y.C.L. (2004). Performance measurement and adoption of balanced scorecard: A survey of municipal governments in the USA and Canada. *International Journal of Public Sector Management, 17* (3), 204-221.

Chang, F.S. and Wiebe, H.A. (1996). The ideal culture profile for total quality management: a competing values perspective, *Engineering Management Journal*, (8)2, pp. 19-26.

Chapman, M. (1997). Social anthropology, business studies, and cultural issues, *International Studies of Management and Organization, Vol. 26* No. 4, pp. 3-29.

Chapman, R., and Al-Khawaldeh, K. (2002). TQM and labour productivity in Jordanian industrial companies. *The TQM Magazine, 14* (4), 248-262.

Chatman, J.A. and Jehn, K.A. (1994). Assessing the relationship between industry characteristics and Organizational Culture (OC): How different can you be? *The Academy of Management Journal, 37*(3), 522-553.

Chenhall, R.H. (2005). Integrative strategic performance measurement systems strategic alignment of manufacturing, learning and strategic outcomes: an exploratory study. *Accounting, Organizations and Society, 30,* 395-422.

Cheng, T.C.E., and Lai, K. (2005). Effects of quality management and marketing on organizational performance. *Journal of Business Research, 58,* 446-456.

Chin, khor Saw, Sofian Saudah (2011). The Impact of Human Capital and Total Qualty Management on Carporate Performance. *Journal of Contemporary Research In Business, Vol. 3,* No. 3, pp. 1091-1100.

Chin, K.S., Pun, K.F., Xu, Y., and Chan, J.S.F. (2002). An AHP based study of critical factors for TQM implementation in Shanghai manufacturing industries. *Technovation, 22*(11), 707-715.

Choi, T.Y., and Eboch, K. (1998). The TQM paradox: Relations among TQM practices, plant performance, and customer satisfaction, *Journal of Operations Management, 17*(1), 59-75.

Chong, V.K., and Rundus, M.J. (2004). Total quality management, market competition and organizational performance. *The British Accounting Review, 36,* 155-172.

Chow, Kamal M. Haddad, Anne Wu, (2003). Corporate culture and its relation to performance: a comparative study of Taiwanese and US manufacturing firms, *Managerial Finance, Vol. 29* Issue: 12, pp. 65-76.

Ciampa, D. (1992).Total Quality. Reading, MA, Addison-Wesley.

Claver, E., Tari, J.J. and Molina, J.F. (2002). Areas of improvement in certified firms advancing towards TQM, *International Journal of Quality & Reliability Management, Vol. 19* Nos 8/9, pp. 1014-36.

Clegg, B., Gholami, R., and Omurgonulsen, M. (2012). Quality management and performance: A comparison between the UK and Turkey.

Co akes, S.J. and Steed, L.G. (2003). SPSS: Analysis without anguish: Version 11.0 for Windows. Brisbane: Jacaranda Wiley.

Coilard, R. (1989). Totul Qualitt. Success Tlttough Peol/e. London: IpM.

Coleman, S. and Douglas, A. (2003). Where next for ISO 9000 companies?, *The TQM Magazine,* Vol. 15 No. 2, pp. 88-92.

Combs J.G., Crook T.R., Shook C.L. (2005). The dimensionality of organizational performance and its implications for strategic management research. In Ketchen D.J. and Bergh D.C. (Eds.), *Research methodology in strategy and management,* Vol. 2, pp. 259-286.

Cooke, R.A. and Szumal, J.L. (2000). Using the organizational culture inventory to understand the operating cultures of organizations, *Handbook of Organizational Culture and Climate,* Sage, Thousand Oaks, CA.

Cortina, J.M. (1993). What is coefficient alpha? An examination of theory and application. *Journal of Applied Psychology, 78*(1), 98-104.

Coronado, R.B. and Antony, J. (2002). Critical success factors for the successful implementation of Six Sigma projects in performances, *The TQM magazine,* Vol. 14, No. 2, pp. 92-9.

Costello A.B. and Osborne J.W. (2005). Best Practices in Exploratory Factor Analysis: Four Recommendations for Getting the Most from Your Analysis. *Practical Assessment, Research & Evaluation, 10*(7):1-9.

Cotteleer, M.J., and Bendoly, E. (2006). Order Lead-Time Improvement Following Enterprise-IT Implementation: An Empirical Study, MIS Quarterly (30:3), pp. 643-660.

Crosby, P.B. (1979). Quality is Free, New York, McGraw Hill.

Cross, K.F. and Lynch, R.L. (1988). The SMART way to define and sustain success. *National Productivity Review,* Vol. 8, No. 1, pp. 23-33.

—— (1992). For good measure, *CMA Magazine,* April, pp. 20-3.

Cruickshank, M. (2003). Total Quality Management in the higher education sector: Literature review from an international and Australian perspective. *TQM and Business Excellence,* 14 (10), 1159-1167.

Cruz, N.M., Pérez, V.M. and Cantero, C.T. (2009). The influence of employee motivation on knowledge.transfer. *Journal of Knowledge Management, 13*(6): 478 490.

Cua, K.O., McKone, K.E., and Schroeder, R.G. (2001). Relationships between implementation of TQM, JIT, and TPM and manufacturing performance. *Journal of Operations Management,* 19, 657-694.

Curkovic, S., Melnyck, S., Calantone, R.J., and Handfield, R.B. (2000). Validating the Malcolm Baldridge National Quality Awrad framework through structural equation associate. *International Journal of Production Research, 38*(4), 765-791.

Curry, A., and Kadasah, N. (2002). "Focusing on key elements of TQM: Evaluation for Sustainability". *The TQM Magazine,* 14(4), 207-216.

Cusick, P., (2005). *A passion for learning: The education of seven eminent Americans.* New York: Teachers College.

D'Iribarne, P. (1997). The usefulness of an ethnographic approach to the international comparison of organizations. *International Studies of Management and Organization,* 26(4): 30-47.

Dahar, M.A., Faize, F.A., and Niwaz, A. (2010). A case study of the university college of education Chiniot Punjab (Pakistan) with reference to total quality management. *European Journal of Social Sciences,* 16(4), 511-525.

Dale, B.G. (2002). European quality challenges for the new millennium. *Measuring Business Excellence,* Vol. 6, No. 4, pp. 28-32

—— (2003). *Managing Quality,* 4th ed., Blackwell Publishers, Oxford.

—— and Plunkett, J.J., (1990). *Managing Quality,* Hertfordshire: Philip Allan.

Damanpour, F. (1992). Book Review: Corporate Culture and Organizational Effectiveness. *Journal of Management,* 18: 175-6.

Darandari, E., Al-Qahtanim, S., Allen, I., Al-Yafi, W., Al-Sudairi, A. and Catapang, J. (2009). The Quality Assurance System for Post-Secondary Education in Saudi Arabia: A Comprehensive, Developmental and Unified Approach. *Quality in Higher Education,* 15(1), 39-50.

Darley, W.K., and Blankson, C. (2008). African culture and business markets: implications for marketing practices, *Journal of Business and Industrial Marketing, Vol. 23* No. 6, pp. 374-383.

Darwish, Ahmed M. (2008). Egypt: from e-government to e-governance the road to fast pace development ICEGOV '08 Proceedings of the 2nd international conference on Theory and practice of electronic governance Pages 1-3 ACM New York, NY, USA ©2008.

Das, A., Handfield, R.B., Calantone, R.J., and Ghosh, S. (2000). "A contingent view of quality management: The impact of international competition on quality". *Decision Sciences,* 31, 649-690.

——, Kumar, V. and Kumar, U., (2011). The role of leadership competencies for implementing TQM: An empirical study in Thai manufacturing industry. International *Journal of Quality and Reliability Management,* 28(2), 195-219.

— —, Paul, H., and Swierczek, F.W. (2008). Developing and validating total quality management (TQM) constructs in the context of Thailand's manufacturing industry. *Benchmarking: An international journal,* 15(1), 52-72.

Davenport, T.H. (1993). *Process Innovation: Reengineering Work Through Information Technology,* Boston: Harvard Business School Press.

David, F.R. (1995). *Strategic Management*. 5th edition. New York: Prentice Hall.

Davis, D. (2000). *Business research for decision making.* 5th ed. USA: Duxbury.

Davis, J.L. (2007). *Firm-Level Entrepreneurship and Performance: An Examination and Extension of Relationships and Measurements of the entrepreneurial orientation (EO) Construct.* University of Texas at Arlington, Arlington.

Davis, J.H. and Ruhe, J. (2003). Perceptions of country corruption: antecedents and outcomes, *Journal of Business Ethics, Vol. 43* No. 4, pp. 275-88.

Davis, R.A., Marcos, S., and Stading, G.L. (2005). Linking firm performance to the Malcolm Baldrige National Quality Awrad implementation effort using multi attribute utility theory. *Managerial Finance,* 31(3), 19-33.

Dean, J.W., and Bowen, D.E. (1994). Management theory and total quality: Improving research and practice through theory development. Academy of Management. *The Academy of Management Review,* 19(3), 392-418.

Delaney, J., and Huselid, M. (1996). The impact of human resource practices on perceptions of organizational performance. *Academy of Management Journal,* 39, 949-969.

Dellana, S.A. and Hauser, R.D. (1999). Toward Defining the Quality Culture. *Engineering Management Journal,* 11(2): 11-15.

Deming, W.E. (1986). *Out of crisis*. Cambridge, MA: Massachusetts Institute of Technology Press.

Demir, H. and Yavuz, A. (2009). Cadastral services in Turkey within the framework of new public management, *African Journal of Business Management,* Vol. 3 No. 10, pp. 582-90.

Demirbag, M., Koh, S.C.L., Bayraktar, E., Tatoglu, E. and Zaim, S. (2007). The impact of supply chain practices on performance of SMEs. *Industrial Mangement & Data Systems,* Vol. 107, No. 1, pp. 103-24.

— —, Tatoglu, E., Tekinkus, M., and Zaim, S. (2006). An analysis of the relationship between TQM implementation and organizational performance: Evidence from Turkish SMEs. *Journal of Manufacturing Technology Management,* 17(6), 829-847.

Denison, D.R. Corporate culture and organizational effectiveness. New York: Wiley; 1990

— —, Mishra AK. (1995). Toward a theory of organizational culture and effectiveness, *Organ Sci;* 6(2):204-23.

— —, S. Haaland, and P. Goelzer. (2004). Corporate Culture and Organizational Effectiveness: Corporate Culture and Organizational Effectiveness: Is Asia Different from the Rest of the World? *Organizational Dynamics* 33 (1): 98-109.

Dent, J.F. (1990). Strategy, organizations and control: Some possibilities for accounting research. *Accounting Organizations and Society,* 15 (1/2), 3-25.

Detert J.R., Schroeder R.G., and Mauriel, J.J. (2000). A framework for linking culture and improvement initiatives in organizations. *Academy of Management Review,* 25(4), 850 863).

Diefenbach, T. (2007): The Managerialistic Ideology of Organisational Change Management. In: *Journal of Organisational Change Management,* 20(1): 126-144.

Dilbert, M., Bayyurt, N., Zaim, S. and Tarim, M. (2005). Critical factors of total quality management and its effect on performance in health care industry: A Turkish experience. *Problems and Perspectives in Management,* 4, 220-234.

Ding, L., Velicer, W.F., and Harlow, L.L. (1995). Effects of estimation methods, number of indicators per factor, and improper solutions on structural equation modeling fit indices. *Structural Equation Modeling: A Multidisciplinary Journal,* 2(2), 119-143.

Dixon, J.R., Nanni, A.J. and Vollmann, T.E. (1990). *The New Performance Challenge: Measuring Operations for World-class Companies,* Dow Jones-Irwin, Homewood, IL.

Djerdjour, M. (2000). Overview of the quality movement in the South Pacific Islands. *The TQM Magazine,* 12(1), 62-66.

Don E. Kash, (2010). Technological innovation and culture: research needed for China and other countries. *Journal of Science and Technology Policy in China,* Vol. 1, Issue 2, pp. 100-115.

Dooyoung, S., Kalinowski, J.G., and El-Enein, G. (1998). Critical implementation issues in total quality management. *SAM Advanced Management Journal,* 63(1), 10-14.

Douglas, T.J., Judge Jr, Q.W. (2001). Total Quality Management and competitive advantage: The role of structural control and exploration. *Academy of Management Journal,* 44, 158-169.

Dow, D., Samson, D., and Ford, S. (1999). Exploding the myth: do all quality management practices contribute to superior quality performance? *Production and Operations Management,* 8, 1-27.

Drew, E. and Healy, C. (2006). Quality management approaches in Irish organizations, *The TQM Magazine,* Vol. 18, No. 4, pp. 358-71.

Dwyer, S., Mesak, H., and Hsu, M. (2005). An exploratory examination of the influence of national culture on cross-national product diffusion. *Journal of International Marketing,* 1-27.

Earley, P. and Erez, M. (1999). *The Transplanted Executive.* Oxford University Press, New York, NY.

Eccles, R.G. (1991). The performance measurement manifesto. *Harvard Business Review,* Vol. 69, pp. 131-6.

Edvinsson, L. and Malone, M.S. (1997). Intellectual Capital: Realizing Your Company's True Value by Finding Its Hidden Brainpower, 1st ed., *Harper Business,* New York, NY.

EFQM (1999). Self-assessment guidelines for companies, European foundation for quality management. Belgium: Brussels.

Ehlers, U.D. (2009). Understanding quality culture. *Quality Assurance in Education 17*(4), 343-363.

Ein-Dor, P., Segev, E., and Orgad, M. (1993). The effect of national culture on IS: Implications for international information systems. *Journal of Global Information Management,* 1(1), 33-39.

El-Messery, Mamdouh A., G.A. Ismail, and Anwaar K. Arafa. Evaluation of municipal solid waste management in ssociat rural areas. *The Journal of the Egyptian Public Health Association* 84.1-2 (2009): 51.

Epstein, M.J. and Manzoni, J. (1997). The balanced scorecard and tableau de bord: translating strategy into action, *Management Accounting,* Vol. 79, No. 2, pp. 28-36.

Eriksson, H., Hansson, J. (2003). The impact of TQM on financial performance. *Measuring Business Excellence,* Vol. 7, No. 1, pp. 36-50.

Erumban, A.A. et de Jong, S.B. (2006). Cross-country differences in ICT adoption: A consequence of culture? *Journal of World Business,* 41, pp. 302-314.

Eskildsen, J.K., Kristensen, K., and Westlund, A.H. (2004). Work motivation and job satisfaction in the Nordic countries. *Employee relations,* 26(2), 122-136.

——, and Antvor, H.G. (2010). The relationship between job satisfaction and national culture. *The TQM Journal,* 22(4), 369-378.

European Commission (2002). Reforming the Commission. An administration at the service of half a billion Europeans. Brussels.

European University Association (EUA) (2006). Quality Culture in European Universities: a bottom-up approach (Brussels, EUA).

Fang, T. (2003). A critique of Hofstede's ûfth national culture dimension. *International Journal of Cross Cultural Management,* 3(3): 347-368.

—— (2005-2006). From 'onion' to 'ocean': Paradox and change in national cultures. *International Studies of Management and Organization,* 35(4): 71-90.

—— (2010). Asian management research needs more self-conûdence: Reûection on H (2007) and beyond. *Asia Paciûc Journal of Management,* 27(1): 155-170.

Faucheux, C., Amado, G., and Laurent, A. (1982). Organizational development and change. *Annual Review of Psychology,* 33: 343-370.

Feigenbaum, A.V. (1986). Total quality control 3rd, New York: McGraw-Hill.

Feisthammel D. et Massot P. (2005). Fondamentaux du pilotage de la performance, le tableau de bord adapté à la réalité des activités, AFNOR.

Feng, J., Prajogo, D.I., Tan, K.C., and Sohal, A.S. (2006). The impact of TQM practices on performance: A comparative study between Australian and Singaporean organizations. *European Journal of Innovation Management,* 9(3), 269-278.

Feng, M. (2006). "The relationship between motivation and effort in the implementation of ISO management systems and organisational performance", PhD thesis, Department of Management and Marketing, University of Melbourne, Melbourne.

Fernie, S. and D. Metcalf (1995). Participation, Contingent Pay, Representation and Workplace Performance: Evidence from Great Britain. *British Journal of Industrial Relations,* 33, 3, 379-415.

Fields. Dail and Paul M. Roman, (2010). Total Quality Management and Performance in Substance Abuse Treatment Centers, Health Research and Educational Trust DOI: 10.1111/j.1475-6773.2010.01152.x

Finkelstein, S., and Hambrick, D.C. (1996). Strategic Leadership: Top executives and their effects on organizations. New York: West.

Fitzgerald, L., Johnston, R., Brignall, S., Silvestro, R. and Voss, C., (1991). Performance Measurement in Service Businesses, London, CIMA.

Flynn, B.B., (1994). The relationship between quality management practices, infrastructure and fast product innovation. *Benchmarking for Quality Management and Technology,* 1(1), 48-64.

—— (2001). Further evidence on the validity of the theoretical models underlying the Baldrige criteria. *Journal of Operations Management,* 19(3), 617-652

—— and Saladin, B. (2006). Relevance of Baldridge constructs in an international context: a study of national culture. *Journal of Operations Management,* Vol. 24, No. 5, pp. 583-603.

— —, Schroeder, R.G., Sakakibara, S., (1994). A framework for quality management research and an associated measurement instrument. *Journal of Operations Management* 11 (4), 339-366.

— —, Schroeder, R.G., and Sakakibara, S. (1995). The impact of quality management practices on performance and competitive advantage. *Decision Sciences,* 26(5), 659-691.

Ford, D.P. and Chan, Y.E. (2003). Knowledge sharing in a multi-cultural setting: a case study. *Knowledge Management Research and Practice,* Vol. 1, No. 1, 11-27.

Ford, J.D., and Schellenberg, D.A. (1982). Conceptual Issues of Linkage in the Assessment of Organizational Performance. *The Academy of Management Review,* 7(1), 49-58.

Forrester, G. (2011). Performance management in education: milestone or millstone?. *Management in Education, 25*(1), 5-9.

Forstenlechner, I., and Rutledge, E. (2010). Growing Levels of National Unemployment in the Arab Gulf: Time to Update the 'Social Contract'. *Middle East Policy,* 17(2): 38-51.

Forza, C., and Flippini, R. (1998). TQM impact on quality conformance and customer satisfaction: A causal model. *International Journal of Production Economics,* 55, 1-20.

Fotopoulos, C.B. and Psomas, E.L. (2009). The impact of soft and hard TQM elements on quality management results. *International Journal of Quality and Reliability Management,* Vol. 26, No. 2, pp. 150-63.

Frazer, L. and M. Lawley (2000). *Questionnaire Design and Administration.* Brisbane, John Wiley & Sons Australia.

French, W. (Ed.), Bell, C. (Ed.), and Zawacki, R. (Ed.). (1994). *Organization development and transformation: Managing effective change (4th ed.).* Homewood, IL: Richard D Irwin. Retrieved from *EBSCOhost.*

Fuchsberg, G. (1993). Baldrige award may be losing some luster. *The wall Street Journal,* B-1 April 9.

Fuentes-Fuentes, M.M., Albacete-Saez, C.A., and Liorens-Montes, F.J. (2004). The impact of environmental characteristics on TQM principles and organizational performance. *The International Journal of Management Science,* 32, 425-442.

Fukuyama, F. (1995). *Trust: The Social Virtues and the Creation of Prosperity.* London: Hamish Hamilton. 44.

Fussell, S.R., Kraut, R.E., and Siegel, J. (2000, December). Coordination of communication: Effects of shared visual context on collaborative work. In Proceedings of the 2000 ACM conference on Computer supported cooperative work (pp. 21-30). ACM.

Fynes B. [1998/1999]. Quality Management Practices: A Review of the Literature. *Irish Business and Administrative Research,* Vol. 19/20, No. 2, pp. 113-138.

Gable, R.K., and Wolf, M.B. (1993). *Instrument development in the affective domain: Measuring attitudes and values in the business and school setting.* (2nd ed.). New York: Springer.

Gadenne, D. and Sharma, B. (2009). An investigation of the hard and soft quality management factors of Australian SMEs and their association with firm performance. *International Journal of Quality and Reliability Management,* 26(9), 865-880.

Galloway, L. *et al.* (2000). Operations Management in Context (Oxford: Butterworth Heinemann).

Gatchalian, M.M. (1997). People empowerment: The key to TQM success. *The TQM Magazine,* 9(6), 429-433.

Ghalayini, A.M., Noble, J.S. and Crowe, T.J. (1997). An integrated dynamic performance measurement system for improving manufacturing competitiveness, *International Journal of Production Economics,* Vol. 48, pp. 207-25.

Ghobadian, Abby, Speller, and Simon. (1994). Gurus of quality: A framework for comparison. *Total Quality Management,* 5 (3), 53-69.

Glenn, E.S. and Glenn, C.G. (1981). Man and Mankind: Conflict and Communication Between Cultures, Norwood, NJ, Ablex Grandzol, J.R., and Gershon, M., (1998). A survey instrument for standardizing TQM modeling research. *International Journal of Quality Science,* 3(1), 80-105.

Gomes, R.C., and Miranda Gomes, L.D.O. (2011). Performance Measurement and Stakeholder Perceptions: Assessing Performance through the Dimensions of Stakeholder Expectations, (Article) *Brazilian Administration Review.* (BAR, & 2), 133-149.

Gomez-Mejia, L.R., Balkin, D.B., and Cardy, R.L. (2004). *Managing human resources.* Upper Saddle River: Prentice Hall.

González-Benito, O., González-Benito, J., (2005). Cultural vs. operational market orientation and objective vs. subjective performance: perspective of production and operations. *Industrial Marketing Management,* 34, 797-829.

Gooderham, P., and Nordhaug, O. (2001). Are cultural differences in Europe on the decline? *Economic Business Forum,* (8), 48-53.

Gordon, G., 2000b, Building creative internal and external partnerships: experiences, issues and com ponents. *Education Through Partnership,* 4(1) pp. 71-76.

Gordon, G.G., and DiTomas, N. (1992). Predicting corporate performance from ssociation al culture. *Journal of Management Studies,* 29(6), 793-798.

Gotzamani, K., Theodorakioglou, Y.D. and Tsiotras, G.D. (2006). A longitudinal study of ISO 9000 (1994) series' contribution towards TQM in Greek industry. *The TQM Magazine,* Vol. 18, No. 1, pp. 44-54.

Govindarajan, V. and Gupta, A.K. (1985). Linking control systems to business unit strategy: Impact on performance. *Accounting, Organizations and Society,* 10 (1), 51-66.

Grandzol J.R., and Gershon M., (1998). A survey instrument for standardizing TQM modeling research. *International Journal of Quality Science,* 3(1), 80-105.

Graves, D. (1972). A Cross-Cultural Comparison of Managerial Behavior in England and France. *International Studies of Management and Organization,* 2(1), 105-116.

Grip, A.D and Saverman, J (2010). The effects of training on own and co-workers productivity: Evidence fropm a field experiment; retrieved from http://wharton.upenn.edu/awfe2010conferencepaper/savermann on October 6Th2011 http://wiki.answers.com/Qtraining&development-meaning-definition-human-resource management. Http://training and development:naukrichub.com http://.your dictionary.com/workers. Retrieved on October 5th, 2011.

Groeschl, S. and Doherty, L. (2000). Conceptualising culture., *Cross Cultural Management,* Vol. 7, No. 4, pp. 12-17.

Groocock, J.M., and Groocock, J.M. (1986). *The chain of quality: market dominance through product superiority*. New York: Wiley.

Gudykunst, W.B., Matsumoto, Y., Ting-Toomey, S., Nishida, T., Kim, K., and Heyman, S. (1996). *The influence of cultural individualism-collectivism, self-construals, and individual values on communication styles across cultures.*

Gunasekaran, A. and McGaughey, R.E. (2003). TQM in supply chain management, *The TQM Magazine,* Vol. 15, No. 6, pp. 361-3.

Gustafsson, A., Nilsson, L., and Johnson, M.D. (2003). The role of quality practices in service organizations. *International Journal of Service Industry Management, 14* (2), 232-244.

Hackman, J., and Wageman, R. (1995). Total Quality Management: empirical, conceptual, and practical issues. *Administrative Science Quarterly, 40,* 309-342.

Hafeez, K., Malak, N. and Abdelmeguid, H. (2006). A framework for TQM to achieve Business excellence. *Total Quality Management,* Vol. 17, No. 9, pp. 1213-29.

Hafeez Khalid, Ru•evièius Juozas "Total quality management and excellence: A framework for managing governance, Verslo ir teisës aktualijos/Current Issues of Business and Law ISSN 1822-9530 print/ISSN 2029-574X online 2011, 6(1), 7-10 http://www.vta.ttvam.eu.

Hair, J.F., Anderson, R.E., Tatham, R.L. and Black, W.C. (2010). *Multivariate Data Analysis*. 7thEd. Prentice Hall: USA.

Hair, J., Black, W., Babin, B., Anderson, R. and Tatham, R. (2006). Multivariate data analysis. 6 Ed. Pearson international, Prentice Hall, New Jersey.

Hair, J.F., Celsi, M.W., Money, A.H., Samouel, P., and Page, M.J. (2011). *Essentials of Business research methods*. ME Sharpe.

Hall, E.T. (1960). The silent language in overseas business. *Harvard Business Review,* May June.

—— (1959). *The silent language* (Vol. 3). New York: Doubleday.

—— (2000). Context and meaning. In L.A. Samovar and R.E. Porter (Eds.), *Intercultural Communication: A Reader,* 9th ed. (pp. 34-43). Belmont, CA: Wadsworth Publishing Co.

—— and Hall, M.R. (1990). *Understanding Cultural Differences*. Yarmouth, ME: Intercultural Press Inc.

Hall, Edward T. (1976). *Beyond Culture*. Garden City, NY: Anchor Press/Doubleday.

Hammer, M.H. and Champy, J. (1993). *Reengineering the Corporation: A Manifesto for Business Evolution,* Harper Business, New York, NY.

Hampden-Turner, C. and Trompenaars, F. (1997). Response to Geert Hofstede. *International Journal of Intercultural Relations,* 21(1), 149-59.

Hansson, B. (2007). Company-based determinants of training and the impact of training on company performance: Results from an international HRM survey. *Personnel Review,* 36(2), 311-331.

Harari, O. (1993). Ten reasons TQM doesn't work. *Management Review,* 82(1), 33 38.

Harmon, P. (2003). *Business Process Change: A Manager's Guide to Improving, Redesigning and Automating Processes,* Morgan Kaufmann Publishers, San Francisco, CA.

Harrington, D., and Williams, B. (2004). Moving the quality efforts foreward: The emerging role of the middle manager. *Managing Service Quality,* 14, 297-308.

Harvey, L. (2009). Deconstructing quality culture, EAIR Conference in Vilnius 2009, http://www.qualityresearchinternational.com/Harvey%20Vilnius.pdf (last accessed 24.08.2010).

—— and Green, D. (1993), Defining quality. *Assessment and Evaluation in Higher Education,* 18(1), pp. 9 34.

Hatch, M.J. (1993). The dynamics of organizational culture. *Academy of Management Review,* Vol. 18, pp. 657-93.

—— and Schultz, M. (2002). The dynamics of organizational identity. *Human Relations,* Vol. 55, No. 8, pp. 989-1018.

Haubrich, D. and McLean, I. (2006). Evaluating the Performance of Local Government: A Comparison of the Assessment Regimes in England, Scotland and Wales. *Policy Studies,* Vol. 27, No. 4, pp. 271-293.

Hayes, N. (2000). Doing Psychological Research. Surrey: Open University Press.

Hellsten, U., Klefsjö, B. (2000). TQM as a management system consisting of values, techniques and tools. *The TQM Magazine,* Vol. 12, No. 4, pp. 238-244.

Hendrick, K.B., and Singhal, V.R. (2001). Firm characteristics, total quality management, and firm performance. *Journal of Operations management,* 19, 269 285

—— (1997). Does implementing an effective TQM program actually improve operating performance? Empirical evidence from firms that have won quality awards. *Management Science,* 43, 1258-1273.

Hepworth, P. (1998). Weighing it up–A literature review for the balanced score card. *The Journal of Management Development,* 17 (8), 559-563

Herbig, P., Dunphy, S. Culture and innovation. *Cross Cult Manag 1998;* 5(4):13-22.

Herskovits, E. (1989). Man and his Works, Knopf, New York NY.

Hillstrom, L.C. (2009). "Balanced scorecard", in Helms, M.M. (Ed.), *Encyclopedia of Management,* eNotes.com, Seattle, WA, available at: www.enotes.com/management-encyclopedia/balanced-scorecard (accessed 14 December 2009).

Hinterhuber, H.H. (1995). Business process management: the European approach. *Business Change and Re-engineering,* Vol. 2, No. 4, pp. 63-73.

Hirzel, M. (2008). Erfolgsfaktor Prozessmanagement, in Hirzel, M., Kühn, F. and Gaida, (Eds), *Prozessmanagement in der Praxis,* Gabler, Wiesbaden, pp. 11-22.

Hoang, D.T., Igel, B., and Laosirihongthong, T. (2006). The impact of total quality management on innovation: findings from a developing country. *International Journal of Quality and Reliability Management,* 23(9), 1092-1117.

Hofstede Geert (1991). Cultures and organizations: Software of the mind. McGraw-Hill book company. London.

Hofstede, G. (1983). Dimensions of national cultures in fifty countries and three regions. In J.B. Deregowski, S. Dziurawiec, and R.C. Annis (Eds.), *Expiscations in cross-cultural psychology* (pp. 335-355). Lisse, Netherlands: Swets & Zeitlinger.

—— (1983). The cultural relativity of organizational practices and theories. *Journal of International Business Studies, 14*(2), 75-89.

—— (2001). *Culture's Consequences: Comparing Values, Behaviors, Institutions, and Organizations Across Nations,* 2nd edn, Sage: Thousand Oaks, CA.

——(2006). What did GLOBE really measure? Researchers' minds versus respondents' minds. *Journal of International Business Studies,* 37(6): 882-896

——, and Bond, M.H. (1988). The Confucius connection: From cultural roots to economic growth. *Organizational Dynamics,* 16(4): 4-21.

——, and Hofstede, G.J. (2005). *Cultures and organizations: Software of the mind,* 2nd ed. NewYork: McGraw-Hill.

—— (1980). *Culture's Consequences: International Differences in Work Related Values* (Sage, Beverly Hills, CA).

— — (1994). Values survey module 1994 manual. Institute for Research on Intercultural Cooperation: Maastrict, The Netherlands.

— — (1993). Cultural constraints in management theories. *Academy of Management Executive*, 7(1), 81-94.

Holden, N.J. (2002). Cross-cultural management: A knowledge management perspective *Hort. Sci*. 117:260-264.

Holzer, H.J., Block, R.N., Cheatham, M., and Knott, J.H. (1993). Are Training Subsidiesfor Firms Effective ? *The Michigan Experience, Industrial and Labour Relations Review*, Vol. 18, pp. 1-20.

Hooley, Graham John Fahy, Gordon Greenley, Jozsef Beracs, Krzysztof Fonfara, and Borls Snoj (2003). Market Orientation In the service sector of the of the transition economies of central Europe. *European Journal of Marketing*, 37 (1-2) 86-106.

Hoskins EJ, Abdul al-Hamid Noor F., Ghasib SH. Implementing TQM in a military hospital in Saudi Arabia. *Jt Comm J Qual Improv* 1994; 20: 454-64.

Hossain, M., and Leo, S. (2009). Customer perception on service quality in retail banking in Middle East: the case of Qatar. *International Journal of Islamic and Middle Eastern Finance and Management*, 2(4), 338-350.

House, R., Hanger, P., Quintanilla, A., Dorfman, P., Dickson, M., Javidan, M. *et al.* (1999). *Culture, leadership, and organizational practices*, in Mobley, W.H., Gressner, M.J. and Arnold, V.H.

House, R.J., Hanges, P.J., Javidan, M., Dorfman, P. and Gupta, V. (2004). *Culture, Leadership, and Organizations: The GLOBE Study of 62 Societies*, Sage Publications: Thousand Oaks, CA.

HRmarketer.com (2005). Looking for ways to Boost your company's Bottom-Line Results? Research shows big impact of positive, PR Newswire.

Huang, T.C. (2000). Are the human resource practices of effective firms distinctively different from those of poorly performing ones? Evidence from Taiwanese enterprises. *International Journal of Human Resource Management*, 11, 436-451.

Hunt, V.D. (1995). *Quality management for government: A guide to federal, state and local implementation*. Milwaukee, Wisconsin: ASQC Quality Press.

— — (2005). Managing change: a barrier to TQM implementation in service industries. *Managing Service Quality*, Vol. 15, No. 5, pp. 452-69.

— —, Stolen, J.D. (1998). Total quality management contrasts in manufacturing and service Industries. *International Journal of Quality and Reliability Management*, *15*(2),138-161.

Hurley, R.F. and Hult, G.T.M. (1998). Innovation, Market Orientation and Organizational.

Hüseyin Selçuk Kýlýç (2011). a Fuzzy AHP based performance assessment system for the Strategic Plan of Turkish Municipalities, *International Journal of Business and Management Studies*, Vol. 3, No. 2, 2011 ISSN: 1309-8047 (online).

Hussain, F., Lucas, C., and Ali, M.A. (2004). *Managing Knowledge Effectively. Managing Knowledge Effectively*. [Online] Available: http://www.tlainc.com/articl66.htm (June 21, 2010).

Husted, B. (1999). Wealth, Culture, and Corruption. *Journal of International Business Studies*, XXX (2): 339-60

Idris, F and M Ali, K.A., (2008). The impacts of leadership style and best practices on company performances: Empirical evidence from business firms in Malaysia. *Total Quality Management and Business Excellence*, *19*(1-2), 163-171.

Idris, F., Abdullah, M., Idris, M.A., and Hussain, N. (2003). Integrating Resource based viewand Stakeholder theory in developing the Malaysian Excellence Model: A conceptual framework. *Singapore Management Review*, 25(2), 91 109.

Idris, Fazli (2011). Total quality management (TQM) and sustainable company performance: the examining the relationship in Malaysian firms, *International Journal of Business and Society*, Vol. 12, No. 1, 31-52.

Idris, M.A. and Zairi, M. (2006). Sustaining TQM: a synthesis of literature and proposed research framework, *Total Quality Management*, Vol. 17, No. 9, pp. 1245-60. Eng., 21(4), pp. 17-21.

Inglehart, R.F. (1997). Modernization and postmodernization: Cultural, Economic and polit.

Inkson, K., Khapova, S.N. and Parker, P. (2007). Careers in cross-cultural perspective, *Career Development International*, Vol. 12, No. 1, pp. 5-8.

Inzerilli, G., Laurent, A. (1983). Managerial Views of Organization Structure in France and the U.S.A. *International Studies of Management and Organization* 13(1/ 2): 97-118.

Irani, Z., Beskese, A., and Love, P.E.D. (2004). Total Quality Management and corporate culture: Construct of organizational excellence. *Technovation*, 24, 643 692.

Ishikawa, K. (1985). What is total quality control? *The Japanese way*. London: Prentice Hall.

Jaafreh, A.B., and Al-abedallat, A.Z. (2012). The Effect of Quality Management Practices on Organizational Performance in Jordan: An Empirical Study. *International Journal of Financial Research*, 4(1), p. 93.

Israel, G.D. (1992). *Determining sample size*. University of Florida Cooperative Extension Service, Institute of Food and Agriculture Sciences, EDIS.

Ittner, C.D., Larcker, D.F., Nagar, V., and Rajan, M.V. (1999). Supplier selection monitoring practices, and ûrm performance. *Journal of Accounting and Public Policy*, 18, 253-281.

Ivancevich, J.M. and Matteson, M.T. (2002). Organizational Behavior and Management, McGraw-Hill, Boston, MA.

Jaeger, A.M. (1986). Organization development and national culture: Where's the fit?. *Academy of Management Review*, 178-190.

James, M.E. (2008). An Empirical Investigation into the Extent of Quality Management Practices in the Jamaican Manufacturing Industry. University of Phoenix.

Javidan, M., Stahl, G.K., Brodbeck, F. and Wilderom, C.P.M. (2005). Cross-border transfer of knowledge: cultural lessons from project GLOBE. *The Academy of Management Executive* 19(2): 59-76.

Jimenez-Jimenez, D. and Martinez-Costa, M., (2009). The effectiveness of TQM: The key role of organizational learning in small business. *International Small Business Journal*, 27(1), 98-125.

Jing, F.F., and Avery, G.C. (2008). Missing Links in Understanding the Relationship between Leadership and Organizational Performance. *International Business and Economics Research Journal*, 7(5), 67-78.

Jitpaiboon, T. and Rao, S.S. (2007). A meta-analysis of quality measures in manufacturing System. *International Journal of Quality and Reliability Management*, 24(1), 78-102.

Johannessen, J.A., Olaisen, J., and Olsen, B. (1999). Strategic Use of Information Technology for Increased Innovation and Performance. *Information Management and Computer Security* 7(1), 5-22.

Johns, G. (2006). The essential impact of context on organizational behavior. *Academy of Management Review, 31*: 386-408.

Johnston, Hank, and Bert Klandermans. Eds. (1995). *Social Movements and Culture.* Minneapolis: University of Minnesota Press.

Jones, Efferey P. Seraphim, Daniele, (2008). TQM implementation and change management in an unfavorable environment, *Journal of Management Development,* Vol. 27, Issue: 3, pp. 291-306.

Jones, G.R. (2004). Theory of Organization Theory, Design, and Change, Texas A&M University, USA, Person Prentice Hill, Texas, USA.

Judson, A.S. (1990). *Making Strategy Happen, Transforming Plans into Reality,* Basil Blackwell, London.

Jung, J.Y., and Hong, S. (2008). Organizational citizenship behaviour (OCB), TQM and performance at the maquiladora. *International Journal of Quality and Reliability Management,* 25(8), 793-808.

Juran, J. and Gryna (1980). *Quality Planning and Analysis,* McGraw-Hill, New York, NY.

—— (1993). *Quality planning and analysis.* New York: McGraw-Hill.

Juran, J.M. (1988). *Juran on planning on quality.* New York: Free Press.

—— (1995). *A history of managing for quality: The evolution, trends, and future directions of managing for quality.* ASQC Quality Press: Wisconsin USA.

Jusoh, D., Ibrahim, N., and Zainuddin, Y. (2008). The performance consequence of multiple performance measures Usage: Evidence from the Malaysian manufacturers. *International Journal of Productivity and Performance Management,* 57(2), 119-136.

Kaiser, H. (1974). An index of factorial simplicity. *Psychometrika, 39,* 31-36.

Kanji, G.K. (1996). Can total quality management help innovation? *Total Quality Management, 7*(1), 3-9.

—— (1998). Measurement of Business Excellence, *Total Quality Management,* Vol. 9(7), pp. 633-643.

—— (2002). *Measuring business excellence.* London: Routledge.

Kanungo. Shivraj, Jain. Vikas (2011). Organizational Culture and E-Government Performance: An Empirical Study. *International Journal of Electronic Government Research,* Volume 7, Issue 2..

Kaplan, R.S. and Norton, D.P. (1992). The Balanced Scorecard – measures that drive performance. *Harvard Business Review,* Vol. 70, No. 1, pp. 71-9.

—— (2000). The strategy-focused organization. USA: Harvard Business School Press.

—— (1993). Putting the balanced scorecard to work. *Harvard Business Review,* September-October, pp. 134-47.

Karia, N., and Ahmed, Z.A. (2000). Quality Practices that pay: Empowerment and teamwork. *Malaysian Management Review, Vol. 35* No. 2, pp. 66-76

Kartha, C.P. (2004). A Comparison of ISO 9000:2000 Quality System Standards, QS9000, ISO/TS 16949 and Baldrige Criteria. *The TQM Magazine, 16*(5), 331 340.

Karuppusami, K., and Gandhinathan, R. (2006). Pareto analysis of critical success factors of total quality management. *The TQM Magazine,* 18(4), 372-385.

Kaynak, H. (2003). The relationship between total quality management practices and their effects on firm performance. *Journal of Operations Management,* 21, 405-435

— —, and Hartley, J.L. (2005). Exploring quality management practices and high tech firm performance. *Journal of High Technology Management Research,* 16, 255-272.

Keegan, D.P., Eiler, R.G. and Jones, C.R. (1989). *Are your performance measures obsolete Management Accounting,* June, pp. 45-50.

Kekale, T., and Kekale, J. (1995). A mismatch of cultures, a pitfall of implementing a total quality approach. *International Journal of Quality and Reliability Management, 12*(9), 210-229.

Kelley, Lane and Clayton Reeser. (1973). The persistence of culture as a determinant of differentiatedattitudes on the part of American managers of Japanese ancestry. Acoderrry of Ma11agetrrer7t Jourrlal, 16: 67-76.

Kelman, S. and Friedman, J.N. (2009). Performance improvement and performance dysfunction: anempirical examination of distortionary impacts of the emergency room wait-time target in the English National Health Service. *Journal of Public Administration Research and Theory,* Vol. 19, No. 4, pp. 917-46.

Kempner, T. (1987). *The Penguin management handbook.* Chichester: John Wiley & Sons.

Keng, B.O., Abu Bakar, N., Veeri, A., Vellapan, L., and Alex Kim, Y.L. (2005). Does TQM influence employees job satisfaction? An empirical case analysis. *International Journal of Quality and Reliability Management,* Vol. 24, No. 1, 2007 pp. 62-77.

Kennerley, M. and Neely, A. (2003). A framework of the factors affecting the evolution of performance measurement systems, *International Journal of Operations and Production Management,* Vol. 22, No. 11, pp. 1222-39.

Kerlinger, F.N. and Lee, H.B. (2000). *Foundations of behavioral research.* 4th ed. Harcourt College Publishers: Orlando, US.

Kerr, M. (1996). Developing a corporate culture for the maximum balance between the utilization of human resources. *Canada-United States Law Journal,* 22169. Retrieved from EBSCO host.

Khairul Anuar, M.A. (2002). *Hubungan amalan pengurusan kualiti cemerlang dengan kepuasan pelanggan dalaman dan prestasi organisasi pihak berkuasa tempatan di Semenanjung Malaysia.* Desertasi PhD. Universiti Utara Malaysia. Sintok.

— —, Rushami, Z.Y. and Zakaria, A. (2001). The relationship between quality management practices and productivity in revenue and cost management: A study of Local Authorities in Peninsular Malaysia. *Malaysia Management Journal, 5* (1&2), 35-46.

Khamalah, J.N. and Lingaraj, B.P. (2007). TQM in the service sector: a survey of small business, *Total Quality Management,* Vol. 18, No. 9, pp. 973-82.

Khan. Muhammad. Aslam and Afza. Hasan l (2011). High level of education builds up strong relationship between organizational culture and organization performance in Pakistan. *The International Journal of Human Resource Management,* Vol. 22, No. 7, April 2011, 1387-1400.

Kýlýç, Hüseyin Selçuk. "A Fuzzy AHP Based Performance Assessment System for The Strategic Plan of Turkish Municipalities." *International Journal of Business and Management Studies* 3.2 (2011): 77-86.

Kish, Leslie. (1965). *Survey Sampling.* New York: John Wiley and Sons, Inc.

Klein, A., Waxin, M., F. Radnell, E., (2009). The impact of the Arab national culture on the perception of ideal organizational culture in the United Arab Emirates: An empirical study of 17 firms, *Education, Business and Society: Contemporary Middle Eastern Issues,* Vol. 2, Issue: 1, pp. 44-56.

Kline, R.B. (1998). *Principles and practice of structural equation modeling*. New York: Guildford press.

Kloot, L. and Martin, J. (2000). Strategic performance management: A balanced approach to performance management issues in local government. *Management Accounting Research,* 11, 231-251.

Kluckchorn, E. and Strodbeck F. (1961). *Variations in Value Orientations,* Harper & Row, New York.

Koehler, J.W. and Pankowski, J.P. (1996). *Quality Government: designing, developing and implementing TQM*. Florida: St. Lucie Press.

Koh, S.C.L., Demirbag, M., Bayraktar, E., Tatoglu, E. and Zaim, S. (2007). The impact of supply chain practices on performance of SMEs. *Industrial Management and Data Systems,* Vol. 107, No. 1, pp. 103-24.

Kontoghiorghes, C., and Gudgel, R. (2004). Investigating the association between productivity and quality performance in two manufacturer settings. *The Quality Management Journal 11*(2), 8-20.

Kotter, J., and Heskett, J. (1992). *Corporate culture and performance*. New York: Free Press.

Kotter, J.P. (1995). Leading change: why transformation efforts fail. *Harvard Management Review* 73(2), 59-67.

Krasachol, L., and Tannock, J.D.T. (1999). A study of TQM implementation in Thailand. *International Journal of Quality and Reliability Management, 16*(5), 418 432.

Kreitner, R., and A. Kinicki. (2008). Organizational Behavior, 8th Edition. New York: McGraw-Hill/Irwin.

Krejcie, R.V., and Morgan, D.W. (1970). Determining sample size for research activities. *Educ Psychol Meas.*

Kroeber, A.L., and Kluckhohn, C. (1952). Culture: A critical review of concepts and definitions. Cambridge, MA: Harvard University Peabody Museum of American Archeology and Ethnology.

—— and T. Parsons (1958). The concepts of culture and of social systems. *Amer. Soc. Rev.* 23: 582-583.

Krumwiede, K.R., and Charles, S.L. (2006). Finding the right mix. How to match strategy and management practices to enhance firm performance. Strategic Finance, 87, 37-43. Retrieved September 7, 2008, from ProQuest database.

Kuchinke, K. (1999), Leadership and culture: work-related values and leadership styles among one company's US and German telecommunication employees. *Human Resource Development Quarterly,* Vol. 10, No. 2, pp. 135-154.

Kumar, S., Gupta, Y.P. Statistical control at Motorola's Austin Assembly Plant. *Interfaces 1993;* 23 (2): 84-92.

Kumar, V., Choisne, F., Grosbois, D., and Kumar, U. (2009). Impact of TQM on company's performance. *International Journal of Quality and Reliability Management,* 26(1), 23-37.

Lagrosen, S. (2003). "Exploring the impact of culture on quality management". *The International Journal of Quality and Reliability Management,* 2-(4/5), 473-487.

– –, and Lagrosen, Y. (2003). Quality configurations: a contingency approach to quality management. *International Journal of Quality and Reliability Management, 20*(7), 759-773.

– – (2005), The Effects of Quality Management: A Survey of Swedish Quality Professionals'. *International journal of Operations and Production Management* Vol. 25, No. 10, pp. 940-952.

Lai, K. (2003). Market orientation in quality-oriented organizations and its impact on their performance. *International Journal of Production Economics,* 84, 17 34.

Lakhal L., Pasin F., and Limam, M., (2005). Quality Management practices and their impact on Performance. *International Journal of Quality &Reliability Management, 23*(6), 625-646.

Lakhe, R.R. and Mohanty, R.P. (1995). Understanding TQM in service systems. *International Journal of Quality and Reliability Management,* 12 (9), 139-153.

– – (1994). 'Total quality management: concepts, evolution and acceptability in developing economies', *International Journal of Quality and Reliability Management,* Vol. 11, No. 9, pp. 9-33.

Lau, C.M., and Ngo, H.Y. (1996). One country many cultures: organizational cultures of firms of different country origins. *International Business Review, 5*(5), 469-486.

– – (2004). 'The HR System, Organizational Culture, and Product innovation', *International Business Review,* 13, 685-703.

Lau, R.S.M., Zhao, X., and Xiao, M. (2004). Assessing quality management in China with MBNQA criteria. *International Journal of Quality and Reliability Management,* 21(7), 699-713.

Laurent, A. (1983). The cultural diversity of western conceptions of management. *International Studies of Management and Organization,* 8(2), 75-96.

Lawrence, P.R., and Lorsch, J.W. (1967). Differentiation and integration in complex organizations. *Administrative Science Quarterly,* 12(1), 1-47

Learning: An Integration and Empirical Examination. *Journal of Marketing 52*(3) (July): 42-55.

Leary, M.R. (2004). *Introduction to behavioral research methods* (4th ed.). Pacific Grove, CA: Brooks/Cole.

Lemak, J.D., Reed, R., and Satish, P.K. (1997). Commitment to total quality management: Is there a relationship with firm performance? *Journal of Quality Management,* 2(1), 67-86.

Lenartowicz, T., and Roth, K. (1999). A framework for culture assessment. *Journal of International Business Studies,* 781-798.

– – (2001). Does subculture within a country matter: A cross cultural study of motivational domains and business performance in Brazil. *Journal of International Business Studies,* 32(2),

Lessen, R., and Neubauer, F. (1994). *European Management Systems.* London: McGraw-Hill.

LeVine, Robert (1984). Properties of Culture: An Ethonographic View, in *Culture Theory: Essays on Mint, Self and Emotion,* eds. R. Shweder and R. LeVine. New York: Cambridge University Press. pp. 67-87.

Li, J.H., Andersen, A.R., and Harrison, R.T. (2003). Total quality management principles and practices in China. *International Journal of Quality & Reliability Management,* 20 (9), 1026-1050.

Li, S., Ragu-Nathan, B., Ragu-Nathan, T.S. and Rao, S.S. (2005). Development and validation of a measurement for studying supply chain management practices. *Journal of Operations Management,* Vol. 23, pp. 618-41.

Lim, B. (1995). Examining the Organizational Culture and Organizational Performance Link. *Leadership and Organization Development Journal,* 16, 5, 16 21.

Lin, L.H. (2009). Effects of national culture on process management and technological innovation. *Total Quality Management and Business Excellence,* 20, 1287-1301.

Llorens Montes, F.J. and Verdu Jover, A.J. (2004). Total quality management, institutional isomorphism and performance: The case of financial services. *The Service Industries Journal,* 24 (5), 103-119.

Loehlin, J.C. (1992). Latent variable models: An introduction to factor, path, and structural analyses. Hillsdale, NJ: Lawrence Erlbaum Associates.

Lok, P. Crav^ ford, J. (2004). The Effect of Organisational Culture and Leadership Style on Job Satisfaction and Organisational Commitment: A cross national Comparison. *Journal of Management Development,* 23(4), 321-338.

Lumpkin, G.T., and Dess, G.G. (1996). Clarifying the entrepreneurial orientation (EO) construct and linking it to performance. *Academe of Management Review,* 21(1), 135-172.

Lundberg, C.C. (1988). Working with culture. *Journal of Organizational Change Management,* 1(2), 38-47.

Luthans, F., Welsh, D.H.B. and Rosenkrantz, S.A. (1993). What do Russian managers really do? A cross-cultural comparison of successful and effective managers, *Journal of International Business Studies,* 24, 741-761.

Lynch, R.L. and Cross, K.F. (1991). Measure up: The Essential Guide to Measuring Business Performance, Mandarin, London.

Madu, C.N., Kuei, C. and Lin, C. (1995). A comparative analysis of quality practice in manufacturing firms in the U.S. and Taiwan. *Decision Sciences, 26* (5), 621 635.

Mahesh, C. (1993). Total quality management in management development. *Journal of Management Development, 12*(7), 19-49.

Mahmood, W, Y, W., Mohammed, H.A., and Misnan, S.M. (2006). *Development of quality culture in the construction industry*. pp. 1-11.

Maiga A.S. and Jacobs F.A. (2005). Antecedents and consequences of quality performance. *Behavioral Research in Accounting,* No. *17,* pp. 1-17.

Maltz, A.C., Shenhar, A.J. and Reilly, R.R. (2003). Beyond the Balanced Scorecard: refining the search for organizational success measures. *Long Range Planning,* Vol. 36, No. 2, pp. 187-204.

Manal Yunis, Joo Jung, Shouming Chen, (2013). TQM, strategy, and performance: a firm-level analysis. *International Journal of Quality and Reliability Management,* Vol. 30, Issue 6, pp. 690-714.

Maroun, Nabih, *et al. How to Succeed at Education Reform: The Case for Saudi Arabia and the Broader GCC Region*. Abu Dhabi, Ideation Center, Booz & Company (2008).

Martinez-Costa, M., and Jimenez-Jimenez, D. (2009). The effectiveness of TQM: The key role of organizational learning in small business. *International Small Business Journal, 27*(1), 98-125.

Martinez-Lorente, A.R., Dewhurts, F.W., and Gallego-Rodriguez, A. (2000). Relating TQM, Marketing and business performance. *International Journal of Production Research,* 38(14), 3227-3246.

Martinsons, M.G., and Westwood, R.I. (1997). Management information systems in the Chinese business culture: An explanatory theory. *Information and Management,* 32(5), 215-228.

Maskell, B. (1989). Performance measurement for world class manufacturing. *Management Accounting,* May, pp. 32-3, June, pp. 32-3, July/August, pp. 48 and 50, September, pp. 64-6.

Maskell, B.H. (1991). *Performance Measurement for World Class Manufacturing: A Model for American Companies,* Productivity Press, Cambridge, MA.

Mathews, B.P., Ueno, A., Kekäle, T., Repka, M., Pereira, Z.L., and Silva, G. (2001). European quality management practices: The impact of national culture. The *International Journal of Quality and Reliability Management,* 18(6/7), 692-707.

Mathews, J.A. (1992). The cost of quality. *Newsweek,* September 7, 48-49.

Matzler, K., Hinterhuber, H., Daxer, C., and Huber, M. (2005). The relationship between customer satisfaction and shareholder value. *Total Quality Management and Business Excellence,* 16, 671-680. Retrieved June 25, 2008.

Maul G.P., Gillard JS. Solving chronic problems with simple tools. *Quality Progress* 1994; 51-5.

Maull, R., Brown, P. and Cliffe, R. (2001). Organisational culture and quality improvement. *International Journal of Operations and Production Management,* Vol. 21, No. 3, pp. 302-326.

Maznevski, M.L., Gomez, C.B., DiStefano, J.J., Noorderhaven, N.G. and Wu, P.C. (2002). Cultural dimensions at the individual level of analysis: the cultural orientations framework, *International Journal of Cross Cultural Management,* Vol. 2 No. 3, pp. 275-95.

MBNQA (Malcolm Baldrige National Quality Award), (2004). Criteria for Performance Excellence. Gaithersburg, MD: United States Department of Commerce, Technology Administration, National Institute of Standards and Technology.

McCormack, K.P. and Johnson, W.C. (2001). Business Process Orientation-Gaining the E Business Competitive Advantage, St. Lucie Press, FL.

McCrae, R.R., Terracciano, A., Realo, A. and Allik, J. (2008). Interpreting GLOBE societal practices scales, *Journal of Cross-cultural Psychology,* Vol. 39, No. 6, pp. 805-10.

McFadden, F. R,1993, Six sigma quality program, *Quality Progress,* June, 37-41.

McGuire, D., and Hutchings, K. (2006). A Machiavellian Analysis of Organizational Change. *Journal of Organizational Change Management,* 19(2), 192 209.

McLeod, H. (2006). Images of home: Visual memories of interior decoration and 'modernization'. *BCATA Journal, 48*(2), 40-43.

McSweeney, B. (2002). Hofstede's model of national cultural differences and their consequences: A triumph of faith—A failure of analysis. *Human Relations, Israel Science Foundation, Jerusalem* 55: 89-118.

Mead, R. (1998). *International Management,* 2nd ed., Wiley-Blackwell, London.

Medsker, G.J., Williams, L.J., and Holahan, P.J. (1994). A review of current practices for evaluating causal models in organizational behavior and human resources management research. *Journal of Management,* 20(2), 439-464.

Mehmet M., Xiaowen H., and Roger G. Schroeder (2010). The Effect of Quality Management on Mass Customization Capability. *International Journal of Operations and Production Management,* 30 (9), 900-922.

Mehra, S., Hoffman, J.M., and Sirias, D. (2001). TQM as a management strategy for the next millennia. *International Journal of Operations and Production Management*, 21(5/6), 855-876.

Meier, Kenneth J., and Laurence J. O'Toole, Jr. (2002). Public Management and Organizational Performance: The Impact of Managerial Quality. *Journal of Policy Analysis and Management*, 21 (Fall), 629-643.

Melhem, Y. (2004). The antecedents of customer-contact employees' empowerment. *Employee Relations*, 26 (1), 72-93.

Mellat-Parast, M., Adams, S.G., and Jones, E.C. (2007). An empirical study of quality management practices in the petroleum industry. *Production Planning and Control*, 18(8), 693-702

Menou, M. (1983). Cultural barriers to the international transfer of information. *Information Processing and Management*, 19(3), 121-129.

Mensah, J., Osei (2012). The status of total quality management (TQM) in Ghana A comparison with selected quality awards winners from Turkey. *International Journal of Quality and Reliability Management* Vol. 29, No. 8, 2012 pp. 851-871.

Mercer Tenisha (1996). Study Confirms it: Corporate culture matters. *Cranes Detroit Business* Nov, 1996.

Merchant, K.A. (1985). *Control in business organizations*. Boston: Pitman.

Metters, R. (2008). A case study of national culture and offshoring services. *International Journal of Operations and Production Management, 28*(8), 727-747.

Micheli, P. and Manzoni, J.F. (2010). Strategic performance measurement: benefits, limitations and paradoxes, *Long Range Planning*, Vol. 43, No. 4, pp. 465-76.

Mimouni, F., and Metcalfe, B.D. (2012). 7. Leadership development philosophy and practice in Saudi Arabia. *Leadership Development in the Middle East*, 169.

Min, Pyong Gap. (1992). The Structure and Social Function of Korean Immigrant Churches in the United States. *International Migration Review 26*, 4, 1370-1394.

Minkov, M. (2007). What makes us different and similar: A new interpretation of the World Values Survey and other cross-cultural data. Sofia, Bulgaria: Klasika i Stil.

Miroshnik, V. (2002). Culture and international management: A review. *Journal of Management Development*, Vol. 21, No. 7, pp. 521-544.

Mitchell, T.R. (1979). Organizational behavior, *Annual Review of psychology*, Vol. 30, pp. 243-281.

Miyagawa, M. and Yoshida, K. (2005). An empirical study of TQM practices in Japanese-Owned manufacturers in China. *International Journal of Quality and Reliability Management*, Vol. 22, No. 6, pp. 536 53.

Moawad, Ahmed, (2011). Presentation in the Millennium Development Goals (MDGs) for Water and Sanitation Sector in Egypt, water and sanitation reform in Egypt world (water week in Stockholm August (2011).

Mobley, W.H., Wang, L. and Fang, K. (2005). Organizational Culture: Measuring and Developing It in Your Organization. *Harvard Business Review China*, 3, 128 139.

Mohd Nizam, A.R. and Tannock, J.D.T. (2005). TQM best practices: Experiences of Malaysian SME. *Total Quality Management*, 16 (4), 491-503.

Molina-Azorin, J.F., Tari, J.J., Claver-Cortes, E., & Lopez-Gamero, M.D. (2009). Quality management, environmental management and firm performance: A review of empirical studies and issues of integration. *International Journal of Management Review*, 11(2), 197-222.

Molina-Azorin, J.F., Tari, J.J., Claver-Cortes, E., and Lopez-Gamero, M.D. (2009). Quality management, environmental management and firm performance: A review of empirical studies and issues of integration. *International Journal of Management Review,* 11(2), 197-222.

Moorhouse Adrian, (2006). "Think outside the black box: how Employee Relations links to Performance" WWW.PEOPLEMANAGEMENTCO.UK

Morden, T. (1999). Models of National Culture—A Management Review, *Cross Cultural Management 6(*1), 19-44.

Motwani, J. (2001). Critical factors and performance measures of TQM. *The TQM Magazine,* Vol. 13, No. 4, pp. 292-300.

Moynihan, Donald P., and Sanjay K. Pandey. (2005). Testing how management matters in an era of government by performance management. *Journal of Public Administration Research and Theory* 15: 421-39.

Mrayyan, B., and Hamdi, M.R. (2006). Management approaches to integrated solid waste in industrialized zones in Jordan: A case of Zarqa City. *Waste Management, 26*(2), 195-205.

Murphy, G.B., Trailer, J.W., and Hill, R.C. (1996). Measuring Performance in Entrepreneurship Research. *Journal of Business Research,* 36, 15-2.

Myers, M.D., and Tan, F.B. (2002). *Beyond models of national culture in information system research.* In E.J.

Myers, R.H. (1990). *Classical and modern regression application.* 2nd edition. Duxbury press. CA.

Nair, A. (2006). Meta-analysis of the relationship between quality management practices and firm performance-implications for quality management theory development. *Journal of Operations Management,* 24, 948-975.

Nagi, E., and Hamdan, M. (2009). Computerization and e-Government implementation in Jordan: Challenges, obstacles and successes. *Government Information Quarterly,* 26(4), 577-583.

Naj, A. (1993). Some manufacturers drop efforts to adopt Japanese manufacturing techniques. *The Wall Street Journal,* A-1 May 7.

Naman, J.L., and Slevin, D.P. (1993). Entrepreneurship and the concept of fit: A model and empirical tests. *Strategic Management Journal,* 14, 137-153.

Neely, A. (1999). The performance measurement revolution: why now and what next? *International Journal of Operations and Production Management,* Vol. 19, No. 2, pp. 205-28.

—— and Crowe, P. (2001). The performance prism in practice. *Measuring Business Excellence,* Vol. 5, No. 2, pp. 6-12.

Neely, A., Adams, C. and Kennerley, M. (2002). *The Performance Prism: The Scorecard for Measuring and Managing Business Success,* Prentice Hall Financial Times, London.

Nelson, R. and S. Gopalan (2003). Do organizational cultures replicate national cultures? Isomorphism, rejection and reciprocal opposition in the corporate values of three countries. *Organization Studies* 24/7: 1115-1151.

Newman, K.L. and Nollen, S.D. (1996). Culture and congruence: The fit between management practices and national culture, *Journal of International Business Studies,* Vol. 27, Issue 4, pp: 753-779.

Newman, W.H., Summer, C.E., and Warren, E.K. (1977). *The Process of Management.* Englewood Cliffs, NJ: Prentice Hall.

Ng'ang'a Muya James, Justus Nyongesa Wesonga (2012). The Impact of Organisational Culture on Performance of Educational Institutions. *International Journal of Business and Social Science* Vol. 3, No. 8, April 2012] pp 211-217.

Nicholson-Crotty, Sean, and Laurence J. O'Toole, Jr. (2004). Public Management and Organizational Performance: The Case of Law Enforcement Agencies. *Journal of Public Administration Research and Theory* 14, 1 (January): 1-18.

Nickels, M.A. (2009). Workforce.com, (May 22, 2006). Special report: Traning and Development). Roger Kaufman-Florida State University Donald Nickels, M.A.

Niven, P.R. (2003). *Balanced Scorecard Step-by-Step for Government and Nonprofit Agencies*, Wiley, Hoboken, NJ.

Nor Hazilah, A.M. (2004). Quality management in the public sector: An empirical survey of the Ministry of Health Hospitals in Peninsular Malaysia. Unpublished PhD dissertation: Universiti Malaya.

Noronoha, C. (2003), National culture and total quality management: Empirical assessment of a theoretical model. *The TQM Magazine*, Vol. 15, No. 5, pp. 351 355.

Norreklit, H. (2000). The balance on the balanced scorecard a critical analysis of some of its assumptions. *Management accounting research*, 11(1), 65-88.

Nunnally, J., (1978). *Psychometric methods*. New York: McGraw.

Nunnally, J.C. and Bernstein, I.H. (1994). *Psychometric Theory*, McGraw-Hill, New York, NY.

Nyhan, R.C. and Martin, L.L. (1999). Comparative performance measurement. *Public Productivity & Management Review*, Vol. 22, No. 2, pp. 348-64

O'Reilly, S.Y., Griûn, W.L. and Ryan, C. (1991). Residence of trace elements in metasomatized spinel lherzolite xenoliths: a proton microprobe study. *Contributions to Mineralogy and Petrology* 109, 98-113.

O'Toole, Laurence J., Jr. and Kenneth J. Meler. (2003). Plus ça Change: Public Management Personnel Stability, and Organizational Performance. *Journal of Public Administration Research and Theory* 13 (January), 43-64.

Oakland, J. (2000). *Total Quality Management: Text With Cases*, 2nd ed., Butterworth Heinemann, Oxford.

Oliver, N. (1998). Employee commitment and total quality control, *International Journal of Quality and Reliability Management*, 7, pp. 21-29.

Olsen, J.P. and Maassen, P. (2007). European debates on the knowledge institution: The modernization of the university at the European level, in: P. Maassen and J.P. Olsen (Eds.) *University Dynamics and European Integration* (Dordrecht, Springer).

Olve, N., Roy, J. and Wetter, M. (1999). *A Practical Guide to Using the Balanced Scorecard*, Wiley, Chichester.

Ooi, K.B., Bakar, N.A., Arumugam, V., Vellapan, L., and Loke, A.K.Y. (2007). Does TQM influence employees' job satisfaction?An empirical case analysis. *International Journal of Quality and Reliability Management*, 24, 62-77.

Oppenheim, A.N., (2000). Questionnaire Design, Interviewing and Attitude Measurement. Continuum (London).

Otley, D.T. (1980). The contingency theory of management accounting: Achievement and prognosis. *Accounting, Organizations and Society*, 5 (4), 413 428.

— — (1999). Performance management: A framework for management control systems research. *Management Accounting Research*, 10 (4), 363-382.

Oyserman, D., Coon, H.M., and Kemmelmeier, M. (2002). Rethinking individualism and collectivism: Evaluation of theoretical assumptions and meta-analyses. *Psychological Bulletin,* 128: 3-72.

Ozcan Ümit. (2006). Municipal Partnership in Turkey: Local Administration Reform Programme Funded by the EU and Implemented by the Ministry of Interior with the Support of UNDP (2006).

Ozcan Ümit, Bahloul Hachemi (2006). Municipal Partnership in Turkey: Situation analysis Funded by the EU and Implemented by the Ministry of Interior with the Support of UNDP. Turkey.

Padovani, E., Yetano, A. and Levy Orelli, R. (2010). Municipal Performance Measurement and Management in Practice: Which Factors Matter?, *Public Administration Quarterly,* Vol. 34, No. 4, pp. 591-635.

Pagell, M., Katz, J.P., and Sheu, C. (2005). The importance of national culture in operations management research. *International Journal of Operations and Production Management,* 25(3/4), 371-394.

Pallant, J. (2005). SPSS Survival Manual: A step by step guide to data analysis using SPSS version 12. Maidenhead, Berkshire: Open University Press.

Palo, S., and Padhi, N. (2005). How HR professionals drive TQM: A case study in Indian organization. *The TQM Magazine,* 17, 467-486.

Parast, M.M. (2006). The Effect of Quality Management Practice on Operational and Business Results in the Petroluim Industry in Iran. University of Nebraska, Lincoln, Nebraska.

Park, N.K. (2003). A guide to using event study methods in multi-country settings". *Strategic Management Journal,* forthcoming.

Parsons, Talcott and Edward A. Shils (eds.) (1951). Toward a General Theory of Action.

Paul, P., Roy, A., and Mukhopadhyay, K. (2006). The impact of cultural values on marketing ethical norms: A study in India and the United States. *Journal of International Marketing,* 28-56.

Pavlov, A., and Bourne, M. (2011). Explaining the effects of performance measurement on Performance: An organizational routines perspective. *International Journal of Operations and Production Management, 31*(1), 101-122.

Perera, H.S.C. and Kuruppuarachchi, Impact of TQM and Technology Management on Operations Performance (August 24 2010). *The IUP Journal of Operations Management, Vol. IX,* No. 3, pp. 23-47.

Peschel, D. (2008). Total quality management and the Malcolm Baldrige National Quality Award: Benefits and directions for banking institutions. *Business Renaissance,* 3(4), 49-66.

Pettigrew, Andrew M. (1979). On Studying OrganizationalCultures. *Administrative Science Quarterly,* 24 (December), 570-81.

Pfau, L.D. (1989). Total Quality Management Gives Companies a Way to Enhance Position in Global Marketplace.

Phatak, A. (1986). International Dimensions of Management, PWS-Kent, Boston, MA.

Pinho, J.C. (2008). TQM and performance in small medium enterprises: the mediating effect of customer orientation and innovation, *International Journal of Quality and Reliability Management,* 25(3): 256-275.

Porter, L.J. and Parker, A.J. (1993). Total quality management: The critical success factors. *Total Quality Management,* Vol. 4, No. 1, pp. 13-22.

Powell, T.C. (1995). Total quality management as competitive advantage: A review and empirical study. *Strategic Management Journal,* 16 (1), 15-37.

Prajogo, D.I. (2005). The relationship between total quality management practices and organizational culture. *International Journal of Operations and Production Management,* 25 (11), 1101-1122.

— — (2005). The comparative analysis of TQM practices and quality performance between manufacturing and service firms. *International Journal of Service Industry Management,* Vol. 16, No. 3, pp. 217-28.

Prajogo, D.I. and McDermott, C.M. (2005). The relationship between total quality management practices and organizational culture. *International Journal of Operations and Production Management,* Vol. 25, No. 11, pp. 1101-22.

— —, and Sohal, A.S. (2001). TQM and innovation: A literature review and research framework. *Technovation,* 21, 539-558.

— — (2003). The relationship between TQM practices, quality performance, and innovative performance. *International Journal of Quality and Reliability Management,* 20(8), 901-918.

— — (2006). The relationship between organizational strategy, total quality management (TQM), and organizational performance-the mediating role of TQM. *European Journal of Operation Research,* Vol. 168, No. 1, pp. 35-50.

Prybutok, V.R. and Ramasesh, R. (2005). An action research based instrument for monitoring continuous quality improvement. *European Journal of Operational Research, 166* (2), 293-309.

Pun, K.F. (2001), Cultural influences on total quality management adoption in Chinese enterprises: an empirical study. *Total Quality Management,* Vol. 12, No. 3, pp. 323-342

— — (2002): Development of an integrated total quality management and performance measurement system for self-assessment: A method. *Total Quality Management, 13*(6), 759-777.

Quazi, H.A. and Padibjo, S.R. (1998). A journey toward total quality management through ISO 9000 certiûcation—A study on small- and medium-sized enterprises in Singapore. *International Journal of Quality and Reliability Management,* 15, 489-508.

Rad, A.M.M. (2006). The impact of organizational culture on the successful implementation of total quality satisfacti. *The TQM Magazine, 18*(6), 600-625.

Rahman, S. (2001a). A comparative study of TQM practice and organizational performance of SMEs with and without ISO 9000 certification. *International Journal of Quality and Reliability,* 18(1), 35-49.

— — (2001b). Total quality management practices and business outcome: evidence from small and medium enterprises in Western Australia. *Total Quality Management and Business Excellence,* 12(2), 201-210.

— — (2004, June). The future of TQM is past. Can TQM be resurrected? *Total Quality Management and Business Excellence,* 15(4), 411-422. Retrieved April2, 2009, from Business Source Elite database.

— —, and Bullock, P. (2005). Soft TQM, hard TQM and organizational performance relationships: An empirical investigation. *Omega,* 33, 73-83.

Ralston, D.A. (2008). The crossvergence perspective: Reflections and projections. *Journal of International Business Studies,* 39(1): 27-40.

— —, Holt, D.A., Terpstra, R.H., Yu, K.C., The impact of national culture and economic ideology on managerial work values: A study of the United States,

Russia, Japan, and China (1997) *Journal of International Business Studies, 28,* pp. 177-208

Ramayah T., Nusrah Samat, May-Chiun Lo, (2011). Market orientation, service quality and organizational performance in service organizations in Malaysia. *Asia-Pacific Journal of Business Administration,* Vol. 3, Issue: 1, pp. 8-27.

Ramli, N., Fun, C.W. and Idris, F. (2009). A Study of Customer Satisfaction of Malaysian Public Library, *Journal Pengurusan,* 28, 23-43.

Ramseook-Munhurrun, P., Munhurrun, V., and Panchoo, A. (2011). Total Quality Management Adoption in a Public Hospital: Evidence From Mauritius. *Global Journal of Business Research,* Vol. 5, No. 3, 67-77.

Rantanen, H., Kulmala, H.I., Lonnqvist, A. and Kujansivu, P. (2007). Performance measurement systems in the Finnish public sector", *International Journal of Public Sector Management,* Vol. 20, No. 5, pp. 415-33.

Rao, S.S., Solis, L.E., and Raghunathan (1999). A framework for international quality management research: Development and validation of a measurement instrument. *Total Quality Management* ,10(7), 1047-1075.

Rashid, A.Z., Sambasivan, M., and Johari, J. (2003). The Inûuence of Corporate Culture and Organizational Commitment on Performance. *Journal of Management Development,* 22, 8, 708-728

Ravasi, D., and Schultz, M. (2006). Responding to organizational identity threats: Exploring the role of organizational culture. *Academy of Management Journal,* 49: 433-458.

Rawabdeh, I.A. (2008). Jordan Quality Award (King Abdullah II Award for Excellence (KAIIAE)): Characteristics, assessment and benchmarking. Benchmarking: *An International Journal,* 15(1), 4-24.

Redding, S. Gordon. (1994). Comparative management theory: Jungle, zoo or fossil 'bed? *Organization Studies,* 15:323-59.

Reed, R., Lemak, D., and Montgomery, J.C. (1996). Beyond process: TQM content and firm performance. Academy of Management. *The Academy of Management Review,* 21(1), 173-202.

— —, and Mero, N., P. (2000). Total Quality Management and sustainable competitive advantage. *Journal of Quality Management, 5,* 5-26.

Reeves, C., and Bednar, D.A. (1994). Defining quality: Alternatives and implications. Academy of Management. *The Academy of Management Review, 19*(3), 419-445.

Richard, P.J., Devinney, T.M., Yip, G.S., Johnson, G., (2009). Measuring organizational performance: towards methodological best practice. *Journal of Management 35* (3), 718-804.

Riley, D. (2002). Simulation modelling: educational development roles for learning technologists. *Research in Learning Technology,* 10(3).

Ringov, D and Zollo, M. (2007). The Impact of National Culture on Corporate Social Performance. Corporate Governance: *The International Journal of Effective Board Performance,* Vol. 7(4): 476-485.

Rivera-Vazquez, J.C., Ortiz-Fournier, L.V., and Flores, F.R. (2009). Overcoming cultural barriers for innovation and knowledge sharing. *Journal of Knowledge, Management,* 13(5), 257-270.

Robbins S P (2006). Organizational Behavior, Up Saddle River, New Yesrey, Prentic-Hall.

Robinson, H.S., Carrillo, P.M., Anumba, C.J. and Al-Ghassani, A.M. (2005). Review and implementation of performance management models in construction engineering organizations. *Construction Innovation,* Vol. 5, pp. 203-17.

Roffe, I. (1999). Innovation and creativity in organizations: A review of the implications for training and development. *Journal of European Industrial Training,* 23(4/5), 224-237.

Rokeach, Milton, J. (1973), *The Nature of Human Values,* New York, The Free Press.

Romanelli, Elaine, and Michael Tushman. Michael L. (1994). Organizational transformation as punctuated equilibrium: An empirical test. *Academy of Management Journal,* 5: 1141-1166.

Roscoe, J.T. (1975). *Fundamental Research Statistics for the Behavioural Sciences,* 2nd edition. New York: Holt Rinehart & Winston.

Rotter, Julian B. (1966). Generalized expectancies for internal versus external control of reinforcement. In *Psychological Monographs: General and Applied,* 80(1): 1-28.

Rungtusanatham, M., Forza, C., Filippini, R., and Anderson, J.C. (1998). A replication study of a theory of quality management underlying the deming method: Insights from an Italian context. *Journal of Operations Management,* 17, 77-95.

Russell-Einhorn, Malcolm (2007). *Legal and Institutional Frameworks Supporting Accountability in Budgeting and Service Delivery Performance", in Shah (Ed.), pp. 183 232.*

Salaheldin, S.I. (2003). The implementation of TQM strategy in Egypt: a field-force analysis. *The TQM Magazine,* 15, 266-274.

—— (2009). Critical success factors for TQM implementation and their impact on performance of SMEs. *International Journal of Productivity and Performance Management,* 58(3), 215-237.

Salem, S.M., Lettieri, P., and Baeyens, J. (2009). Recycling and recovery routes of plastic solid waste (PSW): A review. *Waste Management,* 29(10), 2625-2643.

Salleh, L.M. (2005). High/Low context communication: The Malaysian Malay Style. Proceedings of the 2005 Association for Business Communication Annual Convention.

Samaha, H.E. (1996). Overcoming the TQM barrier to innovation. *Human Resource Magazine, 41*(6), 145-149.

Samat, N., Ramayah, T., and Saad, N.M. (2006). TQM practices, service quality, and market orientation: Some empirical evidence from a developing country. *Management Research News, 29*(11), 713-728.

Samson, D., and Terziovski, M. (1999a). The link between TQM practices and organizational performance. *International Journal of Quality and Reliability Management,* 16(3), 226-262.

—— (1999b). The relationship between total quality management practices and operational performance. *Journal of Operations Management, 17*(4), 393-409.

Sanchez-Rodriguez, C. and Martinez-Lorente, A.R. (2004). Quality management practices in purchasing function: An empirical study. *International Journal of Operations and Production Management, 24* (7), 666-687.

Sanger, M.B. (2008). From measurement to management: breaking through the barriers to state and local performance. *Public Administration Review,* Vol. 68, pp. S70-S85

Saraph, J.V., Benson, P.G. and Schroeder, R.G. (1989). An instrument for measuring the critical factors of quality management. *Decision Sciences, 20* (4), 810-828

Saravanan, R. and Rao, K.S.P. (2006). The impact of employees' characteristics on total quality service implementation: An empirical study. *The Quality Management Journal,* 13(4), 22-35.

Sathe, V., (1985). Managing an entrepreneurial dilemma: nurturing entrepreneurship and control in large corporations 636-656. Frontiers of Entrepreneurship Research Babson College, Wesley, Mas.

Saxenian, A. (1994). Regional advantage: Culture and competition in Silicon Valley and Route 128. Cambridge, MA: Harvard University Press.

Schaffter, R., and Thomson, H. (1992). Successful change programs begin with results. *Harvard Business Review,* (January-February), 80-89.

Schein, E.H., (2004). Organizational Culture and Leadership, third ed. Jossey-Bass.

Schuler, R.S. (2000). The internationalization of human resource management. *Journal of International Management,* 6, 239-260.

Schultz, M. and Hatch, M.J. (1996). Living With Multiple Paradigms: The Case of Paradigm Interplay in Organizational Culture Studies, *Academy of Management Review 21:* 529-557.

Schwartz, S.H. (1994). Beyond individualism/collectivism: New cultural dimensions of values. In U. Kim, H.C. Triandis, Ç. Kagitçibas, S.C. Choi and G. Yoon (Eds.) *Individualism and collectivism: Theory, method, and applications* (pp. 85-119). Thousand Oaks, CA: Sage.

— —, and Bilsky, W. (1990). Toward a theory of the universal content and structure of values: Extensions and cross-cultural replications. *Journal of Personality and Social Psychology,* 58, 878-891.

— — (2008). Cultural Value Orientations: Nature and Implications of National Differences, Israel Science Foundation, Jerusalem.

Scott, V., Saviour, N. and James, B. (1993). The effects of culture on ethical decision-making: An application of Hofstede's typology. *Journal of Business Ethics,* Vol. 12, pp. 753-60.

Sebastianelli, R., and Tamimi, N. (2003). Understanding the obstacles to TQM success. *Quality Management Journal,* 10(3), 45-56.

Seijts, Gerard H., and Michael Roberts. The impact of employee perceptions on change in a municipal government. *Leadership and Organization Development Journal* 32.2 (2011): 190-213.

Sekaran, U. (2003). Research Methods for Business: A Skill-Building Approach. 4th Edition. Singapore. JohnWiley & Sons, Inc.

Seleim and Bontis, Seleim, A. and Bontis, N. (2009). The relationship between culture and corruption: a cross-national study. *Journal of Intellectual Capital,* Vol. 10, No. 1, 2009, pp. 165-184.

Selto, F.H., Renner, C.J., and Young, S.M. (1995). Assessing the organizational fit of a just-in-time manufacturing system: Testing selection, interaction and systems models of contingency theory. Accounting, *Organizations and Society,* 20(7/8),665-684.

Shaffer, T.R., and O'Hara, B.S. (1995). The effects of country of origin on trust and ethical perceptions of legal services. *The Service Industries Journal, 15*(2), 162 185.

Shane, S.A. (1993). Cultural Influences on National Rates of Innovation. *Journal of Business Venturing,* Vol. 8, 59-73.

Shane, S.A. (1992). Why Do Some Societies Invent More Than Others? *Journal of Business Venturing*, Vol. 7: 29-46.

Shenkar, 0. (2001). Cultural distance revisited: Towards a more rigorous conceptualization and measurement of the cultural distance construct. *Journal of International Business Studies*, 32: 519-535.

Shiryan, S. Shee, H. Stewart, D. (2012). Employee Training Effectiveness in Saudi Arabian SME Performance. *International Journal of Business and Social Science*, (3), 14, (46-52).

Shores, R.A., (1992). Improving the quality of management systems. *Quality Progress*, pp. 53-57.

Shortell SM, O'Brien JL, Carman JM, Foster RW, Hughes EF, Boerstler H., O'Connor EJ. Assessing the Impact of Continuous Quality Improvement/Total Quality Management: Concept versus Implementation. *Health Services Research*. 1995; 30(2) : 377-401.

Sia Mal Kong, Kanesan Muthusamy, (2011). Using service gaps to classify quality attributes, *The TQM Journal*, Vol. 23, Issue: 2, pp. 145-163.

Sila I and Ebrahimpour M., (2003). Examination and Comparison of the Critical Factors of Total Quality Management across Countries. *International Journal for Production Research*, Vol. 541(2), pp. 235-268.

Sila, I. and Ebrahimpour, M. (2002). An investigation of the total quality management surveysures based research published between 1989 and (2000). *International Journal of Quality and Reliability Management*, 19 (7), 902-970.

Sila, I. (2005). The influence of contextual variables on TQM practices and TQM-organizational performance relationship. *The Business Review*, 4(1), 204-210.

Sila, I., and Ebrahimpour, M. (2005). Critical linkages among TQM factors and business results. *International Journal of Operations and Production Management*, *25*(11), 1123-1155.

Silos, I. (1999). Employee involvement: a component of total quality management, *Production and Inventory Management Journal*, Vol. 40, No. 1, pp. 56-65.

Silvestro, R. (1998). The manufacturing TQM and service quality literatures: Synergistic or Conûicting paradigms? *International Journal of Quality and Reliability Management*, *15*(3), 303-328.

Singels, J., Ruël, G. and van de Water, H. (2001). ISO 9000 series certiûcation and performance. *International Journal of Quality and Reliability Management*, 18, 62 75.

Singh, P.J., and Smith, A.J.R. (2004). Relationship between TQM and innovation: an empirical study. *Journal of Manufacturing Technology Management*, 15(5), 394 401.

Singh, P.J. and Smith, A. (2006). An empirically validated quality management measurement instrument, *Benchmarking: An International Journal*, Vol. 13 No. 4, pp. 493-522.

Sink, D.S. and Tuttle, T.C. (1989). Planning and Measurement in Your Organization of the Future, Industrial Engineering and Management Press, Norcross, GA.

—— (1990). The performance management question in the organization of the future, *Industrial Management*, Vol. 32, No. 1, pp. 4-12.

Sinkovic', G., Currie, D.M. and Bevanda, V. (2011). From IT to BSC: the importance of culture in implementing a performance measurement system in Croatia. *Indian Journal of Economics and Business*, Vol. 10, No. 1, pp. 39-55.

Sitkin, S.B., Sutcliûe, K.M. and Schroeder, R.G. (1994). Distinguishing control from learning in total quality management: a contingency perspective, *Academy of Management Journal*, 19, pp. 537-564.

Skrinjar, R., Vulksic, V.B., Stemberger, M.I. (2008). The impact of business process orientation on financial and non-financial performance. *Bus. Proc. Manage. J. 14*(5): 738-754. [Online]. Available: www.emeraldinsight.com. (Accessed 22 September 2008).

Smircich, L. and Stubbart, C. (1985). Strategic management in an enacted world. *Academy of Management Review*, Vol. 10, No. 4, pp. 724-36

Smith. Keith A. Total Quality Management in the Public Sector: Part 1. *Quality Progress*. (June 1993), 46.

— —, Peterson, M.F. and Schwartz, S.H. (2002). Cultural values, source of guidance, and their relevance to managerial behavior: a 47-nation study, *Journal of Cross-Cultural Psychology* 33(2): 188-208.

— —, Trompenaars, E., and Dugan, S. (1995). The Rotter locus of control scale in 43 countries: A test of cultural relativity. *International Journal of Psychology*, 30, 377-400.

— — (1992). Organisational behaviour and national cultures. *British Journal of Management*, 3, 39-51.

Smith, S. (1988). Trends in TQM, *The TQM Magazine*, pp. 5-6.

Sohail, M.S. and Shaikh, N.M. (2004). Quest for excellence in business education: a study of student impressions of service quality. *The International Journal of Educational Management*, Vol. 18, No. 1, pp. 58 65.

— — and Hoong, T.B. (2003).TQM practices and organizational performance of SMEs in Malaysia: Some empirical observation. Benchmarking: *An International Journal, 10* (1), 37-53.

Sohal, A.S. and Terziovski, M. (2000). TQM in Australian manufacturing: Factors critical To success. *International Journal of Quality and Reliability Management*, 17 (2), 158-167.

Sondergaard, M. (1994). Research note: Hofstede's consequences: A study of reviews, citations and replications. Organization Studies, 15(3), 447-456.

Sousa-Poza, A and Sousa-Poza, A.A. (2000). Taking another look at the gender/job satisfaction paradox. *Kyklos*, Vol. 53, pp. 135-152.

— —, Nystrom, H., and Wiebe, H. (2001). A cross-cultural study of the differing effects of corporate culture on TQM in three countries. *The International Journal of Quality and Reliability Management*, 18(6/7), 744-761.

Spence, A.M. Job-Market Signalling. *Quarterly Journal of Economics*, Vol. 87, (August 1973), pp. 355-379.

Spicer, J. (Ed.). (2005). Making Sense of Multivariate Data Analysis. SAGE Publications, Inc.

Spina, G., E. Bartezzaghi, A. Bart, R. Cagliano, D. Draaijer and H. Boer. (1996). Strategically Flexible Production: The Multifocused Manufacturing Paradigm. *International Journal of Operations and Production Management*, 16: 20-41.

Sproull, N.D. (2004). *Handbook of research methods: A guide for practitioners and Students in the social sciences* (3rd Ed.). New Jersey: The Scarecrow Press.

Srinidhi, B. (1998). Strategic quality management. *International Journal of Quality Science*, 3(1), 38-70.

Srite, M., and Karahanna, E. (2006). The role of espoused national cultural values in echnology acceptance. *MIS quarterly*, 30(3), 679-704.

Stashevsky, S., Elizur, D. (2000). The effect of quality management and participation in decisionmaking on individual performance. *Journal of Quality Management,* Vol. 5, No. 1, pp. 53-65.

Sterman, J.D., Repenning, N.P., and Kofman, F. (1997). Unanticipated side effects of successful quality programs: Exploring a paradox of organizational improvement. *Management Science,* 43(4), 503-521.

Stone, D.L. and Eddy, E.R. (1996), A model of individual and organizational factors affecting quality-related outcomes. *Journal of Quality Management, 1,* 1, 21-48.

Strohhecker, J. (2007). Does a Balanced Scorecard Management Cockpit Increase Strategy Implementation Performance? Frankfurt School of Finance and Management. http://www.systemdynamics.org/conferences/2007/proceed/papers/STROH532.pdf, Access Date: 17.12.2007.

Sudman, Seymour. (1976). Applied Sampling. New York: Academic Press.

Sullivan, L.P., (1987). Quality Function Deployment QFD: The beginning, the end, and the problem in-between, A collection of presentations and QFD case studies, American Supplier Institute.

Sun, H. (2000). A comparison of quality management practices in Chanhai and Norwgian manufacturing companies. *International Journal of Quality and Reliability Management,* 17(6), 636-660.

— —, Li, S., Ho, K., Gersten, F., Hansen, P. and Frick, J. (2004). The trajectory of implementing ISO 9000 standards versus total quality management in Western Europe, *International Journal of Quality and Reliability Management,* Vol. 21, No. 2, pp. 131-53.

Sureshchandar, G.S., Rajendran, C. and Ananthraman, R.N. (2001). A holistic model for Total quality service. *International Journal of Service Industry Management,* 12 (4), 378-412.

Sveiby, K.E. (1997). *The New Organizational Wealth: Managing and Measuring Knowledge-based Assets,* Berrett-Koehler, San Francisco, CA.

Swamidass, P.M., and Newell, W.L. (1987). Manufacturing strategy, environmental uncertainty and performance: A path analytic model. *Management Science,* 33 (4), 509-524.

Swift, J.A. *et al.* (1998). *Principles of Total Quality* (Boca Raton, FL: St. Lucie Press).

Tabachnick, B.G., and Fidell, L.S. (2001). *Using Multivariate Statistics.* Boston: Allyn and Bacon.

Taguchi, G., (1986). *Introduction to Quality Engineering, Asian Productivity Organization* (Distributed by American Supplier Institute Inc., Dearborn, MI).

Taguchi, G., Clausing, D. (1993). Robust quality. *Harvard Business Review;* 65-75.

Takruri, Y.A. (2011). Corporate Governance in Jordan. *International Journal of Governance,* 1(3), 592-598.

Talib, F., Rahman, Z., and Qureshi, M.N. (2011). A study of total quality management and supply chain management practices. *International Journal of Productivity and Performance Management,* 60(3), 268-288.

— — (2012). an empirical investigation of relationship between total quality management practices and quality performance in Indian service companies. *International journal of quality and reliability management,* 30(3), 280-318.

Tamimi, N. (1995). An empirical investigation of critical TQM factors using exploratory factor analysis. *International Journal of Production Research.* 33: 3041-3051.

— — (1995). A tool for assessing industry TQM practice versus Deming philosophy. *Production and Inventory Management Journal,* 36, 27-32.

Tams, S., and Arthur, M.B. (2007). Studying careers across cultures: distinguishing international, cross-cultural, and globalization perspectives. *Career Development International,* 12(1), 86-98.

Tan, K.C. (2001). A structural equation model of new product design and development. *Decision Sciences,* 32(2), 195-226.

Tan, P.K.L. (1997), An evaluation of TQM and the techniques for successful implementation. *Training for Quality,* Vol. 5, No. 4, pp. 150-159.

Tang, H.K. (1998). An integrative model of innovation in organizations. *Technovation,* 18(5), 297-309.

Tari, J.J. (2005). Components of successful total quality management. *The TQM Magazine, 17*(2), 182-194.

Tata, J., Prasad, S., and Thorn, R. (1999). The influence of organizational structure on the effectiveness of TQM programs. *Journal of Managerial Issues,* 11(4), 440-453

Tennant, C., Wu, Y. (2005). The application of business process reengineering in the UK, *The TQM Magazine,* Vol. 17, Issue 6, pp. 537-545.

Thiagarajan, T. and Zairi, M. (1997a). A review of total quality management in practice: Understanding the fundamentals through examples of best practice application-Part I. *The TQM Magazine,* 9 (4), 270-286.

— — (1997b). A review of total quality management in practice: Understanding the fundamentals through examples of best practice application-Part II and III. *The TQM Magazine,* 9 (5), 344-356. 319

— — (1997c). A review of total quality management in practice: Understanding the fundamentals through examples of best practice application-Part III. *The TQM Magazine,* 9 (6), 414-417.

— — and Dale, B.G. (2001). A proposed model of TQM implementation based on an empirical study of Malaysian industry. *International Journal of Quality and Reliability Management*, Vol. 18, No. 3, pp. 289-306.

Thomas, D.C. (2002). Essentials of International Management: A Cross-Cultural Perspective, Sage Publications, Thousand Oaks, CA.

Tompenaars F., Hampden-Turner C. (1998). Riding the Waves of Culture: Understanding Diversity in Global Business, 2nd edition (New York: McGraw-Hill), p. 183.

Trailer, J.W., and Hill, R.C. (1996). Measuring Performance in Entrepreneurship Research. *Journal of Business Research,* 36, 15-23.

Triandis, H.C. (1990). Cross-cultural studies of individualism and collectivism. In J.J. Berman (Ed.), Nebraska symposium on motivation, 1989: Vol. 37. Cross-cultural perspectives. Lincoln: University of Nebraska Press.

— — (1972). The analysis of subjective culture. New York; john Wiley.

— — (1995). Individualism and Collectivism. Boulder, Colorado: West view Press.

— — and Albert, R.D. (1987). "Cross-cultural Perspectives", in F.M. Jablin, L.L. Putnam, K.H. Roberts, and Porter, L.W. (Eds.), Handbook of organizational communication: An interdisciplinary perspective (pp. 264-296). Newbury Park, CA: Sage.

Tricker, R.I. (1988). *Information resource management: A cross cultural perspective. Information and Management,* 15(37-46).

Trompenaars, F. and Hampden-Turner, C. (1997). Riding the waves of culture:

Understanding cultural diversity in business (2nd edn). London: Nicholas Breazley.

Tseng, S.M. (2010). The correlation between organizational culture and knowledge conversion on corporate performance. *Journal of Knowledge Management*, 14(2), 269-284.

Tsui, A.S., Zhang, Z.X., Wang, H., Xin, K.R., and Wu, J.B. (2006). Unpacking the relationship between CEO leadership behavior and organizational culture. *The Leadership Quarterly*, 17(2), 113-137.

Tung, R.L., and Verbeke, A. (2010). Beyond Hofstede and GLOBE: Improving the quality of cross cultural research. *Journal of International Business Studies*, 41(8): 1259-1274.

Tutuncu, O. and Kucukusta, D. (2008). "The role of supply chain management integration in quality management system for hospitals", *International Journal of Management Perspectives*, Vol. 1, No. 1, pp. 31-9.

Ugboro, I.O. and Obeng, K. (2000). Top management leadership, employee empowerment, job satisfaction, and customer satisfaction in TQM organizations: an empirical study, *Journal of Quality Management*, 5(2), 3rd Quarter, pp. 247-272.

Ul Hassan, M., Mukhtar, A., Qureshi, S.U., and Sharif, S. (2012). Impact of TQM Practices on Firm's Performance of Pakistan's Manufacturing Organizations. *International Journal*, 2.

Vande Ven, A.H. and Drazin, R. (1985). The concept of fit in contingency theory. *Research in Organizational Behavior*, 7, 333-365.

Van de Ven, A.H. and Ferry, D.L. (1980). *Measuring and assessing organizations*. Wiley: New York.

Van der Post, W.Z., De Coning T.J., and Smit, E. vd M. (1998). The relationship between organizational culture and financial performance: some South African evidence. *South African Journal of Business Management*, 29(1), 30-40.

Vanichchinchai, A. and Igel, B. (2009). Total quality management and supply chain management: similarities and differences. *The TQM Magazine*, Vol. 21 No. 3, pp. 249-60.

Venkatraman, N. (1989b). The concept of fit in strategy research: Toward verbal and statistical correspondence. *Academy of Management Review, 14* (3), 423-444.

Vidal, J. (2003). Quality assurance, legal reforms and the European Higher Education Area in Spain, *European Journal of Education*, 38, pp. 301-313.

Voss, C. and Blackmon, K. (1996). The impact of national and parent company origin on world-class manufacturing ûndings from Britain and Germany. *International Journal of Operations and Production Management*, 16(11), 98.

Vouzas, F.K. and Gotzamani, K.D. (2005). Best practices of selected Greek organizations on their road to business excellence, *The TQM Magazine*, Vol. 17, No. 3, pp. 259-66.

Vouzas, F. and Psyhogios, A.G. (2007). Assessing managers' awareness of TQM. *The TQM Magazine*, Vol. 19, No. 1, pp. 62-75.

Waldman, D.A. (1994). The contributions of Total Quality management to a theory of work performance. *Academy of Management Review*, 19, 510-536.

Walsh. Aidan, Hughes. Helen, Daniel, Maddox P., (2002). Total quality management continuous improvement: is the philosophy a reality? *Journal of European Industrial Training*, Vol. 26, Issue: 6, pp. 299-307.

Weerakkody, V., El-Haddadeh, R., and Al-Shafi, S. (2011). Exploring the complexities of e-government implementation and diffusion in a developing country: Some lessons from the State of Qatar. *Journal of Enterprise Information Management,* 24 (2), 172-196.

Weerakon, T.S. (1996). Organizational performance: A stakeholder concept. Proceedings of International Research Conference on Quality Management, 80-90.

Weick, K.E. (1996). Drop your tools: An allegory for organizational studies. *Administrative Science Quarterly,* 41(2), 301-313.

Westland, A.H., Gustafsson, C., Lang, E., and Mattsoon, B. (2005). On customer Satisfaction and financial results in Swedish real estate market. *Total Quality Management and Business Excellence,* 16, 1149-1159.

White, M., Hill, S., McGovern, P., Mills, C. and Smeaton, D. (2003). High performance: Management practices, working hours and work-life balance. *British Journal of Industrial Relations,* 41:2, 175-195.

Wichowsky, Amber, and Donald P. Moynihan. (2008). Measuring how administration shapes citizenship: A policy feedback perspective on performance management. *Public Administration Review* 68: 908-20.

Wiklund, J., and Shepherd, D. (2005). Entrepreneurial orientation (EO). and small business performance: a configurationally approach. *Journal of Business Venturing, 20,* 71-91.

Wilkinson, A., (1992). The other side of quality: "Soft" issue and the human resource dimension. *Total Quality Management,* 3(3), 323-329.

——, Redman, T., Snap Ed and Marchington, M. (1998). Managing with Total Quality Management, First Adition, Macmillan Press Ltd., London.

Williams, D.W. (2004). Evolution of performance measurement until 1930, *Administration and Society,* Vol. 36, No. 2, pp. 131-65.

Williams, R., Wiele, T., Iwaardeen, J., and Visser, R. (2004).TQM: Why it will again become a top management issue. *International Journal of Quality and Reliability Management,* 21 (6), 603-611

Witcher, B. (1994). The adoption of total quality management in Scotland. *The TQM Magazine,* 6 (2), 48-53.

Woolliams, P. The Trompenaars database. In F. Trompenaars and C. Hampden-Turner (Eds) (1997). *Riding the waves of culture: Understanding cultural diversity in business* (2nd edn). London: Nicholas Brealey.

Wruck, Karen H., and Michael C. Jensen (1994). Science, specific knowledge, and Total Quality Management. *Journal of Accounting and Economics,18*: 247-287.

Wu, H.Y., Wiebe, H.A. and Politi, J. (1997). Self-assessment of total quality management programs. *Engineering Management Journal,* 9 (1), 25-31.

Yang, C.C. (2003). The establishment of a TQM system for the health care industry. *The TQM Magazine, Vol. 15* No. 2, pp. 93-8.

—— (2006). The impact of human resource management practices on the implementation of total quality management: an empirical study on high-tech firms. *The TQM Magazine,* 18(2), 162-173.

Yasin, M.M., Alavi, J., Kunt, M. and Zimmerer, T.W. (2004). TQM practices in service organizations: An exploratory study into the implementation, outcomes and effectiveness. *Managing Service Quality,* 14 (5), 377-389

Yeganeh, H. and Su, Z. (2007). Comprehending core cultural orientations of Iranian managers. *Cross Cultural Management: An International Journal,* Vol. 14, No. 4, pp. 336-353.

Yong, J., and Wilkinson, A. (1999). The state of total quality management: Are view. *The International Journal of Human Resource Management,* 10(1), 137-161.

— — (2002). The long and winding road: The evolution of quality management. *Total Quality Management,* 13(1), 101-121.

York, K.M. and Miree, C.E. (2004). Causation or co variation: an empirical re-examination of the link between TQM and ûnancial performance. *Journal of Operations Management,* 22, 291-311.

Yusof, S.M. and Aspinwall, E.M. (1999). Critical success factors for total quality management implementation in small and medium enterprises. *Total Quality Management,* 10(4-5), S803-S809.

— — (2000). Total quality management implementation frameworks: comparison and review. *Total Quality Management, 11*(3), 281-374.

Yusuf Y.G.A., and Dang (2007), Implementation of TQM in China and Organization Performance: An empirical investigation, *Total Quality Management,* 18(5): 509-530.

Zadry, R.H. (2005). The integration of total quality management and theory of constraints implementation in Malaysian Automotive suppliers. A thesis submitted in fulfillment of the requirements for the award of the degree of Master of Engineering (Mechanical). 1-211.

Zahra, S.A., and Covin, J. (1995). Contextual influences on the corporate entrepreneurship-performance relationship: A longitudinal analysis. *Journal of Business Venturing,* 10, 43-58.

— —, and Garvis, D.M. (2000). Entrepreneurship and firm performance: The moderating effect of international environmental hostility. *Journal of Business Venturing,* 15(5), 469-492.

Zairi, M. (1996). Effective Benchmarking: Learning from the Best, Chapman & Hall, London.

— — (1996). Economic development and globalcompetitiveness: why should Arab managers take note of total quality management. The Fourth Arab Management Conference, 16-18 July, University of Bradford, UK, pp. 408-23.

— — (1997). Business process management: A boundaryless approach to modern competitiveness, *Business Process Management Journal,* Vol. 3, No. 1, pp. 68-80.

— — and Thiagarajan, T. (1997). A review of total quality management in practice: understanding the fundamentals through examples of best practice applications - Part III. *The TQM Magazine,* Vol. 9, No. 6, pp. 414-17.

Zakaria, A. (1999). *Budgetary Slack in Total Quality Management Environment.* Unpublished PhD dissertation: Universiti Utara Malaysia.

Zakuan, N.M., Yusof, S.M., Laosirihongthong, T. and Shaharoun, A.M. (2010). Proposed relationship of TQM and organizational performance using structured equation modeling. *Total Quality Management,* Vol. 21, No. 2, pp. 185-203.

Zaman website, "Turkish column says *Egypt* needs" Istanbul, in English 22 Apr 2012/BBC Monitoring/(c) BBC Monitoring European. London: Apr 22, 2012.

Zeffane, R., and Al Zarooni, H.A.M. (2008). The influence of empowerment, commitment, job satisfaction and trust on perceivedý: managers' performance. *International journal of Business excellence,* 1(1), 193-209.

Zehir. Cemal, Ertosun. Öznur, Zehir. Songül, Müceldili. Büsra, The Effects of Leadership Styles and Organizational Culture over Firm Performance: Multi-National Companies in Istanbul. *Procedia Social and Behavioral Sciences,* 24 (2011) 1460-1474.

Zigan, K., and Zeglat, D. (2010). Intangible resources in performance measurement systems of the hotel industry. *Facilities*, 28(13/14), 597-610.

Zikmund, W.G. (2000). Business Research Methods (6 edition). USA: Harcourt.

— — (2003). Business Research Methods (7th ed.), South-Western, Ohio.

Zhang, X. and Maruping, L.M., (2008). Household technology adoption in a global marketplace: Incorporating the role of espoused cultural values. Information Systems Frontiers 104.

Zhang, Z., Waszink, A., and Wijngaard, J. (2000). An Instrument for measuring TQM implantation for Chinese manufacturing companies. *International journal of quality and Reliability Management*, Vol. 17, No. 7, 2000, pp. 730-755.

Zhang Z.H. (2000). Implementation of total quality management: an empirical study of Chinese manufacturing firms. PhD unpublished thesis, University of Groningen, Groningen.

Zhou, P., Bundorf, K., Chang, J., Huang, J.X., and Xue, D. (2011). Organizational culture and its relationship with hospital performance in public hospitals in China. *Health Services Research*, 46 (6pt2), 2139-2160.

Zwick, Thomas (2005). Continuing Vocational Training Forms and Establishment Productivity in Germany, *German Economic Review*, 6 (2).

Index